Primitive Tribes of Orissa
and their Development Strategies

Primitive Tribes of Orissa

and their Development Strategies

by

Nityananda Patnaik

D.K. Printworld (P) Ltd.
New Delhi

Cataloging in Publication Data — DK

[Courtesy: D.K. Agencies (P) Ltd. <docinfo@dkagencies.com>]

Patnaik, N. (Nityananda), 1926 -

Primitive tribes of Orissa and their development strategies / by Nityananda Patnaik.

xxiii, 304 p. 23 cm.

Includes bibliographical references (p.)

Includes index.

ISBN 8124602727 (Hardbound)

ISBN 8124602735 (Paperback)

1. Tribes – Indian – Orissa. I Title.

301.095 413 21

ISBN : 81-246-0272-7 (Hardbound)

ISBN : 81-246-0273-5 (Paperback)

First Published in India in 2005

Published and printed by:

D.K. Printworld (P) Ltd.

Regd. Office : 'Sri Kunj', F-52, Bali Nagar

New Delhi - 110 015

Phones : (011) 2545-3975; 546-6019

Fax : (011) 2546-5926

E-mail : dkrpintworld@vsnl.net

Web : www.dkprintworld.com

Preface

A NEW strategy called Tribal Sub-Plan was evolved in the Fifth Five-Year Plan. Accordingly the areas inhabited by the tribal communities by more than 50 per cent concentration were identified. The Block was taken as the unit for delineation of the tribal areas.

Being very large in coverage, the area which came under the Tribal Sub-Plan in a State was divided into smaller planning units called Integrated Tribal Development Agency.

Considering the level of development, certain tribal communities were identified as very Primitive. The criteria adopted for the identification of the Primitive tribes were of three categories, namely (1) Pre-agricultural level of technology, (2) level of literacy below 5 per cent and (3) low growth rate or stagnant population.

Based on these criteria, 13 tribal communities were identified as the Primitive Tribes in the State of Orissa. These communities are (1) The Birhor, (2) The Bondo, (3) the Chuktia Bhunjia, (4) The Didayi, (5) The Dongria Khond, (6) The Juang, (7) The Hill Kharia, (8) The Kutia Kondh, (9) The Lanjia Saora, (10) The Lodha, (11) The Mankidia, (12) The Paudi Bhuinya and (13) The Saora including Lanjia Saora.

It was felt that unless some detailed account of the socio-economic and cultural characteristics of these communities are available, it would be difficult to formulate any scientific and realistic plans for the development of these communities. The ethnographic account of many of these Primitive Tribes are already available in a haphazard manner in different reports and publications. But these accounts are of general nature and not related to the problems and typical features which are required for formulating suitable strategies for their development.

The socio-economic data on different Primitive Tribes, which are presented in this book, are basically problem oriented and focused on such facts as are needed in planning strategies for their development. Guided by this end in view, different aspects of the Primitive Tribal Groups have been gathered through fieldwork using latest techniques of data collection.

I hope this book which is a compilation of the socio-economic data specific to different Primitive Tribal Groups will be of immense help to evolve appropriate strategies and formulate suitable plans for their development.

Nityananda Patnaik

Contents

PART 2
TRIBAL DEVELOPMENT

Acknowledgements

ACKNOWLEDGEMENTS are due to various organizations and institutions and also many scholars and specialists with whose support and help the study of the Primitive Tribes was undertaken on various occasions and at different times.

For the study on the Birhors, acknowledgement is due to PA Karanjia ITDA, for furnishing information regarding location of a Birhor Tanda at Kendumundi in Mayurbhanj district.

The Juangs and the Paudi Bhuinyas were studied with the assistance of Ministry of Home Affairs, GOI, Tribal and Rural Welfare Department, Govt. of Orissa and National Institute of Community Development, Hyderabad. Consultancy assign-ment was given to the NICD by the Tribal and Rural Welfare Department of the Govt. of Orissa at the instance of Ministry of Home Affairs, GOI, for preparations of an Integrated Tribal Development Plan for tribal regions of Keonjhar district by employing techniques of growth centre concept and central place theory. The author being then the Director of Anthropology at the NICD, was assigned the Project for the formulation of the plan.

Acknowledgement is due to Swiss Federal Institute of Technology (ETH) Zurich, Switzerland, for the financial assistance provided to the Social Science and Development Research Institute (SSADRI) for the work on the Project on Local Management of Forests as determined by the environmental perception and traditional knowledge in the wider Himalayan context with particular reference to Juangpirh and Bhuinyapirh of Keonjhar district.

The fieldwork for the study of the Didayi tribe was undertaken by the author himself with the help of Mr. Dubek who provided valuable data about the tribe. Credit is due to him for sharing his knowledge for the study conducted in Oringi Didayi village in Kunda, Kamberu hill ranges.

Acknowledgements are due to Research Assistants, Shri P.K. Mohanty and Shri T. Sahoo, with whose help the study on the Bhuinya tribe was undertaken by the author himself while in service as the Director of THRTI, Govt. of Orissa.

Acknowledgement is due to SIDA for providing financial assistance for the anthropological study on the Kutia Khond and Dongria Khond under the Project on the Study of the Techniques of Shifting Cultivation as practised by the tribes of Orissa.

Shri R.N. Sahoo, Special Officer, Bonda Development Agency, needs special mention for offering logistic assistance to the author for his anthropological fieldwork on the Bondo tribe while in service as Director THRTI, Government of Orissa.

The fieldwork among the Saoras and the Lanjia Saoras was undertaken for collection of socio-economic information about the tribe with particular reference to the study on Shifting Cultivation by the author himself in his capacity as Consultant under SIDA.

Acknowledgement is due to the Department of Culture, Government of India for providing a research grant for the study of the Hill Kharia with particular reference to their material culture.

The study on the Lodhas was taken up during the implementation of the Mayurbhanj Pilot Project sponsored by the ILO. The author collected anthropological data about the Lodhas in Suliapada village in Mayurbhanj district.

Shri Manoranjan Patnaik is appreciated for his logistic support and co-ordination.

The data processing was done in the computer section of Social Science and Development Research Institute (SSADRI). The over-all supervision and credit for computerization, layout design and format of the report goes to Mr. Pradeep Satapathy and Smt. Nilanjana Patnaik. They deserve thanks for their efforts.

List of Abbreviations

ITDA	:	Integrated Tribal Development Agency
ITDP	:	Integrated Tribal Development Project
LAMPS	:	Large Size Multipurpose Co-operative Society
MADA	:	Modified Area Development Agency/Approach
NICD	:	National Institute for Community Development
THRTI	:	Tribal Harijan Research Tribal Institute
SIDA	:	Swedish International Development Agency
TSP	:	Tribal Sub-Plan
SCA	:	Special Central Assistance
PTGs	:	Primitive Tribal Groups
NIRD	:	National Institute of Rural Development
ST	:	Scheduled Tribe
SC	:	Scheduled Caste

List of Tables and Maps

Tables

Maps

List of Visuals

The Bondo

The Dongria Khond

The Juang

The Hill Kharia

The Kutia Khond

The Paudi Bhuinya

The Saora (Lanjia Saora)

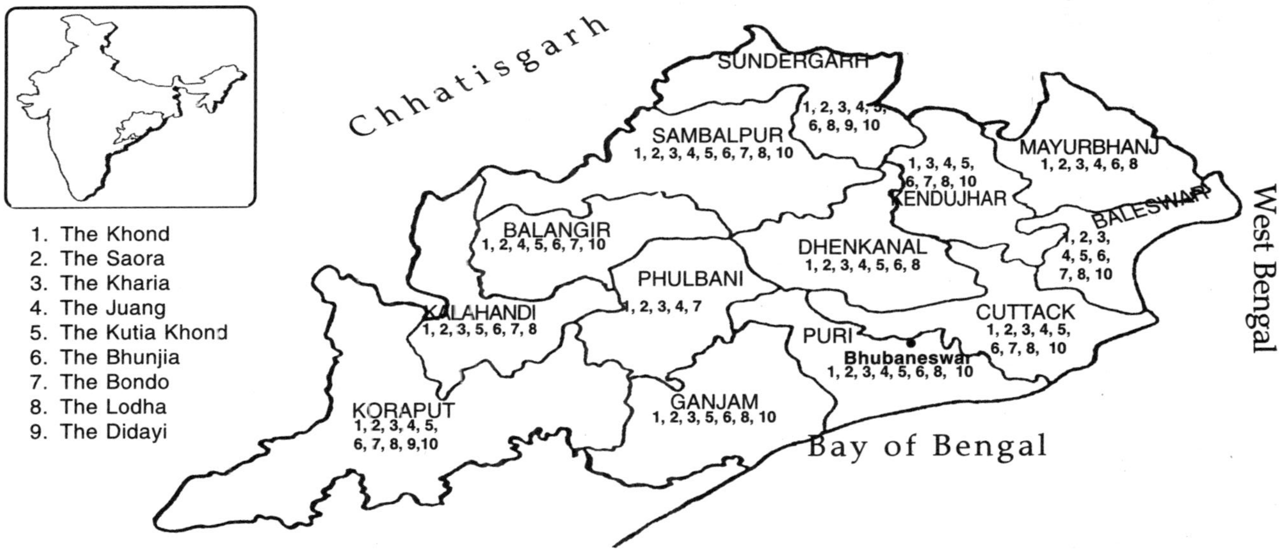

Map. 1. Distribution and Ranking of Scheduled Tribes in different districts of Orissa as per 1981 census.

Introduction

THE largest concentration of tribal communities anywhere in the world, except in Africa, is in India. There are more than 250 different tribal groups in India most of which are divided into several sub-groups. Some tribal communities are most numerous exceeding lakhs in population. In contrast, there are many tribal communities which are even less than 1000 in population and yet some other tribes which have a population less than 50 persons.

Like the varying size of population there is a considerable variation also in their culture, language, economic life and level of literacy. There are industrial workers, settled cultivators, shifting cultivators, artisans, traders, cattle breeders, landless wage earners, hunters and food gatherers.

Generally the tribal societies have some special features. These are :

- The first characteristic of tribal society is the element of its geographical and cultural isolation and resultant stability of the norms of their culture over a fairly long period of time.
- The second characteristic is that the tribes have a group identity and a cultural self image because of the face-to-face character of their society.
- The tribal groups have a limited world-view and have an extremely restricted and limited historical depth. Any probing into the history of a tribe shows that after a few generations, the past turns into mythology.

- The fourth characteristic is that the emphasis in these societies is on tradition.
- The fifth characteristic is that there is a relative absence of range in prescribed and actual norms. In tribal societies there is a great degree of universality in the application of norms and the permissible range of deviation is extremely limited.
- The sixth characteristic is that in tribal societies, there is considerable emphasis on group self-sufficiency.
- The seventh characteristic is that the tribal groups have limited population density and therefore limited innovative potential.
- The eighth characteristic is that there is a general merging of the natural and the supernatural resulting in the blending of the sacred and the secular.

Since the British times different policies and strategies have been adopted for the development of the tribal communities and to bring them into the national stream. Some of these approaches are the policy of "leave the tribals alone" as adopted by the Britishers, followed by the approach of "Detribalization" as adopted by the missionaries, approach of "Social work" as adopted by the social workers, and the Panchaseel approach and special multipurpose tribal development blocks which were adopted after independence.

The tribal communities have experienced various such strategies for their development. The one which is now in operation is the "Tribal Sub-Plan Approach." For the implementation of this approach the tribal areas have been divided into three different zones. These are :

1. Zone of tribal concentration of 50 per cent and above.
2. Zone of dispersed population below 50 per cent.
3. Zone of extremely backward and isolated little communities.

Such planning units as Integrated Tribal Development Agencies (ITDA), Modified Area Development Agencies (MADA) pockets including clusters and micro projects. These different strategies have been discussed in this book.

This book presents a short ethnographic account of the Primitive Tribes of Orissa. 13 such tribal communities have been identified by the Government as Primitive groups based on the following characteristics namely, (1) Pre-agricultural technology, (2) Low level of literacy, (3) Stagnant or diminishing population. It is necessary to highlight the distinct cultural patterns of these Primitive Groups, because these features are needed for the formulation of Micro Projects for the Primitive Tribal Groups in a scientific manner.

The reader may find that while a few pages have been devoted to certain tribes, others have been dealt with in greater detail. The basic idea is to highlight the distinguishing features of each tribe and not to give their detailed enthnographic account.

This publication also gives two case studies, namely, Saora Development Agency and Juang Development Agency showing the degree of impact of the Micro Projects on these two Primitive Tribal Groups. These two studies indicate as to what degrees the Micro Projects have been effective in bringing out the desirous change and development in the living condition of these two Primitive Tribal Groups.

Part I
Primitive Tribes of Orissa

1

General Account of Tribes of Orissa

ANTHROPOLOGICALLY Orissa is one of the most fascinating States of India. There are as many as 62 different tribal communities inhabiting the State. Starting from the primitive hunting and food gathering communities and shifting cultivators to the advanced agriculturists and industrial workers, the tribal communities show a great variety of interesting features in their social structures, cultural patterns, economic pursuits, belief systems, art and dance forms, and magico-religious practices. Some of them are found in inaccessible pockets away from contact with outsiders whereas many others are in areas having good road communications and inhabited by many progressive non-tribal communities.

The communities who are in greater isolation have been able to retain their traditional social and cultural traits and own ways of managing internal affairs, but those who live in close contact with their non-tribal neighbours have undergone great acculturation and adopted the lifeways and workways of their neighbours in place of their own. In between these two groups there are some tribal communities who are in transitional stage. In such a situation they continue to retain their own cultural traits in some aspects and at the same time have borrowed many alien traits from their neighbouring non-tribal communities.

With the development of road communications and increasing inter-regional migration and cultural contact almost all tribal communities so to say are in the process of acculturation in varying degrees. The present work is about those communities which have been identified as primitive tribes and are found in most inaccessible areas and least acculturated.

In defining the term "primitive" Surjit C. Sinha and B.D. Sharma have distinguished the prior stage of economic development from the lower level in the economic structure. Those groups which fall in the former category have been categorized under primitive tribal communities, while those in the latter category are termed as the more backward tribal communities. In this context agricultural economy has been taken as the watershed for identifying primitive tribal communities. Following this premise the pre-agricultural economic groups have been included in the primitive communities.

Amongst the primitive groups the hunting and food gathering communities are at the earliest stage of economic evolution. Next in gradation, from hunting and food gathering, follows the shifting cultivators who have the highest form of technology among the primitive groups who represent a pre-agricultural stage of socio-economic life. When a community takes up plough and animal traction for carrying on agricultural operations, it is considered to have advanced technologically and therefore ceases to be primitive.

It has been seen that many tribal communities in the North-Eastern Hill areas have advanced educationally and socially although their level of technology has not advanced beyond that of the shifting cultivators. In this respect, besides the economic criterion, some more distinguishing features have been taken into consideration for identifying the primitive communities. The level of literacy not above 5 per cent has been taken as an additional characteristic to identify the primitive groups. To these main features a population criterion like a low growth rate, stagnation in growth of population and declining population has been added for a precise identification. Based on these features 13 tribal communities have been identified as primitive and a comprehensive ethnographic account of each of these groups has been given in this book. These tribal communities are : 1. Birhor, 2. Bondo, 3. Chuktia Bhunjia, 4. Didayi, 5. Dongria Khond, 6. Juang, 7. Kharia, 8. Kutia Khond, 9. Lanjia Saora, 10. Lodha, 11. Mankidia, 12. Paudi Bhuinya, 13. Saora.

Physical Setting and Distribution

Orissa extends from 17°49' N to 22°34' N latitude and from 81°27' E to 87°29' E longitude in the eastern coast of India. It is bounded on the north-east by West Bengal, on the north by Bihar, on the West by Madhya Pradesh, on the south by Andhra Pradesh, and on the east by Bay of Bengal. It covers an area of 155,842 sq. km. and comprises 13 districts. Its total population as per 1981 census is 26370271, of which the Scheduled Caste population is 3845543 (14.66 per cent) and Scheduled Tribe population is 5915047 (22.43 per cent). The tribal population varies from district to district in the State. They are in great concentration in some districts and sparsely populated in others. Table 1.1 and Table 1.2 gives the distribution of tribal population in different districts as per 1981 census compared with population as per 1991 census.

Table 1.1 : Distribution of Tribal population in 13 districts of Orissa as per 1981 census

Sl. No.	Name of the district	Total population	Sch. Caste population	% to total population	Sch. Tribe population	% to total population
1.	Balasore	2,252,808	404,197	17.94	154,153	6.85
2.	Bolangir	1,459,113	228,260	15.64	280,381	19.21
3.	Cuttack	4,428,800	817,873	17.66	144,708	3.12
4.	Dhenkanal	1,582,787	250,554	15.82	194,060	12.26
5.	Ganjam	2,669,899	401,116	15.02	253,634	9.47
6.	Kalahandi	1,339,192	211,069	15.76	418,871	31.27
7.	Keonjhar	1,114,622	124.34	11.15	499,567	44.81
8.	Koraput	2,484,005	349,307	14.06	1,371,550	55.21
9.	Mayurbhanj	1,581,873	104,057	6.57	912,320	57.67
10.	Phulbani	717,280	133,071	18.55	279,276	39.83
11.	Puri	2,921,045	377,546	12.92	100,827	3.45

Sl. No.	Name of the district	Total population	Sch. Caste population	% to total population	Sch. Tribe population	% to total population
12.	Sambalpur	2,280,976	350,078	15.34	622,555	27.20
13.	Sundergarh	1,337,871	114,036	8.52	685,765	51.25
	Orissa	26,370,271	3,865,543	14.66	5,951,067	22.43

Table 1.2 : Distribution of Tribal population in different districts as per 1991 census

Sl. No.	Name of the district	Total population	Sch. Caste population	% of SC population to total population	Sch. Tribe population	% of ST population to total population
1.	Sambalpur	2,697,153	471,460	17.47	740323	27.44
2.	Sundergarh	1,573,617	138,157	8.77	798481	50.74
3.	Kendujhar	1,337,026	153,639	11.49	595184	44.51
4.	Mayurbhanj	1,884,580	131,765	6.99	1090626	57.87
5.	Balasore	2,802,417	555,069	19.80	197992	7.06
6.	Cuttack	5,522,659	1,124,160	20.35	182188	3.29
7.	Dhenkanal	1,908,907	313,574	16.42	232519	12.18
8.	Phulbani	863,903	161,876	18.73	322408	37.31
9.	Bolangir	1,707,753	294,875	17.26	316797	18.55
10.	Kalahandi	1,600,385	253,832	15.86	495425	30.95
11.	Koraput	3,012,546	452,133	15.00	1636079	54.30
12.	Ganjam	3,158,764	524,085	16.59	296845	9.39
13.	Puri	3,590,026	554,689	15.45	127347	3.54
	Orissa	31,659,736	5,129,314	16.20	7032214	12.21

Source: Estimated from Census 1991

Broadly there are four distinct geophysical zones in which the tribes of Orissa have been distributed in uneven proportions.

THE NORTHEN PLATEAU

It includes Sundergarh, Mayurbhanj and Keonjhar districts and Bamra and Kuchinda portions of Sambalpur district, and the interior plains of Balasore district and Pallahara region of Dhenkanal district. In this zone, there are as many as 58 tribal groups numbering about 2 million people.

In this zone there are eight major tribes such as Santal, Kolha, Munda, Bhuinya, Oraon, Gond, Kisan and Bathudi, each numbering more than one lakh and there are primitive tribes too, such as the Hill Bhuinya, the Juang, the Kharia, the Lodha, the Mankirdia or the Mankidi and the Birhor, all only a few thousands in strength.

THE CENTRAL TABLE LAND

This zone covers the whole of the Brahmani and the Mahanadi basins. There are only two major tribes, the Gond and the Sabar (acculturated group of the Saora tribe), each numbering more than one lakh. The Primitive tribes found in this zone are the Paudi Bhuinya, the Juang and the Lodha which together count only a few thousands.

THE EASTERN GHAT REGION

The peninsular plateau is bordered on the east by the Eastern Ghats, a tectonic range cut by many rivers into discontinuous blocks of mountains. Broadly it is divided into five sections.

Northern Section

It starts from Nilgiri and stretches up to Boud border rising to a height of 2239 ft. In respect to population no tribe of this zone touches one lakh mark. But the Khond and the Sabar are most numerous in this zone numbering 30517 and 23633 people respectively. This zone includes the primitive sections of the Khond tribe and the Juangs.

Central Section

The Central Section of the Eastern Ghats covers Boudh, Baliguda, Udayagiri areas and the hills of this section are very high, ranging in height from 1000 ft to 4000 ft. The Khond population is 223322 in this section. The population of the Gond, the Kutia, the Saora and the Khond Gouda ranges from 2460 to 9734. The population of the remaining 24 tribes is below one thousand. This zone can be called the Khond zone. The primitive group which is included in this zone is the Kutia Khond, a primitive section of the Khond tribe.

Rayagada Section

This section comprises Parlakhemundi and Rayagada hill areas with an elevation of 1000 ft. Like other sections the mountain ranges of this zone give place to plateaus or broken rugged hill country stretching irregularly towards the west until they merge into the uplands of Madhya Pradesh. These hill areas are inhabited by as many as 42 tribal communities and of them the Khonds and the Saoras are most numerous with 229655 and 132779 people respectively. There are two tribal groups, the Sabar and the Paroja numbering 58634 and 20680 people respectively. Four tribal communities record a population varying between 1355 and 7950 people. All other tribal communities record a population below one thousand. This section includes the Lanjia Saora and the Saoras of Thumba area which are recognized as primitive tribes.

Based on elevation this section is divided into three plateaus.

3000 ft plateau

It covers Koraput and Pottangi areas and have been the home of as many as 33 tribal communities and of them the Khond, the Paroja and the Gadaba are most numerous, recording population above 20,000 while all others below 4000 people.

2000 ft plateau

It covers Jeypore and Nawarangpur sub-divisions. The major tribe inhabiting this zone is Bhottada whose population is above one lakh. There are 40 tribal communities living in this area.

1000 ft plateau

It comprises the Malkangiri sub-division of Koraput district. This area is inhabited by many tribal communities and of them the Koya and the Bhunjia are most numerous. This is the area where the Bonda Paroja live. The Bonda highlanders are considered to be very primitive, and have been of great attraction to the ethnographers and anthropologists.

The Coastal Region (21.2 per cent)

Along the eastern sea-board tract lies a plain, made up partly of deltas formed by the numerous streams which flow from the inland hills and mountains into the Bay of Bengal. It stretches from the Rishikulya river in the south to the Subarnarekha river in the north. The coastal tract is most fertile in the state and has been the home of many hardy and prosperous peasants and fisherfolk.

There are 51 tribal communities numbering 275689 people living in this region. The most numerous tribes among them are the Saora, the Sabar, the Santal, the Khond, the Bhumija, the Kolha and the Munda whose population varies from 14745 to 65268. The tribes of the coastal belt are in close contact with their Hindu neighbours and are in various stages of acculturation and assimilation.

The tribal communities of Orissa may be grouped under five population ranges. Table 1.3 gives the list of tribal communities under such population ranges and their distribution in different districts of the State.

The distribution of the tribal communities under different population ranges shows that there are 15 tribal communities, each being more than one lakh in population and mostly dwell in Sundergarh, Mayurbhanj, Koraput, Sambalpur, Keonjhar, Phulbani and Kalahandi district. These 15 tribal communities are considered major tribes of Orissa.

South-Western Section

This section comprises (a) the plain country and (b) the Donger (a plateau of 2000 ft to 3000 ft high) of Kalahandi district. The Donger portion includes Lanjigarh and Thuamul-Rampur areas, inhabited mostly by the Kutia Khonds who are very primitive. The Khond and the Gond are above one lakh in population and form major tribal group of this section.

The primitive groups fall to different population groups. Table 1.3 gives the distribution of the primitive groups under different population groups.

Table 1.3 : Population groups and primitive communities

Sl. No.	*Name of the tribe*	*Total population (1971 census)*	*Primitive section of the tribe*	*Population*	*Location*
		Less than 100			
1.	Birhor	98	—	—	Sundergarh
		Less than 1000 More than 100			
2.	Mankidia & Mankirdia	393 + 876	—	—	Mayurbhanj Sundergarh
		Less than 10,000 More than 1,000			
3.	Didayi	2,164	—	—	Koraput
4.	Lodha	3,891	—	—	Mayurbhanj
5.	Bonda Paroja	5,338	—	—	Koraput
		Less than 1,00,000 More than 10,000			
6.	Juang	24,384	—	—	Keonjhar Dhenkanal
		More than 1,00,000			
7.	Kharia	1,20,483	Hill Kharia	5,600	Similipal (Mayurbhanj)
8.	Bhuinya	1,88,212	Paudi Bhuinya	4,388	Pallahara (Dhenkanal)
			Paudi Bhuinya		Khuntagaon (Sundergarh)
9.	Saora	3,42,757	1. Lanjia Saora —	3,043	Seranga (Ganjam)
			2. Lanjia Saora —	2,917	Chandragiri (Ganjam)
			3. Saora —	2,734	Thumba (Ganjam)
10.	Khond	8,69,965	1. Kutia Khond	3,835	Belghar (Phulbani)
			2. Dongria Khond	2,666	Bissamcuttack (Koraput)

Racial Affinity and Linguistic Characteristics

Generally speaking the Proto-Australoid type is the dominant racial element among the tribes of Orissa. Agglutinogen tests made on a few tribal groups in the southern and central India show a marked preponderance of the blood group among the tribes of southern India. But such tests on the tribes of central India with which the tribes of Orissa have great affinity, show a considerable preponderance of B over A.

As regards language, the tribes of Orissa fall mainly to two language groups, (1) Austric and (2) Dravidian. The branch of Austric family to which various language groups are included was first isolated by *Mullar* and named by him as "Munda." But later on another linguist P.W. Schmidt named it as "Austric," after his native country. The Dravidian speech family includes such languages as Kui or Kuvi of the Kandha, Gondi of the Gond, Kisan of the Kisan, Malto of the Maler and Kurukh of the Oraon.

The Gadaba tribe is split into two sections — one section speaking Gutob of Mundari family and the other section speaking Ollari which is akin to Parji, Koya, Kolami and Naiki and 74 other Dravidian languages including Brahui of Baluchisthan. The Munda speeches which fall to Austroasiatic language group were in existence in India, even before the Indo-Aryans arrived and what we know of their languages dates from the nineteenth century. The following diagram shows the branches of Munda languages.

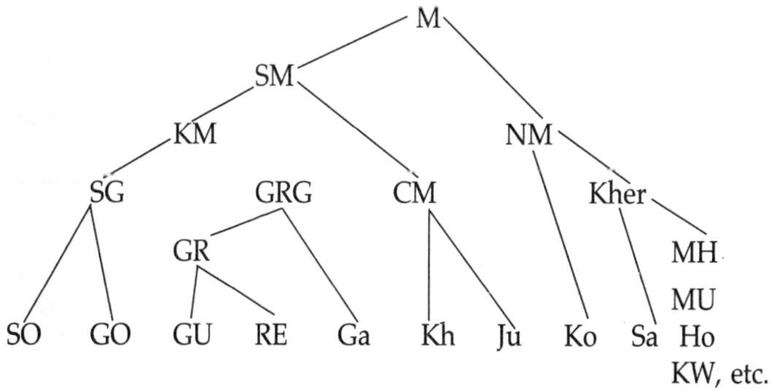

The abbreviations are So=Sora; Go-Gorum; Gu-Gutob; Re=Remo; Ga=Gata, Kh=Kharia; Ju=Juang, Ko=Korku; Sa=Santali; Mu= Mundari; Ko=Korwa; M=Proto-Munda; SM= Proto-South Munda; KM=Proto-Koraput Munda; SG=Proto-Sora Gorum; GRG=Proto-Gutob-Remo-Gata; GR=Proto-Gutob =Remo; CM= Proto-central=Munda; NM=Proto-North Munda; Kher=Proto-Kherwarian; MH=Proto-Mundari-Ho, etc.

The Munda languages are Korku, the Mundari-Ho a branch of Kherwarian, Santali, Kharia, Juang, Gutob (Gadba), Remo (Bondo), Gata (Didayi), Gorum (Parenga), and Soro (Saora). This is not the exhaustive list of Munda groups of languages. It is possible that the unexplored Munda languages will yet be found in the future.

Economic Life

Among the people of Orissa there are some tribal population who are still in a primitive stage of existence, surviving on hunting and food gathering and simple forms of agriculture. Their number is small. The Birhor, the Mankidi and the Hill Kharia fall into this category.

The tribal groups who are in the higher stage of culture and numerically larger and dependent upon shifting cultivation for their sustenance are the Bondo, Didayi, Lanjia Saora, Kutia Khond, Juang and Hill Bhuinya. Among these tribes life is more settled with organized social life and village councils and with development of arts and crafts, music and dancing. The whole social life of the tribes centres round the bachelors' or spinsters' dormitory and religious activities are associated with fertility cult and in some cases are observed in an elaborate manner. The practice of magic, witchcraft, and sorcery is widespread.

Among some tribal communities terracing is widely practised and there where contact has been close as among the Santal, the Munda and many others, plough cultivation has been the primary source of livelihood. A short account of the life-ways of different sections of the tribal people is given below.

HUNTER-GATHERER

The tribes falling under this economic class are not in isolation. They are in contact with other people and in complementary relationship with their neighbours. The important tribes of this category are the Birhor, the Chenchu, the Mallar, the Korwa and the Hill Kharia of Sundergarh and Mayurbhanj districts. Their number does not exceed 10,000 and they have a nomadic style of life. They live in small groups called local bands. Each band is associated with a geographical range. But they do not function as closed social units because inter-group visiting and marriage alliances and reciprocal exchange of goods and services constitute the core features of their socio-economic life. They live in bamboo huts and leaf-shelters. Their fundamental economic base includes a camp life and a division of labour, with males hunting and females gathering roots and tubers from the nearby forests.

The amount of personal property among them is kept at a low level and this constraint on the accumulation of property serves to keep the wealth differences between the individuals to the minimum. This limited wealth differences do not encourage any class system to grow among them and, therefore, their society appears to be more or less of egalitarian type.

The limited resources and the nature of food supply keeps the local bands small. Throughout the world the density of population among the hunters and food gatherers ranges from 1 to 25 persons per 100 square miles. The low population density among the nomadic people explains their greater resistance to the epidemic diseases than what is observed among the farming people in densely populated areas. The constraints that operate among the hunter-gatherer class for population control are malnutrition, disease and prolonged lactation.

The hunter-gatherer band is not a corporate body of persons as they are migratory and do not have ownership right of the resources. Whenever population increases in a local band, it is fissioned into smaller groups which disperse in different directions within the territory of their movement. Due to lack of exclusive rights to resources and variations in food supply from region to region and year to year, there is very little of intra- or inter-band economic competition. The rival groups part company rather than resort to violence which seems to be the simplest device of avoiding conflict and maintaining harmony in the band. This mechanism of fission of the local bands explain the fluidity, composition and flexibility of social organization.

Hunting-gathering refers to a mode of sustenance which is more substantial than what was previously supposed. Some marginal hunters actually work for lesser number of hours and exploit abundant food resources. They show considerable lack of concern about the problem of finding food and hoarding it against future shortages. Perhaps it is this lack of future orientation that has enabled them to live in a stage of mental happiness.

Due to the denudation of the local resources and constant ecological pressure, some hunting and gathering communities are faced with hardship and anxiety. For example, the Birhors not only work hard for their food, but often go hungry in spite of their hard labour. Such communities lead a very precarious life in want of food. They are in contact with the neighbouring people with whom they barter their hunted animals and collected forest produce mainly for rice and other items of daily necessities. The Birhors are the best rope makers and they exchange it for rice with their neighbouring communities.

A specific knowledge about the staple and subsidiary economy of the tribes of this category is essential for their development and adjustment in the national economy. For example, among the nomadic tribes inter-personal conflict is resolved by parting company and the mechanism of fission in the local bands makes its composition fluid. If the nomadic tribes are rehabilitated to a settled life in a colony, the social control of resolving disputes by parting company will no longer be operative and therefore cases of conflicts and quarrels will increase and will be intensified making the life in the colony most uncomfortable. The experiment of rehabilitation of the Chenchus in Andhra Pradesh has shown that the Chenchus started killing one another and cases of quarrelling and murder multiplied in the colony.

The Birhors can most profitably be employed in catching monkeys. There is a great demand in medical research for the Indian Rhesus monkeys. If the skill of the Birhors in catching monkeys could be utilized their economic condition could be improved.

PASTORAL

There is no tribe in Orissa which leads a pastoral life solely for its sustenance. The Koyas were once full-fledged cattle herders. But a change has taken place in their economic life and they have become settled agriculturists and wage earners. Those who live near Balimella have taken to fishing in the reservoir.

SHIFTING CULTIVATION

The total number of forest dwellers practising hunting and gathering does not perhaps exceed a few thousands. But a much larger number of tribes who live in the hills and forests are dependent upon the produce from the slash and burn type of agriculture.

The important tribes practising this primitive agriculture are the Dongria and Kutia Khonds, the Lanjia Saora, the Bonda Paroja, the Juang and the Bhuinya. Some of the salient features of the shifting cultivation are listed below:

1. All activities connected with this type of agriculture are performed mostly by communal labour. A particular hill slope or the area that is to be cultivated in a particular year is chosen at a common village meeting. According to the needs and the consent of the community, plots are parcelled out among the families.

2. A piece of land is used for two or three years when successively different crops are sown and then it is abandoned so that it could recuperate. The recuperative cycle which was previously of a longer duration of six to nine years has been shortened to two to three years because of the necessity arising out of shortage of land and population explosion for repeated clearing and cultivation.
3. Individual ownership of the plots of land on the hill slopes is recognized on a hereditary basis. But when any plot lies fallow it is reverted to the communal ownership.
4. A mixed crop of millets, pulses and vegetables is grown in the hill slopes, and this practice of growing a mixed crop is dictated by their food habits and ecological conditions.
5. All agricultural activities are accompanied by ritual performances. It is the belief of the tribes practising shifting cultivation that if they merely perform the ritual ceremonies and work in a perfunctory manner their crops would suffer and would not yield properly. Therefore, their success in agriculture depends not only on ritual ceremonies but also upon their extensive knowledge of crops suitable for cultivation on the hill slopes, the geographic conditions of the locality, their hard work and reciprocal labour organized with a team spirit.

Shifting cultivation is considered harmful and dis-advantageous. Therefore, this is discouraged for the following reasons: (1) it destroys valuable timber, (2) it makes the hill-streams dry up, (3) it brings about soil erosion and affects rainfall and (4) it is unproductive and unsuited for agricultural development.

Based on these reasons, the government have been discouraging the tribal communities to carry on this harmful practice of cultivation. In spite of intensive efforts on the part of the government to wean the tribals away from shifting cultivation, they show considerable doggedness in sticking to this type of cultivation for the following strong reasons :

1. The plain lands in the tribal areas are in short supply. On calculation we found that there is land ranging from 0.26 to 1.85 hectares per family in the present situation. The tribals have been deprived of all the best lands in the plains by the process of mounting land alienation. One of the conditions which favour land alienation is the lack of land survey and settlement in the tribal areas. The tribals do not have *patta* rights for the lands they cultivate and the land tenure is not under *ryotwari* system. Most of the lands in the tribal areas are in the name of landlords or the erstwhile *muttadar*s and in connivance with them the non-tribal men find easier to take away the lands from the possession of the tribal tenants. In addition to this, the lacunae in law relating to the land alienation have always favoured the cunning non-tribals to circumvent the protective legislation and have access to lands which are cultivated by and in possession of the tribal people.
2. The tribals lack the necessary agricultural inputs such as plough and plough-bullocks, seeds and fertilizers, etc., to carry on cultivation in the plains. Without the necessary capital and other infrastructure which are associated with sound agriculture, it is not possible for the tribals to undertake cultivation in the plains.
3. For the tribal people money is not as great a factor as the satisfaction of their immediate needs. It is due to this peculiar psychology and lack of future orientation that they are satisfied with the meagre produce they get from shifting cultivation. Even though the produce from shifting cultivation is not sufficient to fulfil the minimum food requirements, the tribals do not find any other alternative on which they could depend to improve their economic condition.

4. Most of the tribal people are indebted to the non-tribal traders, merchants and money-lenders. The important reasons for their indebtedness are : (a) unproductive agriculture, (b) expensive festivals and rituals, (c) lack of proper marketing facilities for the forest products which they collect, and (d) the excise laws which prohibit them to brew their liquor by indigenous methods and purchase drink from government-sponsored liquor booths.

Being exceedingly trustworthy, the tribal people believe it as their sacred obligation to pay back their debts whatever might be the burden. But their creditors never wish repayment in cash but aim at the produce raised by the tribals, in settlement of the debts. The rate of the interest also is never stipulated in terms of money for each rupee advanced, a specific quantity of produce in the form of paddy, cereal, pulse, tamarind, etc., is asked towards interest for the fixed time.

The money-lenders by various dishonest methods such as blank promissory notes in which thumb impressions of the tribal debtors are taken without any mention of the amount of the loan, and the use of false weight inflates the debts of tribals, thus keeping them in debt in perpetuity. Compelled by the necessity and obligation as mentioned above, the tribals are forced to cultivate all available tracts, raise produce and pay in kind to the money-lenders.

In a sense, therefore, the money-lenders have impelled the tribals to continue the practice of shifting cultivation. The short-sightedness of the tribals and the greediness of the money-lenders have been responsible for starvation, land-lessness and migration to which the tribal people are subjected. Plots of land or crops are placed under usufruct mortgage for the repayment of loans. This shows that even though the few tribal people who possess some land and put their hard labour in cultivation and growing crops, they do not enjoy the fruits of their labour.

The shifting cultivation has another problem for consideration. Due to repeated cutting and burning of the forests, most of the tracts used for shifting cultivation have become barren. These hill slopes are not conducive to the growth of the forest trees. Large-scale conversion of such tracts into reserved areas does not help very much in augmenting the forest wealth. In fact, what happens as a result is that the tribals are deprived of their only means of living and forced to lead a life of poverty and misery. What is, therefore, necessary is that before banning shifting cultivation sufficient care should be taken to provide the tribals with good land and rehabilitate them in colonies established in suitable places near about their parent habitat.

SETTLED FARMERS

The colonization of the tribals which is suggested as a devise to wean them away from the shifting cultivation and take up wet cultivation in the plains is a very complicated process.

Our experience shows that failure stories have outnumbered the success stories in respect of the colonization scheme. Some Saoras have been rehabilitated in a colony called Thatraj near Rampur in R. Udayagiri block of Ganjam district. They were provided land and necessary inputs for cultivation. Some of them took up cultivation most enthusiastically and thereby were able to improve their economic condition. But certain other Saora families evinced no interest in cultivation and finding no other alternative became agricultural labourers of the farming families of the colony. The reason for this was that those who did well in cultivation were the Kampu Saoras who are the best farmers and those who failed in farming were the Arsi Saoras whose traditional occupation is weaving. Had this occupational difference been recognized earlier this unhappy conversion of a group of skilled artisans to serfdom could have been avoided.

Another instance is drawn from northern Orissa. This is regarding the colonization scheme which was introduced among the Hill

Bhuinyas of Sundergarh district. In this case an organization which is special to the Bhuinya social structure inhibited the success of the scheme. But when correct measures were taken in conformity to the social base of the tribe the scheme was successful.

The chief characteristic of the Bhuinya social structure is its village exogamy. According to this custom marriage within the village is strictly prohibited and therefore some villages are grouped as *Kutumb* (agnatic or consanguinal) and *Bandhu* villages (congnitic or affinal). If by mistake only the Bhuinyas of Kutumba villages are rehabilitated in a colony then they are bound to desert it soon for obvious reasons. But if they are drawn from both the categories of villages they are more likely to stick to the colony than to leave it. From these instances it is obvious that the success of the colonization scheme hinges on many factors, viz., ecological economic, socio-cultural and psychological. The major factors which may favour a colony for its success are as follows :

1. Good flat land in different size is a pre-requisite for any scheme of land colonization.
2. Dereservation of reserved forests is necessary because the nearness of the reserved forests to the living habitation causes a lot of inconvenience to the inmates of the colony.
3. It is necessary to grant rights and concessions to them in regard to free hunting, free collection of forest produce, free removable of timber and grass and free grazing of cattle in the nearby forests. The subordinate staff of the forest department should be made aware of the rules conferring these concessions so that the tribals are not harassed by them.

   The dereservation of the reserve forests close to the place of land colonization is necessary from another point of view. It is our observation that in many places where the land colonization scheme has been implemented the fertile cultivable lands are not in the unreserved areas near the colonies but are in the reserved section of the forest. Finding no better land for cultivation the tribals in many cases have left the colonies and gone back to their parent habitat.

4. Proper selection of the tribals for land colonization is important. The tribals of the villages which surround the place selected for land colonization may be chosen so that they may not find any difficulty in adjusting themselves to the life in the colony because of similarity in environment between their parent villages and the colony.

5. Colonies should be started on co-operative basis and the land under the colony should be on a joint ownership. Revitalization of the traditional pattern of co-operative living and joint ownership of property which are the core features of traditional tribal economic life may help the tribals to live free from indebtedness and land alienation. We have observed among the Hill Maria of Basar that ordinarily they are not indebted to anybody. It is very rarely that they go to the money-lenders who live in the plains. In case someone in the village wants to borrow money to meet some immediate need, the village headman (*Gaita*) goes to the money-lender and borrows money from him on his behalf. The Hill Marias are very keen on repaying the debt quickly because the village as whole considers the debt as their common debt and not a individual debt. At the time of harvest which is done on a co-operative basis a part of the produce is set apart towards the repayment of the debt and it is again the village headman who collects this produce and takes it to the money-lender for repayment of the loan advanced to his villagers.

   The Hill Maria village is a remarkable institution that runs on co-operative principles and it is surprising how these people living in far-off hills and cut-off completely from the civilized world, managed the business of living in such an exemplary manner. They have thus not yet come into the clutches of the money- lenders although the latter are living not far away from them. Therefore, we suggest that the restoration of the co-operative principles in the rehabilitation camps among the tribal communities might help them in leading a life of financial independence and security.

6. Of all the items necessary for successful colonization, irrigation is most important. The tribals attach great importance to irrigation and they show a great skill in water management.

We have observed that in places where there is permanent irrigation, the tribals have shown great skill in wet cultivation, and in those places their economic condition is much better that those who practise shifting cultivation. For example, the yield of paddy per hectare of terraced land under irrigation is about 1,852.25 kg whereas in the case of shifting cultivation without irrigation facilities comes to 416.38 kg.

The Saoras of Ganjam district of Orissa are the best terraced cultivators in the world. By stone packed contour bounding they lay out small terraced fields on the hill slopes and grow paddy. Their water management is skilful. By means of channels they regulate the flow of water from the natural hill streams and irrigate the terraced fields. The availability of irrigation facilities has induced the Saoras to adopt improved agricultural practices. But the use of such practices in axe cultivation is not feasible in a sloping terrain. Due to ecological and human problems, advanced technology and agricultural practices did not diffuse into the tribal areas of Bhadragiri block. Thus, basic to the success of land colonization and agricultural improvement are extensive fertile plain lands, proper reclamation of such lands, water control, soil conservation, seed and livestock improvement, pest control, mechanization of agricultural processes and introduction of plantation crops.

In addition to these measures, provision of employment opportunities and training facilities will enable the inhabitants of the colony to improve their economic condition and foster a feeling of belongingness to the new situation. We suggest that the people in the forest department may be replaced by the tribal people particularly by those who are rehabilitated in the colonies. They may be given training in nursery work, stump planning, alignment and stacking, repair of roads and buildings, seed collection, fire protection, demarcation coups, etc. In addition, a labour contract co-operative society may be organized among the tribals to overcome difficulties in payment of labour charges and provide the idle able-bodied adults with suitable employment throughout the year.

In the case of those who practise settled cultivation and own land on individual basis, a different strategy is to be considered for their development. For this class of tribals a change in land tenure from individual ownership to community ownership is not possible. But the individual ownership right to land among these tribals has encouraged massive land alienation resulting in landlessness and discontent among them. There is, therefore, a need for a detailed study and scrutiny of all legislations affecting tribals' land. All Acts and Regulations relating to land alienation should be examined thoroughly to plug the loop-holes and for some time all transfers of tribals' land to non-tribals should be prevented by streamlining the administration in the tribal areas. Adequate machinery should be created to enforce these legal measures immediately so that no circumvention of protective legislation is possible by the exploiters. The Deputy Commissioner and Collector should have powers *suo moto* or at the instance of the aggrieved tribal land holder to institute enquiries and restore possession of the land without payment of any compensation to the transferee. The Court of Law should be precluded from taking cognizance of such transfers by sale, mortgage, gift or lease or any other agreement or contract and from passing decree thereon.

It is also necessary to launch an educational campaign among the tribals regarding the laws or regulations made for their benefit and make them aware of such laws and render them the necessary financial and legal assistance to accrue full advantage thereof. It is our observation that the present unrest among the tribals is largely due to their unawareness of the constitutional safeguards granted to them entitled on the basis of such protective legislations.

Looking at the problem of colonization from cultural point of view the question of relation to land, types of tribal organization, such as bachelors' dormitory, clan solidarity, ritual and art and belief in supernaturalism, is uppermost in our mind. In most cases the tribes live in villages close together, while their fields are scattered around. A tribal village is a tightly knit community in which most of the members are related, help one another in need, and work together in communal undertakings. For such people the significance of land goes beyond its economic value. In other words, the relationship to land involves personal emotional expression, family ties, religious sentiment, social intercourse, and family established habits of behaviour. Unless these cultural requirements are provided in the new settlement or colony the programme of rehabilitation is likely to be resisted and bound to fail.

Social Organization

FAMILY

Family is the smallest social unit which is present in all the tribal communities. It includes a married couple and their children. When a family comprises only parents and their unmarried children it makes a nuclear family. When a family comprises parents and married sons with their wives and children and also unmarried children it becomes an extended family. There is yet another form of family which is called joint family and in this case the members include the seminal married brothers with their wives and children. The joint family may also include their unmarried brothers and sisters.

Among the tribal communities the nuclear type of family is most prevalent. It is common with most of the tribal communities that as soon as a son is married he lives with his wife in a separate hut which is built either close to his parental hut or in some place away from it. As the tribal huts are very small in size it becomes difficult for two married couples to live in the same hut, and therefore the sons live in separate huts after their marriage.

Among all the tribal communities of Orissa the family is patriarchal and they follow unilateral grouping of kins although the family is bilateral in composition.

After marriage a girl follows her husband and lives with him in his parents' house. The descent is counted in the paternal line and that is why the family is patrilineal. The daughter is regarded as a member of her father's clan so long as she is unmarried. After marriage she leaves her parents' house and lives with her husband in his parents' house and becomes a full-fledged member of her husband's family.

The eldest male member of the family is considered the family head. He is usually the father in a nuclear and extended family or eldest brother in the joint family where the father is dead. Being the head of the family the father exercises considerable authority over all other members of the family who are expected to obey him. In a patriarchal society the father owns the property which is ordinarily not divided during his lifetime. After the death of the father the widow mother neither owns property nor is viewed as the family head. In fact, the authority which is vested in the father descends down to his eldest son.

In all cases of tribal communities of Orissa the family is an economic unit. The male and female members have distinctive duties to perform and both men and women work hard in agricultural and other occupational pursuits following sexual division of labour. All the earnings of the individual members go to the common economic pool of the family.

The family also functions as a ritual unit in religious aspects. The ancestral spirits of a family are propitiated by the head of the family and food and drinks are offered to them for their blessings. Before the new food or crop is eaten it is offered to the ancestral spirits at the family altar. On such occasions the members of the family participate in the worship and consume foods which are offered to the ancestors. No outsider including the married daughters is allowed to take part in the worship on given food offered to the ancestral spirits.

Dormitory Organization

One of the most significant features of tribal societies, particularly primitive communities, is the practice of segregation of unmarried men and women. In many tribal communities dormitories both for the bachelors and for the spinsters are in existence and such youth organizations play an important role in social, economic and educational aspects of tribal life. The tribes such as the Juang and the Bhuinya have well organized dormitory system in their villages. Among the Juangs the bachelors' dormitory is called *Mandaghar* and among the Bhuinya it is called *Majag* or *Darbar*. The *Mandaghar* is the largest hut in the village. It has walls on three sides and is open in front. The wooden posts and side walls are carved with decorative symbols depicting geometric designs and figures of animals. The boys hang in walls their *changu,* a flat percussion musical drum which is used at the time of dancing. In front of the *Mandaghar* is a small open space where dances take place almost every night after the day's work is over.

The unmarried boys of a village sleep at night in the *Mandaghar*. The elders of the village assemble at this place for every important events in their corporate life. Here they settle the distribution of swiddens so that the Gods can overhear everything they do. Fire is always kept alight in the centre of the *Mandaghar* and from this place the sacred fire is taken to kindle the dried bush wood in clearings.

In many villages a dormitory for the unmarried girls is maintained. But in most cases maidens' dormitories have disappeared altogether and the unmarried girls sleep in the house of a widow or old woman. In a large measure the dormitory organization may be considered the centre of social, economic and religious life of the village and the tribal cultural traits and identity are preserved and strengthened by institutions of this type.

MOIETY AND PHRATRY

Every tribe is endogamous, that is, a person marries within his or her tribe. Where a tribe is divided into two moieties or halves, each moiety functions as an exogamous moiety : the *Netam* (*Niji banshi* or consanguinal relatives and *Markam* or affinal relatives). In some cases each moiety is subdivided into exogamous phratries. Among the Koyas there are five phratries: 1. *Kowasi*, 2. *Odi* or *Sodi*, 3. *Madkam*, 4. *Madi* and 5. *Padiam*. As per the rules of exogamy a man cannot marry in the same phratry to which he belongs. He can marry in any other phratry to the exclusion of his own.

Each phratry is again subdivided into several clans. Since phratry is exogamous, marriage either within one's own clan or within any of the clans which belong to the phratry is prohibited. For example, the *Madi* phratry consists of 4 clans such as *Punyam, Emla, Oyami* and *Pusami*. Similarly other phratries are also subdivided into several clans. As the phratry is exogamous these clans are non-intermarrying groups. Persons belonging to these clans can marry in other clans which belong to other phratries. In this case the clan is derivatively exogamous, because the phratry to which it belongs is exogamous.

The next social unit is clan which like the lineage group regulates marriage. Persons belonging to a clan believe to have descended from a common ancestor and therefore think to be related to one another by blood. This is the reason why the clan is exogamous. Generally the clans are totemic in the sense that they are linked with animals and plants towards which an attitude of reverence is prescribed, and such animals and plants are not destroyed and used in food by the clan members.

In some cases the clans are non-totemic and are linked with territorial units called *Muttah*. For example, among the Khonds many consanguinal families constitute together an exogamous division called *Klambu*. The members of a *Klambu* claim descent from a common ancestor and occupy a distinct *Muttah*. The division of *Klambu* for all intents and purposes corresponds to a clan while *Muttah* to a clan territory. All the lands within the territory belong to the members of the *Klambu* who cannot parcel out any land to any outsider either by gift, by mortgage, by sale or by any other means.

In the earlier days the clan-territories were homogeneous. It means that barring a few households belonging to warrior and milkman castes, all other households were of the Khond tribe and they were related to one another by blood. That is why a clan territory was exogamous. But those clan-territories nowadays have become heterogeneous and cases of marriage within the territory are found.

Among the Paudi Bhuinyas the descent group conforming to a clan is called *Khilli,* which is exogamous and totemic. Each *Khilli* is subdivided into a number of lineage groups. The broader group is called major lineage which further splits into a number of smaller segment, called minor lineage. In the case of a minor lineage the families who belong to this lineage can identify their blood relationship with one another quite accurately. A major lineage comprises a number of minor lineage and its members believe to have descended from a common ancestor, but vaguely remember who that ancestor was. In the case of a *Khilli,* which comprises a number of mythically related major lineage groups, the idea of common ancestry is still more mythical and vague.

In the past, marriage within the village was forbidden because the people of a village were agnates and belonged to a single *Khilli*. Among the Paudi Bhuinyas the name of the *Khilli* and that of the village are synonymous. Since the members of a *Khilli* are consanguinal, the *Khilli* is exogamous. Since the people of a village are of a single clan the village therefore is exogamous. Village exogamy as observed among the Bhuinyas were based on *Khilli* or clan exogamy. All people belonging to a single clan are not confined to a single village. They are scattered in different villages. Thus, the villages which comprise the related families of a single clan are grouped together to form *Kutumb* or agnatic villages. According to the rules of clan exogamy, a person cannot marry within the same clan, that is, he cannot marry anyone in any of his *Kutumb* villages. The clans in which he can marry are the *Bandhu* or cognatic clans. Like the *Kutumb* or agnatic clans, the *Bandhu* or cognatic clans are also scattered in different villages. Following the principle of clan exogamy, persons of *Kutumb* villages can have marital relationship with those of their *Bandhu* villages in the Bhuinya society.

LINEAGE

Above the family is the maximal descent group in the lineage which comprises a large number families which are related to one another by blood. This group among the Saoras is called *Birinda,* the members of which trace their descent from a common ancestor. In their society in the absence of clans the *Birinda* regulates marriage. The people of a Saora village are of a single *Birinda*. All people belonging to a *Birinda* are not confined to a single village. They are scattered in different villages. Since *Birinda* is exogamous the villages having people of a single *Birinda* become exogamous. With the migration of people from one village to the other, the Saora villages have become multi-*Birinda* in composition. Though majority of people in some villages belong to a single *Birinda* of patrilineal kin, but there are some matrilineally attached kin members, cognates and affines now found living in these villages. In some other villages there may be families of patrilineal kind and of matrilineal affiliation living together in more or less equal number. Inhabitation of families belonging to both consanguinal and affinal social units in a village has broken down village exogamy and has led to marriage between agnatic and cognatic groups within the same village.

VILLAGE

Among all tribal communities the villages in general do not shift from place to place. Every village has a definite location in space and a definite area confined to a specific boundary. Under unusual circumstances, like frequent occurrences of death which are contributed to the wrath of malevolent spirits, the villages are shifted to new sites. Otherwise the location of villages is more or less permanent. The only exception to this settlement pattern is the Birhor settlement. The Birhor is a hunting and food gathering tribe and is semi-nomadic. The tribe is divided into several groups. Each group comprises 10 to 20 families which are mostly related to one another by blood.

The Birhors move from place to place by groups. Each group selects a place at the edge of a forest and each family of the group builds its hut made of twigs and leaves of *sal* trees. The hut is so simple that it takes only a couple of hours for construction. The leaf hut of Birhors is called *Kumbha*. A wandering Birhor group usually has 10 to 20 *Kumbhas* in a place and these *Kumbha*s constitute a Birhor settlement which is called *Tanda*. The group lives in the *Tanda* for a period of three to four months after which it shifts to another place. Every group has its fixed locations for setting up its *Tanda* and their movement corresponds with change in the seasons. If a group is in a particular place in the rainy season, it is in another place in the summer season and in winter it may again change its *Tanda* to a different locality.

Generally every tribal village is a closely knit social entity with a huge measure of cohesion and continuity. Among the shifting cultivators, like the Juang and the Paudi Bhuinya, all the lands which are used for shifting cultivation belong to the village. These lands are distributed among the villagers by the mutual decision taken at the village *Mandaghar* or *Darbar*. As long as a person carries on cultivation in a particular land he is not dispossessed by any means. But as soon as it lies fallow it comes back to the village for redistribution among the villagers.

The social life in a tribal village is more a village affair than an individual concern. The rituals connected with birth, marriage and death require the co-operation of all the villagers. The unmarried boys and girls are viewed as assets of the village rather than as exclusive possession of their respective parents. The villagers help each other in their respective economic activities. In fact, all the preliminary operations connected with the clearing of the plots for shifting cultivation are done by reciprocal help. The village *Mandaghar* among the Juang and the *Mojang* or *Darbar* among the Paudi Bhuinya are maintained properly and kept under regular repair every year with the co-operation of all the villagers. As in the social sphere, the ritual organization of the village also shows elements of community feeling and sense of solidarity. For example, among the Paudi Bhuinyas the elders of the village decide on which date what rituals would be performed and on the appointed days the *Dehuri* of the village officiates in all the village festivals and performs all the religious activities of the village.

The tribal village is also a quasi-political unit. There is a secular headman in every village. He presides over all village meetings where intra-village quarrels and conflicts are settled and matters relating to the development of the village are decided.

MARRIAGE

All tribal communities are strictly endogamous. Any person marrying outside its own tribe is boycotted and other members of the tribe stop all contacts with him until the person is readmitted into the group. As pointed out above, the tribal community is divided into several social units. The major units are moiety, phratry, clan and lineage. The moiety organization divides a tribe into two halves which are exogamous. The Bhunjia tribe of Orissa has the moiety organization. Among some tribal community a moiety is sub-divided into several phratries which are also exogamous. The exogamy of the phratries is derived because the moiety to which they belong is exogamous. Phratry organization is prevalent among the Koyas of Orissa. Each phratry is subdivided into several clans which are exogamous. A clan comprises a large number of families which are related to one another by blood. Naturally marriage within the clan is prohibited. The study of these divisions show that exogamy and endogamy are not mutually exclusive except with regard to the same unit.

Various forms of marriage are prevalent among the tribal communities of Orissa. Some of the common forms of marriage are, arranged marriage, marriage by exchange, marriage by service, and marriage by elopement. In addition to these types, there are a few other types which are known as marriage by capture and marriage by purchase. Preferential mating is also met with in many tribal communities. One of such type is marriage between siblings of unlike sex, that is, cross-cousin marriage. Marriage between siblings of same sex who are parallel cousins is prohibited.

Both sorrorate and levirate types of marriage are also prevalent among the tribal communities. In the case of the former a man can marry his deceased wife's younger sister. If the wife cannot bear a child then her husband can keep her younger sister as his second wife, even if she is alive. In the case of levirate a younger brother inherits the widow of his elder brother. As this custom is socially approved, disparity of age is no obstacle to levirate or sorrorate types of union.

Among all the tribal communities payment of bride price is most common. According to this custom the bride price is paid to the parents of the bride by the parents of the bridegroom. The amount and the contents of the bride price vary from tribe to tribe. Generally the bride price includes one or two bullocks or some goats, some amount of money in cash and some paddy or rice. Nowadays the bride price is generally paid in cash.

POSITION OF WOMEN

The conditions involved in the relations of men and women are many-sided and therefore it would be wrong to assume anything in regard to the status of women in the tribal society without taking into consideration the whole situation. Some scholars are of the opinion that the position of women in the primitive societies is a little better than that of a slave or a beast of burden. She performs the hardest drudgery and endures all her master's brutality without raising any objection. In their opinion if the primitive society changes into a civilized society there would be an automatic improvement in the position of women. They find a strong correlation between the higher status of civilization and higher status of women.

There are other scholars who think that women are in a low status in hunting and food gathering community whereas they enjoy higher status in farming society. In other words, it is their opinion that as the lower economic activities increase to higher economic activities, the status of women is raised from a lower status to a higher status. A review of the facts regarding position of women in tribal societies of Orissa does not prove the above-mentioned assumptions. There is no tribe in Orissa which treats its women as slaves and where women suffer the brutality of their husbands without seeking redress against such ill-treatments.

The tribes of Orissa who are diverse in their means of sustenance have come to share identical view on women. In other words, in many respects the position of women in a hunting and food gathering community is same as that in an agricultural society. That the higher economic activity raises woman's status and the hunting and food gathering life prejudices her status appears to be non-existent in the tribal society of Orissa. The general sexual inequality is seen to be present in all the tribal societies irrespective of its economic life.

Everywhere the influence of inter-tribal cultural relations is seen to be enormous and the idea about the position of women in all the tribal communities is identical in spite of their differences in economic activities, social organizations and cultural patterns.

Generally the women in different tribal societies enjoy enormous freedom and little authority. They participate freely in dance and songs and even drink and smoke in the presence of their elders. They enjoy great freedom in the choice of their husbands. A women is free to leave her husband if he ill-treats her. Wife-beating is strongly condemned. She carries agricultural and forest produce to the village *hat*s and markets and sell there. The women cook food for their family members, fetch water from the hill stream, go out for collecting roots and berries from the forests and for fishing in the nearby hill streams. A woman helps her husband in many agricultural operations. While her husband is busy in cutting the trees she remains engaged in clearing the fields, making holes in the plots for different seeds. Her works also include transplantation of seedlings, weeding of fields and reaping of crops.

She plays a leading part in marriage ceremonies and dances and sings with her friends and relatives on such occasions. In spite of her freedom and higher position she suffers certain restrictions. She is tabooed during her menstruation period. She is debarred from attending ritual performances. She has no right of inheritance of her father's land and property. On her husband's death she gets her maintenance as a matter of right. The husband's family has to pay a bride-price at the time of marriage. It does not mean that the woman is bought in the tribal society. The payment of the bride-price is only to compensate the loss of income which the girl earns for the family. In the tribal society, the woman is a great economic asset and in many societies works harder than men. Among many tribal communities women perform witchcraft and sorcery. Since these acts are dreaded by public, the tribal sentiment is full of reproach towards those who practise sorcery.

PROPERTY

The concept of property and the mode of ownership of different types of property vary from tribe to tribe. In view of this it is necessary to group the tribes according to their means of sustenance and to examine the mode of ownership of property among the hunters and food gatherers, shifting cultivators, pastoral communities and settled agriculturists. There are one or two hunting and food gathering tribes such as Birhor or Kharia in Orissa, but they do not claim any exclusive right over any tract in which hunting and gathering is practised. Everywhere the tracts belong to the government and is under the management of the Forest Department. The hunters and food gatherers carry on hunting and food gathering in such tracts without any legal sanction for doing so. Generally the hunting and food gathering communities are semi-nomadic. They do not stay permanently in any particular place and therefore do not recognize any inheritable claim to any particular area. However, in respect to the movable properties in the form of chattels it is known that personal titles are more clearly established and every man and woman has personal property. Right of women to such possessions as clothes and ornaments is not challenged.

Some interesting customs are observed among the hunters in regard to the sharing of animals killed. Whenever a Didayi kills an animal, all the men taking part in the hut share the kill equally. However the man whose arrow killed the animal receives slightly a bigger share, preferably the whole hind leg and the skin. The Naik, the head of village, irrespective of whether he takes part in the hunt or not gets a share of the kill. All the households in the village and any visitor to the village receive a share of the kill. The *Pallasi,* priest of the village, gets the head of the animal killed.

The pattern of land ownership among the shifting cultivators varies from tribe to tribe. In some cases collective ownership is recognized and in other cases individual owner-ship is practised. Among the Bondos, the tribal opinion recognizes private ownership of the hill clearings. A piece of clearing has become a personal possession which must be preserved and can be inherited. The Bondos sell their clearings among themselves and mortgage them without of course any legal sanction. Similarly every palm tree in Bondo country belongs to someone as private property although no law of the State recognizes this right of possession among them. The palm trees are bought and sold among themselves and this practice has also no legal sanction. If a man has two trees and two sons, each gets one. If he has three trees, each gets one and the produce of the third is equally divided between them.

In the past the Didayi had full freedom to get any forest tract for shifting cultivation (*Bri*). But nowadays they have to take permission from the Forest Department which allots a particular tract in the forest for *Bri* cultivation. The tracts so allotted are divided into several plots which are distributed among the Didayi families by the officers of the Forest Department. The *Bri* plots are in the name of the head of the family and his sons carry on cultivation in such plots even after the death of their father.

Among the Juangs and Hill Bhuinyas, who are staunch shifting cultivators, the lands under shifting cultivation are held in common by the villagers and form the exclusive joint property of the village. The encroachers are punished by way of giving compensation. The village council decides which tract of the forest would be taken up in a particular year for shifting cultivation. The plots in the tract are distributed among the villagers by mutual consent. As long as a man has the cultivating possession of a plot of land under shifting cultivation no one else can dispossess him from the plot. But as soon as he stops cultivating the plot, the land automatically gets reverted to the joint possession of the village.

Among the Khonds, an interesting territorial organization which is known as *Muttah* is noticed particularly in Phulbani district and Rayagada sub-division of Koraput district. The attachment of the

Khonds to a particular tract or territory is due to some mystical reasons. A *Muttah* may consist of 10 to 12 villages. Each *Muttah* has a name and a distinct boundary.

In a *Muttah* the Khonds are in majority and Oriya castes and scheduled castes in minority. The name of the *Muttah* coincides with that of the clan to which the Khond inhabitants belong. The term *Klambu* is used in *Kui,* the mother tongue of the Khond clan, and it is to the *Klambu* and not to the non-Khonds that the soil of the entire *Muttah* belongs.

Formerly a clan-territory was homogeneous, but nowadays it has become heterogeneous. But the alien elements in a clan-territory are not recognized as owners of the land and therefore have no right to worship the *Dharani* (Mother Goddess). Similarly, any type of ritual pollution of the original Khond (*Jombo Tana*) does not affect the alien Khond (*Koda Tana*) and vice versa. Any incestuous offence committed by a member of any tribal and non-tribal community residing in the *Muttah* pollutes the whole *Muttah.*

No tribal community in Orissa is fully pastoral. All the tribal communities domesticate such animals as cattle, goats, sheep, buffaloes and pigs. But the practice of herding is a supplementary occupation, the main occupation in most cases being agriculture.

There is no tribe in Orissa which shows communism in the goods of every kind. However, collective ownership is met with in some cases particularly among the shifting cultivators. In their case the land which is used for shifting cultivation does not belong to any individual but to the village. Joint ownership of property is also noticed in most cases and it is due to joint inheritance from the father. Personal property right in respect of land as well as movable properties is most common among the settled cultivators. In other words, personal titles or private ownership are more clearly established in all kinds of properties, both movable and immovable, among the settled cultivators and pastoral people.

As regards the incorporeal property, private ownership rather than collective ownership is recognized, irrespective of economic gradation of tribal communities. The magic formulae, which serve to banish diseases, lure games, consecrate charms and exercise evil spirits are the monopoly of the magician who does not divulge the formulae to other people. All incantations of the sorcerers are trade secrets. It is believed that to divulge the formulae is to destroy its efficacy. Among the hill Saoras, there are *Shamans* and sorcerers who are excellent icon painters. They are most knowledgeable about the magical formulae and incantations which serve to cure illness and drive away evil spirits. The sorcerers have proprietorship in such magical performances and no one else claims to have any right to such occult controlling mechanisms and magical formulae which are in the exclusive possession of the magicians.

Among all the tribal communities the inheritance of property is patrilineal. After the death of the father the sons divide the paternal property equally among themselves. There is no discrimination on the basis of seniority. Though there's equality in the division of land among the sons the office of the headman or that of the priest descends to the eldest son. Greater freedom is noticed with regard to the acquired belongings. A man is reckoned as the master of what his personal efforts have produced. In some cases the custom of effective utilization is practised in respect of distribution of property. Articles of dress or artefacts made and used by women, such as earthen wares, vessels and ornaments generally pass into the hands of their daughters because they could make use of these objects effectively.

Political Organization

Every tribal group has its political organization which moulds and modifies behavioural pattern of the tribal people in conformity to the traditional norms of their society. In every tribal village there is a village council presided over by the village secular headman to settle disputes and decide matters concerning the welfare of the village.

Other important persons of the village are the Assistant to the secular and religious headmen of the village. Among the Birhors every *Tanda* has a leader who is obeyed by virtue of his personality and quality of leadership. Next in the order of importance is the *Naya,* the priest, and the *Mati,* sorcerer of the settlement.

Both the Juangs and the Paudi Bhuinya have an elaborate form of political organization. Both the tribes have a territory which goes by the name *Pirh*. Each *Pirh* is subdivided into several sub-*pirhs*. Each sub-*pirh* comprises a number of villages varying from three to six villages. At the village level there is a *Pradhan* who is the hereditary secular chief of the village. Equally important is the hereditary priest called *Buita* who presides over all religious ceremonies and ritual activities. Among the Paudi Bhuinyas the secular headman is called *Naek* or *Padhan* and the religious head is called *Dihuri*. Every Paudi Bhuinya village has a village council which comprises village elders known as *Bhal Bhai* as members. The secular head of the village presides over the council and the religious head remains present in all the sittings of the council to assist the secular headman in all deliberations.

As pointed out above, a group of villages forms a small territory which is called sub-*pirh* and all such smaller territories taken together make a wider territorial organization which is called *Pirh* organization. Each sub-*pirh* has its own council which is presided over by a headman called *Sardar*. The *Padhan*s of the villages which make a sub-*pirh* organization are the members of the sub-*pirh* council. Every sub-*pirh* has its own tutelary deity which is worshipped on the occasion of annual hunt called *Jatalpuja*. At the *pirh* level there is an apex territorial organization which comprises the *Sardar*s of all the smaller territorial organization as members. The seniormost among them presides over the *pirh* council whenever it sits to deliberate matters concerning the whole tribe.

The political organization which is found among the Saoras is somewhat different. The entire Saora country was divided in the past into several administrative units called *Muttah* and each *Muttah* head was called *Bissoyi,* a low country man appointed by the landlord or *Zamindar* who was the chief of the entire Saora country. In each Saora village there is a secular headman called *Gomango* and religious headman called *Buya* and both of them take leading part in the village meeting. The Saora pay *mamools* to the Gomango and also provide labour to him whenever necessary for thatching his houses and tilling his fields. Every *Gomango* pays some tributes both in cash and in kind to the *Bissoyi* who in turn pays certain amount of *peshkush* to the landlord.

Similar *Muttah* organization is prevalent among the Khonds. Every Khond village has a priest who is called *Jani*. Next in position is *Bish Majhi* who collects revenue from the village. These two leaders and the village elders constitute the council at the village level. A group of villages make a *Muttah* which represent the inter-village council. The *Muttah* head is known as *Mandal* who settles inter-village matters.

With the introduction of statutory *gram panchayat* and elective system after independence, the traditional political organization as outlined above among different tribal groups has been considerably weakened. However, the secular and religious headmen are still effective and continue to perform their respective duties with wholehearted co-operation from the people.

Religion and Magic

The universe in which man lives is full of adverse forces which are more powerful than him. He is ought to take the necessary steps in time for his adaptation to the universe and for his security against these forces. Otherwise it would be extremely difficult for him to lead a healthy and peaceful life in the universe. Religion and magic deal with the measures which man takes to control these forces. In the evolutionary sequence of development it is thought that the religious and magical aspects of human society and culture had developed long before the agricultural and pastoral pursuits of man began.

The simple definition of religion is the belief in spiritual beings. The religion of the primitive man is animistic. By animism it means that every creature is endowed with a soul capable of continued existence after its death and disintegration. It is also concerned with a spiritual world which is inhabited by both benevolent and malevolent deities. The belief in spirits leads to various types of ritual activities and active worship.

Many primitive communities believe in animation of inanimate objects. Such attribution of life to the inanimate objects is called animatism. Many scholars think that animatism is antecedent to animism. Whether it is animism or animatism the basic forces of religious belief has grown out of the twin concept of *Mana* and its counterpart taboo. The term *Mana* stands for supernatural power which attaches itself to persons and things and which can be transmitted from one individual to the other. The term taboo means restrictions imposed upon individuals to come in contact with things charged with such supernatural powers. The scheme of things as expressed in the religious and magical beliefs of any people comprises their world-view or cosmology.

Various measures are adopted by man to solve the problems created by the supernatural beings and to control the spirits. The elaborate manner in which the problems are tackled takes the form of rituals and ceremonies. The man resorts to prayer in some cases and occult mechanism and magical performances in other cases to propitiate the deities and control the spirits. Almost all tribal communities have their respective ritual functionaries who perform the ritual activities both at the household level and at the village or community level. Generally the religious headman takes recourse to prayer and supplicates the deities by offering food and prayer. While the approach of the priest to the concerned deities in his prayers is humility and submission, the attitude of the magician in his magical performances is demand and aggression. The magic spell is held to exercise a compulsion over whatever power summons whereas the prayer is a supplication that may or may not be granted at the will of the Being addressed.

Those who take the course of prayer and supplication are called religious headman and in most cases the post of a religious headman is hereditary. As regards the magic it takes various forms. There are broadly two types of magic, black magic and white magic. The former is of the wicked character practised by witch doctors through various methods of witchcrafts whereas the latter is purely beneficent practised by sorcerers and *shamans* to counteract witchcraft. The magical methods are of two types : Imitative (Homeopathic) and Contagious. The Imitative magic is based on the concept that imitation of any action results in identical action. But in the case of the Contagious magic, a contact with the object or any part of the object, which is the target of the magic, is necessary for producing desired magical effect on the object in contact. In magical performances both charms (fetish) and spells are used to achieve desired results.

There are two categories of persons who are skilled in controlling supernatural beings, one is a diviner and the other a *shaman*. The diviner resorts to two types of divinations for controlling the supernatural powers. In one case, the devices used for this purpose are independent of the diviner and in the other case the devices enable the diviner to have contact with the divine spirits. The shamanism is different from divination. A *shaman* who practises shamanism is endowed with supernatural powers to cure illness and physical pain and other physical troubles. He is one who by calling his spirit can find out which evil spirit has caused illness in the person and what measures need to be taken for healing and curing. One thing which is common with both the diviner and the *shaman* is their spirit possession. When they are in this state they represent for the time being the concerned spirit which is invoked to appear in them and who speaks through them whatever they want the spirit to reveal.

Art, Dance and Music

Though the primitive tribes are at a lower level of economic development as compared with agricultural and industrial communities, their sense of beauty is in many ways of a superior order. The innumerably varied forms of art objects which reflect beauty show that the primitive mind is endowed with a creative imagination which is of a superlative degree. The tribal communities in general and the primitive tribes in particular enjoy considerable freedom while living in close relationship with nature. The sense of joy and pleasure finds outlet in their artistic workmanship and handicrafts, music and dancing. In short, the aesthetic drive of the tribal communities which has been the source of joy and enjoyment is, so to say, the essence of their life and interwoven with other aspects of their culture.

The artistic skill can be divided broadly into two categories; Graphic art and Plastic art. Drawing, engraving and paintings are the most common items of the graphic art whereas carving and modelling and such other techniques which involve the manipulation of materials to yield three-dimensional forms represent plastic art. The speciality in tribal arts and crafts is that with poor technological equipments the tribal communities are able to produce first rate objects of art, beautify their simple tools and peck out beautiful designs on wood and bamboo. With the locally available simple materials such as bark, wood and grass, they turn out beautiful textiles and ornaments of various types and musical instruments which speak of their fathomless creative impulse and technical skill.

The primitive tribes differ from one another in their art objects, art-forms and art-styles as they do in other aspects of their culture. For example, the combs of various types made by the Juangs from wood and bamboo with beautiful designs engraved on them are their speciality. Similarly the carving of door with traditional designs is a highly specialized quality of the Khonds. Different media are used by different tribal communities to exhibit their respective artistic skills and tastes for beauty. The Santal houses found in northern Orissa and the Saora wall paintings found in southern Orissa can be mentioned to illustrate the point. The Santals use soils of various colours such as white, yellow, red and black to paint the walls of their houses. The combination of colours used for the paintings of walls and the designs of lines, animals and flowers drawn manually on the walls and on the borders of doors make the Santal houses distinct from those of other communities. The wall paintings as seen among the Santals is exclusively for the purpose of beautifying and decorating their houses.

The Saora houses are depicted with wall paintings completely in contrast with those of the Santals. The Saora houses are single roomed and the wall paintings are on either side of the entrance as well as inside the house. The wall painting of the Saora is of the type of icons which represent unidimensional shrines dedicated to different spirits and sometimes modern-wheeled vehicles such as bicycles, jeep, motor car, aeroplane, are drawn as objects belonging to the spirits. The motifs drawn in icons are not for beautifying or decorating walls but for magico-religious purpose of satisfying supernatural beings. Icons are also drawn to satisfy earth goddess so that the fertility of the soil is enriched and the yield of the crop is increased. The drawing of icon is exclusively taken up by the male *Shamans* who are required to observe fasting and abstinence from any sexual act before taking up the work. Among the Santals such restrictions are not required and it is a daily work on the part of the house-wife or any woman of the house to apply colour on the walls and draw designs of various types in order to give the house an attractive look.

The artistic skill of the tribal communities is not confined only to decoration of houses, carving of doors, and engraving of combs, weaving of clothes and making some embroidery on them. Such creative ability is also reflected in their artefacts and handicrafts. For example, the basketry work of the Juangs showing various techniques of weaving is most attractive and durable. The intense sense of beauty which is a special feature of the tribal mind is observed in the arrangement of hairs into a bun decked with combs and flowers and in the adornment of their body with ornaments made of local materials.

The tribal communities are very fond of dancing and singing. Their sense of joy and pleasure finds outlet in music and dance. The music of the tribal society, accompanied by dance in which men and women, young and old participate, carry true emotional appeal. Every festival and every occasion of marriage are observed in accompaniment of music and dancing. After a day's toil both boys and girls gather at a place and spend time in the evening and late hours at night in dancing and singing. The musical instruments which are used by the tribal communities are of various types. Some of these instruments are drums (kettledrum, single or double membraned drums, bowl-shaped drums), tambourine, and other types of percussion instruments cymbals, gongs, harps, flutes, fiddles and dancing rods, which are all made by themselves out of locally available materials. Some people are so creative that, with the help of small pieces of bamboo splits kept between lips, they produce music of sweet melody by closing and opening of lips and moving the tongue inside the mouth. The split-string instrument used by the Bondos is an example of this type.

2

A Short Ethnographic Account of Different Primitive Tribes of Orissa

THE BIRHOR (MANKIDI/MANKIRDIA)

Introduction

MANY tribes of India depend upon hunting and food gathering for their subsistence. The means of livelihood is such that these hunting communities are invariably nomadic. Some of them have very little contact with any other communities while some others are in contact to some extent and have developed a symbiotic relationship with them. The Birhors, a nomadic tribal community of northern Orissa, fall to the category of such a hunting and food gathering group which has reciprocal economic relations with their neighbouring peasants.

The main concentration of the Birhors is in Bihar where their population was 3,464 as enumerated in the 1971 census. Their number in Orissa during the same census period was 98.

It may be noted that the local people identify the Birhors in various ways. In the district of Kalahandi and Sundergarh they are called as Mankidi whereas in Mayurbhanj and Sambalpur districts they go by the name Mankirdia. In fact, both the Mankirdia and the Mankidi are one and the same and they both are none but the Birhors. But in the 1971 census the Birhor, the Mankidi and the Mankirdia have been enumerated separately because they have been enlisted as separate tribal groups in the list of Scheduled Tribes of Orissa. Taken together the Birhors including the Mankidis and Mankirdias numbered 1,307 persons in 1971 census.

Their distribution in different districts of the State according to 1981 census is given in the Table — 2.1.

Table 2.1 : Distribution of Birhors

Sl. No.	*Name of the district*	*Communities*			*Total population*
		Birhor	*Mankidi*	*Mankirdia*	
1.	Bolangir	1	1	142	144
2.	Balasore	11	0	65	76
3.	Cuttack	11	0	1	12
4.	Dhenkanal	0	4	66	70
5.	Ganjam	11	0	0	11
6.	Kalahandi	0	0	25	25
7.	Keonjhar	1	0	224	225
8.	Koraput	3	6	3	12
9.	Mayurbhanj	0	123	256	379
10.	Phulbani	0	0	0	0
11.	Puri	1	0	3	4
12.	Sambalpur	70	30	69	169
13.	Sundergarh	33	38	151	222
	Total	142	202	1005	1349

The reason for calling Birhors as Mankidi or Mankirdia is that they are skilled in catching monkeys. When the monkeys create havoc in the rural areas and destroy crops, fruits and vegetables, the local people employ the Birhors to catch and kill them. The Birhors belong to the Austro-Asiatic language group and according to their mother tongue the Birhor means men (*Hor*) of the forest (*Bir*). They are dark-skinned, short-statured, long-headed, wavy-haired and broad-nosed people.

There are two types of Birhors — the *Uthal,* i.e., nomadic Birhors and the *Jagi,* i.e., settled Birhors. It is to the nomadic section of the tribe that our attention is directed in this report. The Birhors move from place to place in different groups in a specified area within the State.

Each group comprises on an average 10 to 15 households. Some of the households may be related to one another by blood and others by marriage. A Birhor camp is called *Tanda,* which is generally set-up in a place close to the forest and near some market centre and peasant village.

Material Culture

The Birhors demarcates three seasons in a year: rainy season, winter season and summer season. The change of place is frequent in summer season than in other two seasons. In fact, the Birhors stick to a place where they set-up their *Tanda* and stay for all the four months in the rainy season (June to September). Their *Tanda* is located in a place which is very close to a market centre and also to the mountain ranges covered with thick forest. With the destruction of the forests, it is becoming very difficult nowadays to find such place. Under such circumstances nearness to the market centre is given more preference to that of the forest while selecting a place for setting up the *Tanda.*

In winter season the Birhors feel the need for changing the camp two or three times. But such changes are more frequent in the summer season because of the shortage of food supply in a particular place. The barks of Siali creepers which is the main forest produce to which their subsistence and livelihood is intimately attached are available in plenty in rainy season and therefore shifting of *Tanda* is not necessary in this season.

The situation in the summer season is different. In this season the forest growth is affected by the hot sun and forest fires. Moreover, the wanton destruction of the forest by some tribal communities who practise shifting cultivation and by the non-tribal people who gather fuelwood from the forest make it difficult for the Birhors to get the required amount of bark in one place and therefore they are forced to change their camp two or three times.

A list of the places where the Birhors of our observed group generally set up their *Tanda* in different season is given in Table 2.2.

Table 2.2 : Seasonal change of locations of Tanda

Sl. No.	*Name of the place*	*District*	*Season*
1.	Nilgiri	Balasore	Rainy
2.	Kendumundi	Mayurbhanj	Rainy
3.	Melana	Keonjhar	Rainy
4.	Satkosia	Mayurbhanj	Winter
5.	Dhokota	Keonjhar	Winter
6.	Gudabhanga	Mayurbhanj	Winter
7.	Dongadiha	Mayurbhanj	Winter
8.	Hathikocha	Keonjhar	Winter
9.	Nadinocha	Keonjhar	Winter
10.	Marichapal	Keonjhar	Winter
11.	Tamaka	Keonjhar	Summer
12.	Kaliapani	Cuttack	Summer
13.	Angul	Dhenkanal	Summer
14.	Daitari	Keonjhar	Summer
15.	Nandara	Keonjhar	Summer
16.	Patalikota	Keonjhar	Summer
17.	Harichandanpur	Keonjhar	Summer
18.	Janghira	Keonjhar	Summer
19.	Jaikeshi	Keonjhar	Summer

The Birhors make their huts in leaves. A hut which is called *Kumbha* is conical in shape having an oval-shaped base, covering in circumference about 50 ft living space inside. The height of the *Kumbha* at the centre is 5 ft.

There is an entrance in the middle on the long side of the hut which is 3 ft in breadth. The *Kumbha* is divided into three compartments. On the right side of the entrance is a space set apart for the Kitchen. During rains when cooking is not possible outdoors, the food is cooked at this place. The central part is used for sleeping. On its left side there is a place which is used for storing things. In the rear portion of the hut, the goat-pen is present on the right side while the fowlpen is on the left. The pet-dog of the family finds its place either in the sleeping portion or in the rear end of the hut according to its convenience. A door called *Bagdir,* made of twigs woven in leaves, is used to close the entrance when the family members are out for hunting and gathering in the forest.

The *Kumbha* is made of saplings thatched with twigs having leaves. A wooden beam supported by two forked wooden poles which are struck to the ground holds the frame of the *Kumbha* in position. Rafters laid on either side of the beam are covered with twigs and leaves. Wooden splits one inside and the other outside the *Kumbha* are tied to each other by means of Siali barks to keep the rafters intact. The hut is thatched very skillfully to make it rainproof.

A household has its own *Kumbha* in which parents and children sleep at night. In addition to individual *Kumbha*s there are two other types of *Kumbha*s in every Birhor *Tanda*. One *Kumbha* known as *Kudi Ada* is for the unmarried girls.

The *Tanda* is heterogeneous in clan composition and each clan has a small hut of its own set apart as the shrine of the clan deity. The clan members offer food and worship the deity in this place.

As the Birhors lead a nomadic style of life they keep their household belongings to the minimum so that they can move from place to place conveniently. Table 2.3 gives a list of their household articles, domesticated animals, processed products and miscellaneous items of objects which were found in a *Tanda* during our fieldwork. This inventory concerns five Birhor households of a *Tanda* which was located at Kendumundi, a multi-caste village 17 km away from Karanjia on the Karanjia-Thakurmunda road in Mayurbhanj district.

Table 2.3 : Inventory of household belongings

Name of the item	*Guni Mankirdia*	*Ram Das Mankirdia*	*Akala Mankirdia*	*Kailas Mankirdia*	*Kasia Mankirdia*	*Total*
Food-stuffs						
Rice	2 kg	1 kg	3 kg	2 kg	3 kg	11 kg
Oil	100 gm	50 gm	200 gm	100 gm	250 gm	700 gm
Maize	—	—	—	—	1 kg.	1 kg.
Spices	Rs. 2	Re. 1	Rs. 3	Rs. 2	Rs. 3	Rs. 11
Dried monkey meat	1 kg.	—	2 kg	—	1 kg.	4 kg
Processed Products						
Rope	20 mtr	—	—	10 mtr	20 mtr	50 mtr
Broom	1	1	—	—	1	3 nos.
Sling	2	1	1	1	2	7 nos.
Halter	1	2	1	3	2	9 nos.
Mat	1	2	2	2	6	13 nos.
Net (monkey catcher)	1	1	2	1	1	6 nos.
Net (squirrel catcher)	1	1	—	1	1	4 nos.
Adornments						
Ornament	1 pair ear-ring (rolled gold)	—	1 necklace (rolled gold)	—	—	2 sets
Talcum powder	1 pkt. (50 gm)	—	1 pkt. (50 gm)	—	—	2 pkts. (100 gm)
Clothes (in piece)	6	6	8	6	7	33
Comb	—	1	—	—	1	2 Nos.
Animals and Birds						
Goat	1	8	2	3	4	18 nos.
Poultry	—	1	2	—	4	7 nos.
Dog	—	—	2	1	1	4 nos.
Utensils						
Cooking vessels (big)	2	1	2	3	2	10 nos.

Name of the item	*Guni Mankirdia*	*Ram Das Mankirdia*	*Akala Mankirdia*	*Kailas Mankirdia*	*Kasia Mankirdia*	*Total*
Cooking vessels (small)	2	2	2	—	1	7 nos.
Aluminium utensils	—	3	3	4	4	14 nos.
Bell bowl	—	—	—	—	2	2 nos.
Tools and weapons						
Knife	2	2	1	1	1	7 nos.
Axe	2	4	2	2	2	12 nos.
Wooden flattened stick	3	2	—	—	4	9 nos.
Vegetable cutter	—	—	—	—	1	1 no.
Miscellaneous						
Ladle made of coconut shell	—	1	—	—	—	1 no.
Bamboo (big) basket	2	3	2	2	4	13 nos.
Monkey hide	2	1	—	—	2	5 nos.
Bamboo (small)						
Basket	1	1	—	1	3	6 nos.
Bottle	4	3	—	2	1	10 nos.
Bag	1	—	—	—	1	2 nos.
Container						
Made of net	1	—	1	1	—	3 nos.
Snail shell	20	—	—	—	—	20 nos.
Peacock tail	1	—	—	—	2	3 nos.
Low wooden						
Stool	1	—	—	—	2	3 nos.
Fuel	5 kg	—	10 kg	—	5 kg	20 kg
Lamp (earthen)	1	1	—	1	1	4 nos.
Bolster	1	—	—	—	5	6 nos.
Bamboo yoke	1	2	1	1	2	7 nos.

Name of the item	*Guni Mankirdia*	*Ram Das Mankirdia*	*Akala Mankirdia*	*Kailas Mankirdia*	*Kasia Mankirdia*	*Total*
Grain measuring pot	—	1	—	—	2	3 nos.
Sac	—	—	1	1	1	3 nos.
Musical instrument	—	—	3	—	3	6 nos.
Water container	3	—	2	—	2	7 nos.
Halter meant for goat	1	8	2	—	4	15 nos.
Umbrella (cloth)	—	—	1	—	—	1 no.
Glass	—	—	1	—	—	1 no.
Bamboo stick	—	—	1	—	—	1 no.
Torch	—	—	1	—	—	1 no.
Spoon	—	—	2	—	2	4 nos.
Leaf cups and plates	—	—	1	—	10	12 nos.
Plate (Aluminium)	—	—	—	1	5	6 nos.
Match box	—	—	—	—	1 pkt.	1 pkt.
Herbal medicines	—	—	—	—	1 boxful	1 boxful

Economic Life

The main occupation of the Birhors is the making of ropes out of the bark of Siali creepers (Lama Bayer), which are used for different purposes. A list of the types of ropes and cost per unit and the manner of use is given in Table 2.4.

The Birhors also make small baskets (*Tupa*) out of the Siali bark which are used for pressing oil seeds. Except the baskets and the ropes used for tying the buffaloes which cannot be prepared by women, all other types of ropes are made by both men and women. One load of Siali barks is sufficient to turn out ropes and baskets

Table 2.4 : Outturn of ropes made by Birhors

Sl. No.	Local term	Birhor term	Cost per	Use nit	Daily outturn
1.	Sika (sling)	Sikur	Rs. 5.00 per pair	Attached to carrying pole for carrying things on shoulder	2 pairs per head
2.	Pagha	Pagha	Rs. 1.00 per piece	Rope for tethering cattle	20 pieces per head
3.	Barkai (Rope for drawing water)	Barehi	Rs. 4.00 per piece	Used for drawing water by means of water pots from wells	10 pieces per two persons
4.	Pandachhati (Halter for buffalo)	Kadadogha	Rs. 5.00 per two pieces	Rope in which buffaloes are tethered	8 to 10 pieces per head
5.	Chhelipagha (Halter for goat)	Meromioda	5 paise	For tying goats per piece	20 pieces per head
6.	Jaunli	Dhaunri	Rs. 2.00 per four pairs	For tying cattle at the time of harvest	10 to 12 pieces per head

worth Rs. 20 and a person can exhaust a single load of barks in two days. On an average a Birhor turns out finished products of barks, worth Rs. 10 to Rs. 12 per day.

The animals and birds which the Birhors are fond of keeping at home are goats and chickens. They keep these animals and birds to sell in the market for cash and to offer them to their deities on ritual occasions.

The Birhors are skilled monkey catchers, they use nets made of Siali creepers for catching monkeys. They eat the flesh of the monkey and sell the skin for cash. Use of turmeric in the preparation of curry out of monkey's flesh is a taboo among the Birhors. It is believed that the use of turmeric will make them unsuccessful in their monkey hunting. Sometimes they catch birds with the help of snares, and squirrels, hares and deer with the help of traps and nets. The birds and animals caught are generally disposed of in the neighbouring villages or at the market place for cash.

Many Birhors know-how to do the weeding, transplanting and harvesting of paddy and find employment in agricultural labour during such operations. In many places they earn substantial amount of money from these sources. Sometimes they collect roots and tubers, fruits and flowers from the forest for consumption purposes, but there are other types of forest products such as resin which they collect for selling to the local people for cash. They also catch mongoose and peacock and sell them to the local people who like to keep them as pet animals and birds.

The staple food of the Birhors is rice. With the sale proceeds of ropes and forest produce they buy their weekly requirements of rice, corn, millet and other things from the market. They collect various types of green leaves from the nearby places and mushrooms and various types of fruits such as Kendu, Jackfruit and Mango from the forest for their own consumption. Whenever time permits during their trip to forest for collection of barks, they dig out roots and tubers and also collect honey which supplement their principal cereal diet.

In many places cocoons are available in forest and the Birhors are well acquainted with these places. The cocoons add to the income of the Birhors in the form of cash which they use for buying clothes.

Although the Birhors tap different sources for their livelihood they run deficit of their food supply almost every year. During the scarce period they eat mango kernels which are preserved at home for use in such different times.

The weekly budget of a Birhor family may throw more light on their living conditions. For this purpose the weekly income and expenditure of the family of Sandu Mankirdia stationed at Kendumundi is given below. The budget related to the period from 19 to 25 August, 1984. The family of Sandu Mankirdia comprises his old mother, brother and brother's wife and his daughter.

The income of the week was drawn from the following sources.

1. Sale of bark products		
(a) Tuppa	4 jhala (12 pieces)	Rs. 20.00
(b) Sika	3 pairs	Rs. 15.00
(c) Pagha	4 pieces	Rs. 4.00
(d) Pandachhati	3 pairs	Rs. 15.00
(e) Chhelipagha	4 pieces	Rs. 2.00
2. Income from wage earned by Sandu's daughter 9 pailas of paddy		Rs. 11.25
3. Saving from previous week		Rs. 12.00
	Total	**Rs. 79.25**

Items of expenditure are as follows:

1. Foodstuffs		
Rice 6½ kg		Rs. 20.00
Dal		Rs. 0.50
Brinjal		Rs. 2.00
Potato		Rs. 0.50
Onion		Rs. 0.25
Spices		Rs. 0.50
Salt		Rs. 0.50
Mustard oil		Rs. 0.50
2. Drink		Rs. 10.00
3. Items of fried-food and mutton curry taken with wine		Rs. 2.00
4. Tiffin		Rs. 1.25
5. Clothes and ornaments		Rs. 13.00
6. Tobacco		Rs. 0.50
7. Kerosene		Rs. 0.40
	Total	**Rs. 51.75**

The Birhors do not have any staple income from week to week. The maximum amount of weekly income is of the order of Rs. 60 and the minimum Rs. 20. A Birhor family having five members like that of Sandu Mankirdia needs at least 7 kg of rice per week which costs Rs. 20 to Rs. 25. This means that when the weekly income is limited to Rs. 20 to Rs. 25 the Birhors purchase rice much less in quantity than what is required per week in order to buy other items which are badly needed in daily life.

Among the Birhors a man needs three pieces of clothes annually for his use. One piece is worn another piece is used for covering the body and in case the cloth which is worn gets wet it is replaced by the third piece which is kept at home. A piece of cloth costs Rs. 12 to Rs. 15 and a man needs about Rs. 40 annually towards the cost of his clothes. In case of a woman she needs only two pieces in a year which costs Rs. 60. The male folks have now started wearing shirts and the female folks petticoats and blouses which increase the expenses of the Birhors on clothing. A woman wears bangles and hair-pins to keep the tassel in position in the hair bun.

The Birhors use different types of oil for different purposes such as coconut oil is massaged in the body and also for dressing hair, mustard oil for cooking food and *Mohua* oil (Tola) for lighting lamps. The Birhors are conversant with the techniques of extracting oil from *Kusum* and *Mohua* seeds by using wooden oil press. The process of extraction is that they break the seeds into small pieces and boil them. Thereafter the boiled powdered seeds are kept in small baskets. Two fully filled-in baskets are kept one upon the other and both are kept between the two planks of wood which comprises the oil press. One end of these two planks is tied tightly and inserted into a groove made for this purpose in a tree and the other end of the lower plank is kept to rest on a big piece of stone above the ground and the filled-in oil-seeds baskets are pressed by lowering the upper plank so as to tightly press the baskets until the oil comes out. The oil which is extracted from the seeds is collected in an earthen pot which is kept below on the ground.

The Birhors use earthen vessels for cooking food. They also use earthen pitchers for storing water. They buy these earthen vessels from the weekly market from the potters on payment of cash. A big earthen pot costs Rs. 3 and an earthen pitcher costs Rs. 1.50. A household needs two pitchers and two or three earthen pots. They go on using these vessels until they break. Generally, two earthen pitchers and two to three earthen pots which are required in the minimum in a Birhor family having four to five members, last for three to four months. During the transit from one *Tanda* to the other the belongings which are carried by them to the new camp include the earthen vessels.

Aluminium pots and pans are in use in all the Birhor households. One bowl, one plate and two to three cups constitute the aluminium vessels in a Birhor family. Leaf cups are still common in all the Birhor households for taking cooked food. Brass pots and plates are almost conspicuous by their absence among them. Inventory of household articles in a Birhor *Tanda* located at Kendumundi shows that there were only two brass plates found in the whole of that *Tanda*.

Bamboo baskets are needed to store things at home. The Birhors get the baskets at the weekly market from the basket makers on payment in cash. A basket of minimum size costs Rs. 2 and two baskets of this size last for a year or so. The Birhors use mats for sleeping. Palm-leaves are used for weaving the mats which is the work of the women.

The Birhors of Kendumundi *Tanda* don't know the use of bow and arrow and therefore do not have them. The only weapon which has multipurpose use is axe. Local blacksmiths supply these axes and an axe costs about Rs. 5 and lasts for about five to seven years. It is sharpened periodically by the local blacksmiths on the market day and each time it costs 50 paise per sharpening. In some houses people have knives. A knife costs Re. 1 and is used for peeling off the bark from the Siali creepers.

Cloth umbrella is a new household item which may be found in one or two households in a *Tanda*. For instance, there were only two such umbrellas found in two households out of a total of nine households which comprise the Birhor *Tanda* at Kendumundi. The people use country lamps fed with kerosene in all the households. But a few of them use lanterns. The inventory shows that there were two lanterns in the *Tanda* at Kendumundi. The lantern requires kerosene worth 50 paise per night whereas the house can be lighted for two nights with a country lamp at the same costs.

The Birhors have neither mortar and pestle nor country husking lever. Whenever they get the paddy as their wages, they dry it at home and thereafter take it to some house in the nearby village to get it husked.

Our observation of the economic life of the Birhors shows that they lead a life which is full of hazards and hardships and below the level of subsistence. Even though they live hand to mouth they appear to be very joyful and contended. Almost in every evening both the boys and girls join together and spend time in singing and dancing in accompaniment of music from flute and drum.

Social Organization and Social Control

The family which is the smallest social unit among the Birhors is invariably of nuclear type. It comprises father, mother and unmarried children. In some cases either the widow mother or the widower father lives with their married son in his family. The grown up sons and daughters work for the family with their parents until they are married. But they sleep at night in their respective dormitories.

The next higher social unit is clan which regulates marriage. Clan is exogamous and any sexual union within the clan is incestuous. Our study of the Birhor *Tanda* located at Kendumundi shows that it was composed of the following five clans:

1. Singhkili
2. Hembrum
3. Nagpuria
4. Majhi and
5. Sikria.

As the *Tanda* is multi clan in composition, inter-clan marriage within the Tanda is in vogue among the Birhors. The genealogy which was collected from different households of this *Tanda* shows that the male members have brought their wives from several *Tanda*s such as Dhardhara and Mahulidia of Mayurbhanj district, Nilgiri of Balasore district, Dhudaram and Ghatgaon of Keonjhar district, Kaliapani and Tamka of Cuttack district. Cross-cousin marriage is not practised among the Birhors. But marriage of Sorrorate and Levirate type are in vogue.

Whenever the people of a *Tanda* want to shift to a new place all the households of the *Tanda* move *en bloc* and set-up their *Tanda* there. Before the huts are constructed, a ritual is performed by sacrificing two goats and five chickens and offering prayers to ancestors. A man can leave his parent *Tanda* at will and join a new *Tanda* elsewhere. There will be none to obstruct him from leaving the old *Tanda* and joining the new one. He is also at liberty to return to his parent *Tanda* at will where he will be received by the inmates of the *Tanda* cordially. It is a practice that the newcomer offers drink to the people of the *Tanda* and to the *Tanda* headman for their acceptance of his coming and living with them in the *Tanda*.

There is a headman in each *Tanda* who is called *Mukhya* or Big man and this post is normally handed down from father to son. The *Tanda* headman combines with him the functions of religious headman (*Dehuri*) and in this capacity he worships the deity and associates in all the ritual performances. There is no system of any payment to the secular-cum-religious headman for the services rendered by him. But some times he is given wine and tiffin particularly on market days by his *Tanda* members as a gesture of fellow feeling, generosity and hospitality. It is noteworthy that harmony and friendship is maintained throughout among the households in a *Tanda*. If any conflict arises between some households, the *Tanda* headman settles such conflict through the personal intervention and arbitration.

The Birhors follow the practice of social boycott which is called *Chindal* or *Began*. The person who is kept under boycott is not allowed to mix with others and all kinds of help which he was ordinarily getting from others are withdrawn. It is a sort of punishment for a correct measure to bring a deviant or any person suffering from certain ritually unclean illness back to the normal position.

The situation which invokes social boycott is incestuous sexual union between brother and sister or persons belonging to the same clan. Persons who commit such offences are kept segregated until they pay the fines levied on them by other members of his *Tanda*. Generally, the fine comprises 1 kg of rice, some turmeric and Rs. 10 in cash. The ritual involved for readmitting the deviant into the *Tanda* includes clean shaving of his head and giving him a clean bath.

When any person develops maggots in the sore of any part of the body, this person is also put under social boycott until the sore is healed and the above-mentioned ritual is performed accompanied with a common feast in the *Tanda*. The person who was put under boycott meets the expenses of the ritual and feast.

As regards the inter-caste and inter-dining, the Birhors eat cooked food in the houses of Santals and Kolhas but the reverse is not in vogue. The communities which they avoid in this respect are Muslims, Harijans and Kharias. Any breach of the commensal rules leads to social boycott and the consequence arising therefrom.

Life-Cycle

The Birhor idea of life is a continuous process from birth to death through infancy, adolescence, youth, marriage and old-age and lastly death. He regards himself as the supreme creation of earth and has been bound by supernatural influences. The death, which brings life to an end takes him to the unseen world where a man is transformed into spirit and starts influencing the human beings of this world.

BIRTH

The birth of a baby is a matter of great rejoicing among the Birhors. Pregnancy is very much welcome. An impotent woman is considered inauspicious. A couple having children enjoy a higher status than a childless counterpart in Birhor society. The father is addressed as *Aba* and the mother as *Mai* and those who are addressed as such feel proud of themselves whereas those having none to address them as such feel depressed. When a baby is born in a Birhor household, it is believed that one of the ancestors has taken rebirth and therefore the family's fortune and well-being have come back with greater potency and vitality. Among the Birhor a male child is preferred to a female child because the latter leaves her parents after marriage and therefore is of limited economic utility.

Some of the symptoms of pregnancy are stoppage of menses, feeling of weakness and nausea. With the abdominal protuberance, the pregnancy becomes conspicuous. During pregnancy a woman observes some restrictions and is relieved from doing hard work and cooking, more particularly in the advanced stage. Most often she is not allowed to go outside or come in contact with dead body and move near the shrine (*Sal*). She is forbidden to take consecrated meat. While going out of her house she must cover herself completely with her clothes, least enemies or persons with evil eye should do her some harm.

As soon as the woman feels labour pain, an old woman of her lineage having experience in delivery is immediately called for. In difficult cases some herbal medicines are given to the pregnant woman. As soon as the child is born the old woman who was attending on her informs the husband thereafter, and it takes no time for others to know about the birth of the child. The umbilical cord of the child is cut by means of a sharp snail.

After birth, the mother and the child are considered unclean. It is interesting to note that with the birth of a child the whole *Tanda* comes under ritual pollution as does the family in which the birth took place. The whole *Tanda* is considered impure and all the rituals are suspended for a period. On the 7th day the *Dehuri* (priest) comes and performs the ritual which is meant for the final purification of the *Tanda* members and for the preliminary purification of the new child and his parents.

On the 21st day a ritual is observed and only the kin members are invited to participate. On this day the mother is led to the nearby source of water where her women relatives smear her with turmeric paste mixed with *Mohua* oil and all the accompanying women take ritual bath there and return to her house. Coming to the house she throws the old used earthen pots and cooks in new pots which have been brought previously. The father shaves the baby's head with a razor. In the meantime the *Dehuri* worships the clan deity and the supreme deity *Logo Bir* and *Budhi Mai* and a black cock and a white one are sacrificed. The sacrificial meat is cooked and a small feast is arranged. On the following day a name is given to the baby by the elderly women of the *Tanda* and another feast is arranged to feed the assembled relatives and guests.

MARRIAGE

Marriage is considered a significant event in one's life. One cannot think of adult life without being married. The marriageable age in the case of a girl is 14 to 18 years and in the case of a boy is 20 to 25 years.

In a marriage ceremony the bride's parents meet all the expenses and the bridegroom's parents pay the bride price which comprises Rs. 12.00 and three pieces of clothes. The guests and relatives invited to the marriage ceremony contribute according to their might.

There is no specified month in which the marriage takes place. Generally the best time for marriage is after the rains when people have some savings in hand and the guests and relatives are entertained without difficulty. Before marriage the boys and girls have to spend at least two years in their respective dormitories and thereafter the marriage is thought of. Most of the marriage are of arranged type in which negotiation is held between the parents of the bride and the bridegroom to settle details regarding the bride price, the date of marriage, the number of guests and relatives to be invited and the bridal feast.

The day on which the marriage takes place, the bridegroom's party consisting of bridegroom, his friends and relatives come to the bride's house. The marriage is solemnized there in the presence of the *Tanda* elders. The bridegroom smears vermilion on the forehead of the bride which symbolizes solemnization of marriage. The bride's father provide cooked food and drink to the bridegroom's party.

The boys and girls of both the parties, dance and sing in great joy and happiness to the tune of their drums and other musical instruments. After the marriage ceremony is over, the bride and the groom with the party return to the latter's *Tanda* where the father of the groom arranges a feast for them.

DEATH

When the death of a person takes place in any house other members of the house send the news to all the people of their lineage. The natural death according to the Birhors, is that which comes when a person is very old. If any person dies prior to the old age it is believed to be due to the machination of the evil spirits and sorcerers. On getting the death news the near and dear ones come to console the bereaved family and make necessary arrangements for the burial of the corpse. The women-folk smear turmeric paste on the face of the dead body and a piece of new white cloth is covered all over. A wooden frame of the type of a ladder is made and the dead body is laid on it and is carried to the burial ground (*Gachhad*) by four lineage members while others accompany them.

A trench of about 6 ft into 3 ft into 5 ft in dimension is dug by the relatives in the burial ground. It is dug in such a way that the head can be kept in the south-west direction.

The new white cloth is spread on the floor of the trench on which the dead body with face upward is laid. Thereafter the trench is filled up with soil. Big stones are kept on the pit so that the jackals and other animals may not dig out and eat up corpse.

After the burial is over all the pall-bearers and the members who accompanied go to a place where water is available and take bath there. The family observes mortuary pollution for a period of ten days. On the tenth day, the head of the household (male member) goes to the burial ground and calls the spirit to his own hut and sets fire to the small leaf hut erected there for the spirit. An earthen lamp is kept burning and is covered under a winnowing fan in the house till he comes. As soon as the man bearing the spirit enters the house, the light under the winnowing fan goes out which indicates the entry of the spirit of the dead into the hut.

Sometimes in the midday all the lineage members and the pall-bearers get purified by the *Dehuri* (priest) who arranges a ritual in front of the shrine of the clan deity (*Ora bonga*) and sacrifices a cock and offers *mohua* wine and cooked food.

Thereafter, he sprinkles water all over the *Tanda* and the lineage members. In the evening a feast is arranged and the elderly persons of the *Tanda,* lineage members and other invitees participate in the feast. After the feast is over, all the invitees give consolation to the members of the bereaved family and leave for their respective *Tandas*.

Religious Beliefs and Practices

The Birhors believe in many gods and goddesses. According to them some of these supernatural beings are benevolent and others malevolent who create trouble and cause illness and death. They also worship their ancestors at home on several ritual occasions. Generally, ancestor worship is practised with the purpose of enjoying good health and for being successful in hunting and collection of forest produce without meeting any accident.

Logo Bir and *Budhi mai* are the two main and supreme deities of the Birhors. It is believed that their abode lies in the thicket of Similipal hill ranges and they are worshipped in different months particularly in the months of *Aswina* (September-October) and *Pausa* (December-January). In the month of *Margasir* (November-December) the ancestors are worshipped at home and in the month of *Bhadrab* (August-September) a deity called *Karma Thakur* is worshipped. The main idea of worshipping such deities is to get their blessings for the general well-being of the people and for getting food all the time and also for achieving success in their various economic activities without falling into any accident and illness. Table 2.5 and Table 2.6 give description of different deities and the months in which they are worshipped.

Every clan has its own clan deity for which a small leaf hut is constructed in the *Tanda* and food and prayer are offered to the clan deity on all ritual occasions.

The Birhors have fallen victims to family planning programmes. The demography of the tribe does not show any alarming increase in population which warrants limitation of Birhor population. According to the 1971 census the population of the Birhors was only 92. In such a situation there appears no need for the Birhors to adopt family planning practices. But it is found that many Birhors have got themselves sterilized in order to get financial assistance. During our fieldwork we have met with two such instances in the Kendumundi Birhor *Tanda*. Some unforeseen events and drastic consequences took place soon after they were operated upon and people attributed these mishaps to the vasectomy to which these two Birhors ware subjected.

In both the cases they lost their wives within a period of three weeks from the date of operation and thereafter one of them lost all the children and the other who had two sons and one daughter lost all his sons. Both of them were young and capable of bearing children. The Birhors strongly believed that their supreme deity got angry with these two people for undergoing operation and punished them by causing death to the members of their families with the objective of leaving none to continue in the progeny. There was no escape from this divine punishment and as a result the family planning practices are dreaded in the Birhor community. One of the vasectomized victims pathetically expressed during the interview that he was very keen to get married second time but no woman was willing to marry him because in the Birhor society barren women are looked down upon.

Strategy for Development

The Birhors lead a nomadic style of life. As the seasons change they move from one place to the other. But in all the seasons they try to have the *Tanda* very close to forest. The Similipal hill ranges, around which most of their *Tanda*s are situated are vitally linked with their economic life. They collect Siali bark from the forest to make various types of ropes which are in great demand in the farming community. The transactions between the Birhors and the local peasants take place at the weekly markets, it is for this reason that they set up their *Tanda*s near such marketplaces for conveniently disposing of their finished goods and forest produce for cash income.

The Birhors are skilled monkey-catchers. When there was no restriction to catch monkeys in the reserved forests they set nets in some convenient places in the forest to catch monkeys. They eat monkey flesh and sell the monkey skin to the Scheduled Castes for cash. Sometimes when the monkeys create havoc in the villages and destroy crops their help is sought on payment of money to catch and kill the monkeys.

As they live close to the people who carry on agricultural practices, they have observed various agricultural operations and most of them have experience in ploughing land, sowing seeds, transplanting seedlings and other types of agricultural works such as weeding, manuring and harvesting. Both men and women of their community are employed by the farmers on wage basis to help them in various agricultural operations. The income from agricultural labour is seasonal and therefore not very substantial.

The occupations which feature prominently as substantial sources of income among the Birhors are rope making which is their primary source of livelihood, and goat keeping. The Birhors buy young she-goats from the weekly market at a nominal cost of Rs. 40 to Rs. 50 and raise them properly to bear kids which they sell when they attain full growth. These grown up goats are in great demand in the rural areas and, therefore, fetch substantial amount of money to the Birhors. Sometimes they also buy goats of one year old at Rs. 60 to Rs. 80. After rearing them for a year or so, they take them to the marketplace for sale. These goats also fetch them very substantial income which varies from Rs. 140 to Rs. 160 per goat.

It is the opinion of the Birhors that they no longer want to move from place to place. Instead they are very eager to settle down permanently in some place and carry on cultivation of paddy. They have expressed that they need land, plough, bullocks and seeds for this purpose. From our discussions with them we found that they were interested in having tile roofed permanent houses in place of leaf thatched huts.

Sometime back, the Project Administrator of Karanjia Integrated Tribal Development Agency supplied 25 kg of jute to each of the Birhor households of Kendumundi *Tanda*. They accepted the jute and manufactured ropes and sold them at the local market. Since such kind of help did not continue, the Birhors reverted to their old practice of making ropes from Siaḷi barks. They pointed out that as compared

Table 2.5 : Deities and their Worship

Sl. No.	*Name of the deity*	*Direction in which deity's abode is located*	*Name of the worshipper*	*Ritual designation of the worshipper*	*Village to which worshipper belongs*	*Month in which deity is worshipped*	*Articles of offering*	*Purpose of worship*	*Remarks*
1.	*Logo Bir* (the supreme deity)	North-west direction of the village Kendumundi, i.e., somewhere in the Similipal forest	*Dehuri* and other members of all the *Bansa*s	*Dehuri* as also, every head of the household	Male Members of all the *Tanda*s	November December	Ten cocks and two bucks are sacrificed on behalf of all the *Tanda* members	Overall well-being	*Logo Bir* and *Budhi Mai* are the husband and wife and others except *Chandi* are their children. They all have a society of their own. The *Dehuri* of the *Tanda* worships these deities on behalf of all people of the *Tanda.* All the family members of *Logo Bir* serve as custodian of the Birhor society and provide security, food and drink to the people. They also save the people from danger and other calamities. As the people say, "we are moving in dense forest and have no permanent settlement. There is none to help when we are in distress and in danger. You are our everything, we pray you to keep us out of danger and mishap and grant us good health and long life."
2.	*Budhi mai* (Wife of *Logo Bir*)	North-West	*Dehuri* and other members of all the *Bansa*s	*Dehuri* as also, every head of the household	Male members of all the *Tanda*s	November-December	Ten cocks and two bucks are sacrificed on behalf of all the *Tanda* members	Overall well-being	Beings good luck and good health to children

Sl. No.	Name of the deity	Direction in which deity's abode is located	Name of the worshipper	Ritual designation of the worshipper	Village to which worshipper belongs	Month in which deity is worshipped	Articles of offering	Purpose of worship	Remarks
3.	*All Mai* (Daughter heir)	Ditto	Ditto	Ditto	Ditto	Ditto	Ditto	Ditto	Overall well-being. No such specific reason worshipped as the daughter of *Logo Bir* and *Budhi mai.*
4.	*Sita Mai* (Daughter of *Logo Bir*)	Ditto	Ditto	Ditto	Ditto	Ditto	Ditto	Ditto	—
5.	*Bhandar Bir* (son of *Logo Bir*)	Ditto	Ditto	Ditto	Ditto	Ditto	Ditto	Ditto	Brings success in catching monkey.
6.	*Chandi* (Not a member of *Logo Bir* family)	Some where in Simipal hills	*Tanda* priest	*Dehuri*	*Tanda*	All through the year before starting for hunting	white cock		To ensure success in hunting

Table 2.6 : Clan Deity (Ora Bonga) of the Hembrum Clan

Sl. No.	*Name of the deity*	*Direction in which deity's abode is located*	*Name of the worshipper*	*Ritual designation of the worshipper*	*Village to which worshipper belongs*	*Month in which deity is worshipped*	*Nature of offering*	*Main reasons*	*Remarks*
1.	*Karam Bonga*	The shrine (Sal) is in the back-side of the worhship-pers *Kumbhas*	Hembrum	Household head of each *Bansa*/clan (Males only) clan	Elderly male members of each *Tanda* who belongs to Hembrum	August-September	Two bucks *Mohua* wine, Sun-dried rice	For curing illness particu-larly fever	If someone falls ill, he promises before *Karam bonga* to offer sacrifices to get rid of the illness. In an auspicious day in the month of August-September, the *Dehuri* worships the deity at the shrine and offers prayer and food and sacrifices animals and birds as promised earlier by the *Tanda* members.
2.	*Nasan Bonga*	Resides in the same shrine	Do.	Ditto	Ditto	Ditto	Pig	For hea-ling disea-ses, fever, cough, cold, fests and giddiness.	The worship in the case of this deity is same as that of *Karam bonga*
3.	*Rajakodin Bonga*	Ditto	Do.	Ditto	Ditto	November-December	Cock (Sims)	To get rid of typhoid	He is believed to be the supreme clan deity. Cocks are sacrificed to appease him.

N.B. — The tutelary deities are kept inside a cow-dung plastered bamboo basket in the form of small wooden sticks of different sizes covered with *sal* leaves.

with bark-made ropes, the jute-made ropes fetched them a higher price and there was no need for them to move from place to place in search of fibres. As the help from the ITDA did not come forth on a continuing basis they had to go back to their nomadic way of life in order to get the raw materials for making bark-ropes.

The strategy that emerges from this study for the development of the Birhors is their rehabilitation in agricultural colonies which should be set-up close to marketplaces and not far from places where they set-up their *Tanda*s around Similipal hill ranges. Each household should be allotted adequate land with title rights over it. The beneficiaries of each colony should be provided with plough bullocks, seeds, fertilizers and any other inputs required for growing crops. The most important point in any rehabilitation is people's participation in all works concerning the settling up of the colony. Therefore the beneficiaries of each colony should be motivated for their physical and emotional involvement in clearing the land and irrigation works, digging wells, constructing houses, building approach roads and schools. The cost of materials including labour charges should be borne by the government and payment made daily at the end of the work and in no case contractors should be employed for any work in the colony.

The Birhors are excellent rope makers. As they would settle down in a colony permanently they may not get *Siuli* bark in sufficient quantity throughout the year. In that case jute may be supplied to them on a regular basis for making ropes. Goat rearing is another vocation in which they have gained vast experience. Each household should be provided required units of goats for rearing. These two subsidiary occupations will not only fetch them sufficient cash to meet their expenses on clothes and daily necessities but also help effectively in stabilizing their new sedentary mode of living in the colony on a permanent basis.

THE BHUNJIA (CHUKTIA)

Setting

The Bhunjia tribe is found in large concentration in the Nuapada subdivision of Kalahandi district. They are confined to the Sonabera plateau in Komna block of the same subdivision. Their population as per 1981 census was 9075 of which 6839 Bhunjias were enumerated in Kalahandi district and the remaining Bhunjias are scattered in such districts as Koraput, Sambalpur, Sundergarh, Mayurbhanj and Bolangir. Except few Bhunjia villages which are homogeneous, most of the Bhunjia villages are heterogeneous in caste composition. The castes and tribes which live with Bhunjia are the Gond, Gonda and the Kultas.

The Bhunjias are divided into two groups, namely, Chuktia who live in the hills, and Chinda who live in the plains. The Chuktia Bhunjia villages are generally of linear pattern in which there may be one main street with one or more small lanes branching out of it. The individual houses are located on either side of the village street. The Chuktia villages are all situated in the valleys and plateaus and sometimes in the foot-hills.

The layout of the houses of the Bhunjias is of a peculiar type. Two or three or more households take a wide open space and build their own houses there. A Bhunjia household has generally three rooms, such as the living room which is bigger than other two rooms. Cattleshed built adjacent to the living room and the kitchen room which is the smallest and built at a little distance in front of the living room. It is enclosed on all sides. The Bhunjia keep fowls and the fowl pen is located at a little distance from the main house. Houses are not provided with windows. The walls of the houses are made of wooden poles plastered with mud mixed with cowdung. The outer surface of the wall is given a thin plaster with locally available white or red earth. The roof is thatched with wild grass collected from the forest. The cowshed and goat pen are made of wooden planks. It is taboo among the Chuktias to use any kind of tiles or *Khappars* for thatching purposes.

The kitchen shed is held most sacred. No outsider is allowed to come anywhere near the kitchen shed not to speak of any physical contact with it. In case any outsider touches any part of the kitchen shed the entire shed is razed to the ground and the thatch is immediately burnt. Utmost sanctity is observed in matters of cooking food in the kitchen shed. No member of the house is allowed to eat food inside it. Even no charred wood from outside is used in the oven inside it. It is through this idea of observing pollution and purity associated with the kitchen shed and culinary practices that the tribe maintains its identity as a community separate from all other tribal communities.

Economic Life

The Bhunjias depend upon shifting cultivation and low land paddy cultivation for their livelihood. Food gathering and hunting, animal husbandry, fishing and wage earning are supplementary sources of income. As regards shifting cultivation, which is known as *Bewar,* a piece of swidden is cultivated for two years. In the first year crops like *ragi, kangu, suan, kodo, jhudung* are grown, and in second year crops like *gulgi, biri* are grown. The clearing is left fallow after the second year for a period of three to four years to recuperate.

Besides shifting cultivation, the Bhunjias practise low land paddy cultivation. They follow improved agricultural practices like raising seedlings and transplantation, application of pesticide and fertilizer. *Bajra, janhi* and cucumbers are grown in lands which are close to their houses. These crops are followed by mustard crop.

Fruits of various types such as *kendu,* mango, jackfruits, *mohua,* tamarind, *jamun* are collected from the forests. Eggs of jungle hen, peahen and pigeon are also collected for consumption.

Social Organization

The tribe is divided into two exogamous moieties: the *Netam* and the *Markam*. Each moiety is composed of several non-inter-marrying groups known as *Barga*.

All the people of a moiety consider themselves to be related by blood with one another. As the Bhunjia villages are inhabited by people of both the moieties, marriages are held not only outside but also within the village.

Political Organization

Each Bhunjia village is an independent socio-political unit having its own village council and a group of traditional leaders. Their traditional village council comprises a corporate body of elderly male members called *Bhala Bhai*. The traditional office bearers of the village are *Pujari, Chhatriya, Katariya,* and the eldest male members of all *Barga*s. The village council settles disputes and adjudicates matters relating to partition and inheritance of property, adultery, incest and irregular marriage. The village council also fixes the date of seasonal rites and festivals and time for clearing the hill-slopes for *dahi* cultivation.

The Bhunjias have also an inter-village council. The head of the council is called *Kurha* who presides over the council.

Life-Cycle

BIRTH

Among the Bhunjias a male child is preferred to a female child. A pregnant woman observes many restrictions. She does not go to the burial ground and is restricted to do hard work. She is forbidden to take sacrificial meat. Birth takes place at home in the living room. An elderly woman of her lineage acts as the midwife and cuts the umbilical cord with an arrowhead.

On the sixth day, the purificatory rites are observed. On this day the mother is led to the nearby river or the hill stream where she takes her bath along with others who accompany her. Her brother's son makes a new oven within the enclosure of the kitchen shed and cooks food there in new earthen pots. As a purificatory measure all used earthen pots are thrown away from the kitchen shed. After taking bath the mother and others return to the house where they feed the children of the family as well as of the neighbouring households. Thereafter all others take food. On this day the baby is shaved by the nephew with the help of a new blade.

Among the Bhunjias puberty rites are observed. The first rites preparatory to puberty rites takes place when the girl is of 10 years of age. All the girls of this age of the village undergo this ritual together at a time. On this occasion all the girls take a ceremonial bath and walk seven times around an arrow fixed on the ground. A girl who has undergone this ritual is eligible to marry and is forbidden to take food in the house of others and also in marketplaces.

The puberty rite is observed on the 7th day after the first menstruation. On this day the girl is led to the nearby river by her mother's sister where she takes bath. On return she goes straight to the house of her mother's brother's wife (*Ata*). On reaching her house she is given a brass pot filled in with water which she carries to her own house and with the brass pot enters into the kitchen shed and starts cooking food in a new oven made by herself for this purpose. Her entrance into the kitchen shed and preparation of meals by her are symbolic of the fact that she is free from pollution.

MARRIAGE

Of all types of marriage, the arranged type in which negotiation is held between the parents of the bride and bridegroom is held the best. The Bhunjias do not have any custom of paying any bride price. But the payment of dowry is a recent phenomenon in their society. The marriage takes place at the bride's house and it is solemnized by walking around the sacred post accompanied by the traditional priest who perform the marriage ceremony. After the marriage ceremony is over the bridegroom return to his village with the bride and feast is arranged by the groom's father and all the assembled guest and relatives are entertained with the feast.

DEATH

On getting the death news the near and dear one's and the relatives visit the bereaved family to console the members of the family and make arrangements for the burial of the dead body. The dead body is laid on a bamboo frame and carried to the burial ground. A new cloth is spread on the floor of the trench on which the dead body with face upwards is laid and some new clothes are spread upon it. Thereafter the trench is filled in with soil fully packed from top to bottom.

Those who participate in the burial take bath and return to the house of the deceased. They are given new clothes to wear and food to eat. The nephew sprinkles cow's milk all over the house and throws away all the used earthen pots and cooks food in a new pot. After the food is cooked he shaves the head of the eldest son of the deceased. After the shaving is over he puts on a new cloth and goes straight to the burial ground to offer food to the departed soul. On return from the burial ground arrangements are made for entertaining the assembled guests and relatives with food and drink.

Religion and magic

The Bhunjias believe in a supreme deity called *Sunadei*. This deity is installed in a shrine at some convenient place in the village. The functionaries who are connected with the worship of *Sunadei* are mainly of three types, namely, *Pujari* who offers food and prayer, *Chhatriya*, whose duty is to hold umbrella wide open at the time of worship and *Katariya* who sacrifices animals.

Besides the supreme deity the Bhunjias believe in many gods and goddesses. Each of the *Bargas* is associated with the worship of a particular deity. For example, a section of the Bhunjia community is known by the surname *Barge* which worships earth goddess (*Mati Deota*). The people bearing the surname *Barge* are known as *Mathiar*, a term of which is derived from the word *Mati* (earth).

Different sections of people belonging to both the moieties of the tribe have been assigned different deities to worship. Every section has a place of origin and the abode of the deity is located in the place which is assigned to it. For example, *Sunadei* is assigned to the section called *Pujari* whose original habitat is Sunabera village where the shrine of *Sunadei* is located. Similarly *Thakur Deota* is assigned to the section called *Bada Majhi* whose place of origin is traced to Badagarh village and it is at this place the shrine of the *Thakur Deota* is located.

The Chuktia Bhunjias observe certain restrictions in their life as prohibited by their supreme goddess *Sunadei*. These restrictions are (1) use of husking lever (*Dhenki*), (2) use of any kind of charpai or cot and (3) use of tiles or *Khappars* for thatching. The Bhunjias have been observing these prohibitions very strictly.

THE BONDO

Setting

The Bondo with a population of 5895 (1981) is one of the primitive tribes found only in the Malkangiri district of Orissa. They are confined to the hill ranges of Khairput block of this district. Because of the long inhabitation of the tribe in this region, it is known as the Bondo country and the hills present in this region as the Bondo hills. The Bondo belongs to Proto- Australoid racial stock and speaks Remo, a speech which belongs to South Munda group of Austric family. They are sometimes referred to as the Bondo Paraja.

According to a legend, the Bondos were living in this area since ancient times. There is a water place called *Sita Kunda* in Mudulipada, the central Bondo village. During their banishment for 14 years, Ram, Sita and Lakshman used to frequent this area and Sita used to take bath in *Sita Kunda*. One day when she was taking her bath some Bondo women who were passing by saw her taking bath naked and therefore laughed at her. Being insulted Sita got angry and cursed them to go naked with shaven head so that all people would laugh at them.

There are two important villages namely Mudulipada and Andrahal flanked by a distance of 14 km from each other. The Bondos living in Mudulipada and in villages around it are known as Bara Jangar Bondos, the primitive section of the tribe having no contact with any other tribe, whereas those living in Andrahal and in villages around it are in close contact with the Gadaba tribe and considerably influenced by them. In addition to them, there are Bondos living in the plains who are influenced by the neighbouring Hindus. The Bondos are very backward in respect of education. The level of literacy was at 3.61 per cent in 1981 as compared with 13.96 per cent for the total tribal population of the state. The standard of education is so deplorable among the Bondos that there may be hardly one or two matriculates in the community.

The easiest approach to the Bondo country is through the newly constructed 7 km long Khairput, Mudulipada road. In its meandering course it climbs hills to height of about 3000 ft. above the sea level up to a point in a hill range called *Banapacheri* from which it gradually descends to the Bondo villages amidst jackfruits, mango and tamarind trees. The climate of the Bondo country is characterized by pleasant summer, cool winter and heavy rains during monsoon. The Bondo country is heavily deforested on account of the practice of shifting cultivation. No valuable timber is to be seen anywhere in the region.

Material Culture

SETTLEMENT PATTERN

A Bondo village consists of several streets each belonging to a clan all situated close to one another in a cluster. The houses in a Bondo village lie scattered conforming to a pattern of shapeless cluster. From a distance at a higher place the houses appear as if they have been built on terraces one below the other.

HOUSES

The house of a Bondo is of gabled type with slopes on four sides. It has two rooms — the bigger of the two is used for sleeping and cooking food while the another is used as granary. The house has an enclosed verandah on all sides. The front verandah is the place where guests and relatives are entertained and the family members spend time gossiping with visitors. The goat pen and pig sty are provided in the back verandah. The fowls are accommodated in a fowl pen made of bamboo splits. A separate shed is built close to the house for the cattle to be tethered. The walls of the house are made of bamboo splits plastered with mud and the roof is thatched with a kind of grass locally known as *pir* which is grown abundantly in the forest.

DRESS

The dress of the Bondos is so peculiar that they are quite distinguishable from all other tribal communities. The Bondo women have a clear shaven head with band of *Caryota urens* (*Salap*) fitted round it. They wear large number of necklaces of coloured beads and metal neck rings. A self-woven small piece of skirt called *Ringa* put round the waist string keeping the upper part of the body exposed completes the whole dress of the Bondo women. The *Ringa* hardly reaches the thigh and is not of sufficient length to go round the waist, as such the upper part of the body remains uncovered. The adult boys are fond of wearing metal rings in fingers and ears, and metal bangles and like to adorn their hair with combs. The loin clothes of male and skirts of female and also the clothes of children are woven at home by means of indigenous looms. Not cotton yarn but fibrous yarns prepared from the bark of a plant locally known as *Kode* are used for weaving the clothes used by them. The characteristic ornamentation of the bachelors is their head bands made of leaves of the tree called *Ariei*.

Economic Life

The economic life of the Bondos revolves round agriculture. They practise three types of agriculture — shifting cultivation in the hill-slopes, upland cultivation at the foot-hills and paddy cultivation in irrigated terraced lands. In addition to agriculture, they collect roots and tubers, fruits and flowers and also do hunting in the forest. The kitchen gardens which are in close proximity to the houses are used for growing maize, tobacco, vegetables and chilly during the rainy season.

The Bondos have developed an excellent adaptive strategy by which the local resources are harnessed by means of their own skill for their survival. With great ingenuity and imagination they have scooped out lands by the side of the small hill streams in the valley and made them into narrow terraces in which they grow long duration rice of fine quality by transplantation method. Seedlings are raised in seed beds and transplanted in the terraces, and the streams flowing nearby are channellized to irrigate these lands. The variety of rice which is produced in these fields is locally famous for its fragrance.

The swiddens in which shifting cultivation is practised are held in common by different clan groups of a village. Each household freely cultivates a patch of any size as per his capacity within the area demarcated for his clan group. A patch of swidden is cultivated for three years consecutively by rotation of crops and is left fallow till it sufficiently recoups for use again.

Social Organization

The family among the Bondos is of nuclear type and consists of parents and unmarried children. Soon after their marriage the sons build separate houses of their own and live independently. A daughter after her marriage goes to stay with her husband. Both husband and wife enjoy equal position in the family.

The next higher social unit is the clan or *Kuda* which is exogamous. It comprises a number of families who are believed to have descended from a common ancestor. These clans are named after the functionaries of the village such as *Badnaik, Challen, Dhangra Majhi, Muduli, Kirsani,* and *Sisa*. Formerly the villages used to be inhabited by the members of single clan. But in course of time the villages have become multi-clan in composition. Nevertheless each clan in a village acts as cohesive group in all socio-cultural and economic activities.

Marriage is regulated not by clan alone but also by village. Even though the village is multi clan in composition, it is considered a sacred entity and the sacred food offered to the village deities is shared by all who treat one another as brothers and sisters. In such a case marriage within the village is out of question. Besides the village exogamy the Barajanagar group of 12 villages observe exogamy. No marriage takes place between boys and girls belonging to these villages. They marry in villages outside this group of villages.

The next social unit is moiety or *Bansa* which divides the Bondo tribes into two groups, namely the *Hantal* (cobra) and the *Killo* (tiger). The moiety is totemic and the members of a moiety look upon its totemic animal with reverence. A moiety comprises many clans and is ordinarily exogamous. But due to unequal population size marriage within the moiety has become inevitable. As a result the function of the dual organization among the Bondos has been affected.

Political Organization

The Bondos are very much individualistic and go by their own individual views. Nevertheless they are equally democratic in spirit. All the members of the Bondo society act as a cohesive unit and abide by a set of uncodified customary and moral sanctions. Public opinion and group conscience work most powerfully towards conformation of social norms and cultural traditions. In every village there is a village Panchayat comprising secular headman, religious headman and elders of the clans. The village assembly or *Sindibor* is an important place in the village. The decisions arrived at the Panchayat are generally unanimous and strictly adhered to by all concerned.

The officials of a Bondo village are the secular headman (*Naik*) and his assistant called *Challan*. All the elders of the village are members of the village Panchayat. When there is something to be discussed the village messenger or *Barika* informs all the members about it and calls them to attend the Panchayat. The *Barika* is a scheduled caste who lives in the village. He is an important person in the sense that he leads the villages on the occasion of communal hunt which is held in the month of March-April. He acts as a liaison agent between the Bondos of his village and outsiders. He remains in contact with the police and forest officials and keeps the Bondos informed about the cases lodged against them.

Every Bondo village has a religious headman who is known as *Pujari* or *Sisa* and an astrologer-cum-medicine man called *Disari*. The former performs all communal rituals and festivals and the latter fixes auspicious days on which festivals are to be observed. He is also a specialist in herbal medicines and performs magical rites for curing diseases.

The Bondos have a confederacy comprising 12 villages which are included in the Brajanagar cluster of villages. The head of the confederacy is called *Bada Naik* which is selected out of the *Naiks* of the 12 villages. All these *Naiks* assemble in the precinct of *Patkhanda Mahaprabhu* under the sacred Banyan tree at Mudulipada on *Magh* festival day and select the *Bada Naik* of the village. The *Naik* of Mudulipada puts a vermilion mark on the forehead of the newly selected *Bada Naik* and the *Naiks* tie pieces of a red cloth in his forehead. He is seated on the thorns fitted to a chair and lighted lamp and incense waved before him as part of oblations befitting the occasion. His tenure is for a period of three years and is given an acre of lowland to cultivate and enjoy the produce.

Life-Cycle

BIRTH

When a woman conceives and becomes pregnant after marriage, it becomes a matter of great rejoicing and happiness. The pregnant woman is forbidden to go to the burial ground and come out of her house when there is thunder and lightning.

The birth takes place in the living room and the mother-in-law and some women of her clan attend the delivery. After birth the child is rubbed with chaff mixed with turmeric paste and castor oil and is given a bath in tepid water. No food is given to the child except tepid water on the first day. But from the second day onwards the child is given mother's milk. The mother is given hot rice gruel mixed with turmeric and vegetable till the final purificatory ceremony is performed on the 15th day. The umbilical cord is cut by means of an arrowhead and turmeric paste and leaves of a wild creeper is applied to the naval stump to stop bleeding and for healing.

When the boys and girls become nine to ten years of age they are admitted to their respected dormitories, *Selanidigo* in the case of the girls and *Ingersin* in the case of the boys. The youth dormitories occupy the core of the village life. Its main social function is to impart training to youths in dance and music and in the traditional myths and folklores of the tribe. It also strengthens the sense of social unity and cohesiveness and solidarity of the tribe. For the Bondos, the life in the youth dormitory is considered the best period in their life.

MARRIAGE

In the Bondo society the husband is younger in age than the wife. The age of marriage in the case of a boy is 10-12 years whereas in the case of girls it is between 15 and 20 years. There are cases of girls of 32-35 years of age marrying boys of 15-18 years of age. The reason for the peculiar custom is that the wife will have an able and strong husband to take care of her in old age.

Before marriage takes place the girl comes to the boy's house on a four-day visit and works hard to prove her physical capacity. Similarly, the boy goes to the girl's house and stays there for four days and works hard to prove that he is physically capable.

On the day of marriage the women of the boy's clan go to the bride's village to fetch the bride. They stay there one day and return with the bride the next day. On arrival at the groom's house, the bride distributes cooked rice and meat which she brought along with her among the members present at the groom's village. After reception of the girl at the groom's house both the groom and the bride are kept confined in a room temporarily. After sometime they are released from their temporary confinement. This is done in order to give the marriage a social recognition that the boy and girl have become husband and wife as approved by the society.

After the bride is released she is taken to the kitchen room to cook food which is offered to the ancestral spirits and hence forward the bride is recognized as the housewife. All the guests and relatives present there bless her and accept her as a member of the groom's clan.

Among the Bondos payment of bride price is common and it is paid sometime after the marriage is over.

DEATH

The Bondos believe that the death is due to the work of the evil spirits and effects of black magic and witchcraft. They practise both cremation and burial. The corpse is carried only by the clan members to the cremation ground. The eldest son sets fire to the pyre. After the pyre is set on fire the mourners leave the cremation ground and come to a stream where they take bath. The neighbours feed the mourners on their return from the cremation ground.

The purificatory rites are held on the 10th day. On this occasion the relatives and friends gather at the deceased's house. Rice and beef are cooked and offered to the departed soul at the cremation ground. The guests and relatives are also given food and drink and with their help a memorial stone is erected close to the deceased's house observing elaborate rituals at high cost.

Religious Beliefs and Practices

The Bondos believe that their world is full of supernatural powers which direct and control the life and activities of human beings and therefore their attitude towards this power is one of reverence and fear. They perform many rituals and festivals in order to propitiate and supplicate these supernatural beings and ancestral spirits.

Among the Bondos the *Patkhanda Mahaprabhu* is believed to be the supreme being. The deity stands for the Sun and the Moon. He is considered benevolent. *Patkhanda Mahaprabhu* is represented by a sword which is lodged in a banyan tree in the sacred grove at Mudulipada village.

Development and Change

The habitat which the Bondos inhabit is rugged and mountainous and difficult of access on account of lack of road communication. The long isolation of the tribe in this hilly and inaccessible terrain has militated against their progress and development. Ignorance and illiteracy, ill-health and addiction to liquor and homicidal character have all contributed to their backwardness and stagnation. One advantage which the Bondos enjoy is that, unlike other tribal communities like Saoras and the Khonds who are exploited by the Dombs and Panos, they are free from exploitation by any outside agencies. But the *Goti* system which exists among them is responsible for the rich Bondos exploiting the poor Bondos and keeping them in debt bondage in perpetuity.

Since the time of Fifth Five-Year Plan there has been concerted efforts to bring about all round development of the Bondos. Following the new strategy for tribal development, a Micro Project was launched in the Bondo area in the year 1976-77 which covered all hill Bondo villages. With the sincere attempts made by the Bondo Development Officer and his team of workers, the Bondos have adopted many developmental schemes and have become very much interested in improving their socio-economic condition. Apart from the changes in their economic condition, the Bondos have become very friendly and have given up homicidal character to a large extent. They have started growing several new crops like potato, wheat, pulses, ginger and vegetables with the help of improved techniques of cultivation. They have also taken to plantation of many fruit bearing trees such as mango, banana, guava, *lichi, sapeta,* orange, lemon and coconut trees in their backyards. Wells have been dug in Bondo villages and the Bondos no more go to the hill streams for fetching water. Adult literacy classes have started in villages and both men and women are being taught to read and write by a group of dedicated workers. Continuous efforts of the Micro Project staff are yielding results in the matter of weaning the Bondos away from their drinking habits and in bringing about change in their homicidal propensities to a great extent.

THE DIDAYI

Setting and Settlement

The Didayi is one of the primitive tribes of Orissa. It is a small tribe and according to 1981 census their total population was 1977. The name of the tribe as per their language is not Didayi but they identify themselves as *Gatah-Re* and their language is called *Gatah-Sa*. This community has racial affinity with Austro-Asiatic stock and their language belongs to the greater Munda group.

The Didayi are found nowhere else except in the Malkanagiri district of Orissa State. In this district they are confined to the Kondakamberu hill ranges along the river Machkund. The Didayi country has three well marked sub-regions. One of them lies in the left bank of the river Machkund and is relatively a plain land. The second sub-region lying between the river Machkund and the Bondo hills is a rugged and hilly terrain where the elevation varies from 2000 ft to 3500 ft above the sea level. This is the coldest part of the Didayi country. The third sub-region is situated between the Bondo hills and the Jeypore Chitrakonda road and it is partly plain and partly hilly.

Generally the people of the Didayi community used to be very shy of strangers and fearful of the outsiders. They used to run away into the forest at the sight of any outsider coming to their village. In the past the practice was that a man used to watch the movement of strangers by climbing up a tall tree. On seeing some outsider coming towards their settlement he gave signal to the people so that they hid themselves in places which could not be reached by the strangers.

It is believed by the Didayis that the Bondos who live in the neighbouring hills were their elder brothers. In course of time they became separated from one another. The legend says that once they picked up quarrel with one another over some hare meat and in the tug of war they got themselves separated from one another and since then they have been living in two different parts of the same Kindakamberu hill ranges of Eastern Ghats in the Malkangiri district.

Settlement Pattern and House Types

SETTLEMENT PATTERN

As mentioned earlier, the Didayi villages used to shift from one site to the other in tune with the rotation of their shifting cultivation. Now the villages are no more shifting. Formerly almost all the Didayi villages were situated in the mountains, but today many villages are found on the bank of the Machkund river or in the valley of Kondakamberu hill ranges. The foot-hill villages as well as those established in the plains, are comparatively larger than the mountain settlements. Those who live in the plains and foot-hills have permanent cultivable lands whereas their counterparts living in the hills have only lands in the hill-slopes where shifting cultivation is practised.

When a new settlement is established, the site is selected by taking certain conditions into consideration. The first and the most important condition is that there must be a hill stream with water available throughout the year so that the people will have water all the time from this perennial source. There must be some plain land where the houses can be built. The fulfilment of these two conditions is not enough for the final selection of the site for the settlement. The favourableness of the site, determined through certain divinations is equally important.

When a place is finally selected for building houses, the presiding deity is installed and thereafter the priest (*Pujari*), the village headman (*Nayak*) and the assistant to *Nayak* (*Challan*) starts building their respective houses first then others of the village follow them and build their own houses.

The final step is to distribute different patches of forests on the hill-slopes surrounding the hills for taking up shifting cultivation. This is done in a village meeting specially convened for this purpose.

HOUSE TYPES

After some days the construction of the house starts there. Generally a house is of eight cubits long and seven cubits wide. The foundation of the house is dug and the poles are fixed on all sides. The walls are made of wattle plastered with mud. The roof is made of bamboos which rest on the walls. The house is thatched with either straw or grass. A verandah is provided on all sides of the house. Inside the house, below the roof, a loft is provided to store baskets and other households articles in it. Every house is provided with a fence around it.

DRESS

The Didayi women weave the clothes used by them as well as by the male members. They cut the branches of *Keranga* trees in summer and take out the barks of the branches. Very skillfully they then take out finer strands from the barks and twine them into tough threads by means of a spinning wheel. They dye these threads in black colour. After the yarns are ready, a woman who knows weaving is invited home to weave the cloth. The woman takes about a week to finish weaving a piece of *Keranga* cloth. Generally a piece of cloth is 2½ cubits long and 1 cubit wide.

The women wear the *Keranga* cloth around the waist. The upper part of the body is covered with a torn piece of cloth. The men use cloth of lesser width and wear it also around the waist in such a way that one end of the cloth passes down in between thighs covering the genitals. The cloth used by women is called *Kisalo* and cloth used by men is called *Gusi*. Both men and women use cloths of various colours, particularly of green and black colour.

The Didayi women like to wear ornaments. When a female child becomes six months old, her nose and ears are pierced and small copper rings bought from the market are set into the holes. When the girls grow up, these copper rings are replaced by the new rings of bigger size. A woman without ornaments is ridiculed by the public. The Didayi women also wear necklaces of beads and coins.

Economic Life

The main work of both men and women is shifting cultivation (*Bri*). The women go out to the forest daily and collect firewoods, roots and tubers. They get up early morning, finish works at home, cook food and after taking meals leave home to work in the fields under shifting cultivation. The Didayi women are forbidden to plough the fields, thatch the houses and carry heavy load on shoulder. Their custom is to carry things on their heads. Generally the women help men in all sort of works whereas the reverse is not true.

The principal food of the Didayi is rice and *ragi*. They cook the rice in the form of a gruel mixed with rice water which they like the most to eat. When rice is not in sufficient quantity, then *ragi* replaces it. They are in the habit of eating some vegetables such as cucumber, beans and different kinds of green leaves. They also eat pulses and cereals. The tender bamboo shoots are relished very much. When the rice and even *ragi* run out of stock, they depend upon roots and tubers and green leaves collected from the forests. Mushrooms of various types are available in the forest. These are collected by women and prepared in the form of curry mixed with vegetables.

In addition to the swidden plots of land in the hill-slope which are used for shifting cultivation, there are five other types of land in the Didayi area. They are (1) *Tikara* (upland); (2) *Pada* (lower upland); (3) *Lija* (low land); (4) *Dugadi* (kitchen garden); and (5) *Di* (Homestead land). The crops grown in different types of land are given below:

Tikara	-	*Ragi,* millets, pulses and horsegram
Pada	-	Pulses and oilseeds
Lija	-	Paddy
Dugadi	-	Corn, tobacco, beans, cucumber, groud, sweet potato

Di Homestead land

The people of those villages which are situated on the bank of the river Machkund lead a different life. They have been provided nets and boats by which they catch fish from the river and sell them in the nearby markets.

Social Organization

The Didayi tribe is divided into two exogamous groups which may be equivalent to moiety. All members of a moiety are believed to be related to one another by blood and consider members of the other moiety as their affinal relatives. One moiety is called *Unku* (Tiger) and the other group is called *Mala* (Cobra). The *Unku* moiety composed of three totemic groups are exogamous and pay reverence to their respective totemic animals. Some of these totemic groups which may be equivalent to clans are further sub-divided into several sub-clans, the names of which are used as surnames by the members of the respective sub-clans.

Each clan comprises several lineage groups called *Bedia* formed by all blood relatives in a village under the leadership of the *Mna,* the eldest male member of the group and the *Dha,* the second elder male of the group. These elders are responsible for regulating the conduct of the members and also for the marriage negotiations of its members, and represent and protect the interests of the group in the traditional village panchayat.

The smallest social group among the Didayi people is the family which is mostly nuclear in type and monogamous. The family is patrilocal and patrilineal. Among the Didayi people, the father's brother and mother's brother are highly respected. Cross-cousin marriage is prevalent among them.

Political Organization

Every Didayi village is a cohesive political unit. It has a traditional village *panchayat* which comprises the *Nayak* (village headman) and elders of the village. The *Barika* of the village works as the messenger and assistant to the *Nayak* of the village. The village *panchayat* decides matters relating to social and economic aspects of the village. Some of the matters which are referred to the village *panchayat* are fixation and collection of bride price, widow marriage, cases of divorce, incestuous sexual crime, inter-personal disputes, collection of contributions from the households for the festival observed in the village, fixation of dates for observing village festivals and all matters relating to village development.

There is a supreme Panchayat above the village *panchayat*. It is held on any Wednesday in the month of December or January. It is attended by both men and women of the village. The village *Barik* calls all the people in the morning. This meeting is also attended by important elders of non-tribal communities like Oriya *paik*s and *Khandayat*s of neighbouring villages. The *Nayak*s and *Barik*s of neighbouring villages are also invited to attend the meeting. Discussions about all the events which takes place in the village are held by the elders of the village under the leadership of village *Nayak*. The appointment of the village *Nayak, Barik, Challan* replacing the old ones, if necessary, is also discussed in the meeting. The meeting is not presided by the *Nayak* of the village. The President of the meeting is selected from among the elders of the village. Whatever the President says are listened to by others and are decided unanimously. Generally the new *Nayak* and the new *Barik* are recruited from their respective groups.

Bonded labour is prevalent among the Didayi tribe. Those who are poor serve as bonded labourers in the house of rich people. The bonded labour system is also brought to the *panchayat* for discussions. Those who serve as *Goti* are asked in the meeting whether or not they want to continue as *Goti*. In case any *Goti* wants to discontinue then another *Goti* is selected to replace him. It is in this meeting that the new cowherds are appointed to tend cattle of her village. Cases of divorce are also decided in this meeting.

Life-Cycle

BIRTH

When the time for delivering the child comes the women of the neighbouring households are informed to come and help. They help the woman to deliver the child. After the baby is delivered they bathe the child in tepid water and cut the umbilical cord. There is no difference observed in the manner of cutting the cord. It is the same with both male and female child.

The woman who has delivered the child is kept segregated from other members of his family. She does not touch the cooked vessels. The name giving ceremony is performed on the 15th day after the baby is born. On the day of name giving the house is cleaned and all used clothes are washed. No one is allowed to enter the house from morning till night. Both men and women of the household will not talk to any outsiders. Rice and pulses are cooked and these foods are offered to the ancestors on the roof of the house. No one is given the food cooked on this day in the house. Generally the name of the child is given according to the day of the week in which the baby was born. For example, if the baby is born on Tuesday (*Mangal*) the name of the baby is given as *Mangal* no matter it is male or female.

MARRIAGE

Marriage is essential in the life of the Didayis. On any Tuesday in the months of January and February, the parents of the boy send two men (*Raibadia*) to visit the village to which the girl belongs. As soon as the *Raibadia* reaches the village the parents of the girl invite their agnates who start cooking the foods and serve the assembled guests and relatives. The whole night is spent in dancing and singing. Next day early morning after taking some food the girl is taken to the boy's village in accompaniment of dancing and singing.

On getting the information that the bride has been brought to the place where the marriage will take place, the friends of the bridegroom clothe him with new dress and carry him to the place of marriage in accompaniment of dancing and singing. Both, the bride and the bridegroom, are seated in one place and their hands are kept one upon the other. The priest sacrifices a small black chicken at the place and sanctifies the marriage. After the worship is over, the girl is taken to her husband's house. After the dance and music are over the assembled guests and relatives are entertained with food and drinks. The whole night is spent in dancing and singing.

Next morning the *Raibadia* collect the bride price and sit in one place in village street and call the fathers of both as well as their relatives to the place. The *Raibadia* make payment of the bride price to the girl's father in the presence of others and thereafter all proceed to the house of the boy. The parents of the boy arrange a very big feast and entertain all the guests and relatives assembled there with sumptuous food and drinks.

DEATH

The Didayi people cremate the body in the forest. After the body is cremated some rice is cooked and placed in two leaf cups along the path leading to the cremation ground. At night the front verandah is covered with a layer of ash and some cooked rice and a potful of water are kept there. Next morning they examine the ashes and if they find some footprints on it they believe that the soul of the deceased person has come into the house and has eaten the rice and drunk the water.

After six months or one year a feast is given by the deceased family to their agnates and cognates. The unmarried boys and girls of the village cook the food and serve to the assembled guests and relatives. The relatives are also entertained with drinks. Next day the visiting relatives go back to their villages and get their houses washed and cleaned so that they make themselves free from death pollution.

Religion and Magic

The Didayis believe in many supernatural beings and ancestral spirits. They are worshipped on different rituals and festive occasions. The festivals which are observed are as follows.

Name of the festivals	*Month in which observed*	*Purpose*
Nadi Parba	*Magha* (January)	Seeds of various crops are sanctified
Chaita Parba	*Chaita* (March)	New mango eating
Asa Parba	*Asa* (August)	Eating new rice and *ragi*
Posa Parba	*Posa* (December)	Eating new beans and forest fruits

THE DONGRIA KHOND

Setting and Settlements

The Dongria Khonds live in the Niyamgiri hill ranges covering Bissam, Cuttack, Muniguda, Kalyanisinghpur of Rayagada district and Lanjigarh block of Kalahandi district. These hill ranges rise to a height which varies from 1000 to 5000 ft above the sea. Therefore, the Dongria habitat enjoys a cool climate throughout the year and in winter the area becomes very cold. The population of the Dongria Khonds is roughly around 15,000.

The Dongria Khonds have many distinctive features in their settlement pattern, house types, economic life, social organization, political system and religious beliefs and practices which stand them separate from other tribal groups. They speak *Kuvi* unlike the Khonds of their neighbourhood who speak *Kui,* the two being two different dialects of the main Dravidian language stock. They believe that they are descendants of Niayam Raja and therefore feel proud of their royal ancestry.

Village

A Dongria Khond village is situated in a gentle slope at the foot-hills or in a shelf in the steep hills. Every village has a long and wide street running in east-west direction. The houses are built close to one another or either side of the village street. The reason for the alignment of the village in the east-west direction is to ensure sharing of sun light equally by all houses.

Another reason is that the sun dries up the soil and removes dampness of the village street, a condition which deters the spread of diseases.

At the outskirt of the village by the side of the village road is present the *Jatra Kudi,* the abode of the goddess of the village. The ground for dancing is located in some convenient place at the back of the village or near the abode of the goddess. The community-hall-cum-shrine of *Jakir* (Earth Goddess) or *Sadarkudi* is present in some place in the village street. The girls' dormitories are always built at the back of any of the two rows of houses close to the stream or river flowing nearby. There are hills on all sides of the village with plantations of fruit trees in the hill slopes.

House

Before taking up the construction of the house, certain divinations are performed so, as to test the suitability of the site for habitation. After the site is found suitable for habitation, one morning on any Wednesday after bath, the owner of the house digs a pit in the middle of the site which is cleared for the construction of the house and sets the post in the pit. The next work is to get the required number of posts which are used in the construction of the house. In a Dongria Khond house as many as 60 wooden pillars are required and it takes nearly a week or so for a Khond to collect these posts from the forest. The posts are carved with designs and then set in appropriate places.

A Dongria house has the following rooms — a front room (*Duki*) with a narrow verandah in front (*Assan Pinda*), central room (*Ejo*) with overhead loft, an inner chamber (*Kandadaya*), and hearth and ovens in front of the back room (*Dapa*) with a back verandah (*Assan Pinda*) and attached pig sty. In one corner of the front room a fowl pen is provided and in some convenient place a loft is fixed. Similarly, there is another loft over the hearth for storing food materials. Two mortars (*Hena*) are embedded flush with the ground — one in the central living room and another in the back room. It is in these mortars that the grains are pounded by means of pestle. Near the mortar in the living room at some convenient place in the sides a rotary quern (*Jatawali*) is placed. Near it is the raised earthen platform on which the earthen lamp is kept. Another earthen platform (*Ayu Pinda*) is provided near the oven in the hearth on which cooked food, cooking vessels and water pots are kept. The household shrine (*Kondanake*) is installed in the inner chamber. In the side wall facing the living room some shelves are provided. Things which are used in magico-religious performances like winnowing fan and containers of objects used in occultic practices are kept in these shelves.

The walls are made of wooden poles plastered with mud on both sides. The roof of the house is of gabled type in the sense that it slopes down on both sides from the ridge pole. The roof is thatched with a kind of locally grown grass called *Piri*.

Economic Life

The Dongria Khonds depend primarily upon horticulture. The whole of Niyamgiri hill ranges which have been the home of the Dongria Khonds are full of plantations of jackfruit, banana, mango and pineapple in the hillslopes right from the Valley up to the hill-tops. Turmeric is extensively cultivated and there are citrus fruit trees specially orange plants grown along with other fruit trees in the hill-slopes. They used to carry on shifting cultivation extensively. But they have almost given it up and depend upon horticulture for their livelihood.

Social Organization

The territory inhabited by the Dongria Khonds is divided into several *Muttahs*. Each *Muttah* comprises a group of villages and is considered an administrative-cum-social unit. It also serves the functions of an exogamous clan. Some of these exogamous clan territories of the Niyamgiri hill ranges are *Jakasika, Wadaka, Pusika, Sikaka* and *Kadraka*. As the clan territories are exogamous, the marriage among the people of the villages within a particular clan territory is strictly prohibited. But the marriage of the people in any other clan territory other than their own are permitted. Formerly the ethnic composition of any clan territory was homogeneous but in course of time it has become heterogeneous. For example, formerly the *Jakasika Muttah* was inhabited by people of *Jakasika* clan alone. But nowadays people of other *Muttahs* are found living in *Jakasika Muttah*.

One significant feature of the Dongria village is the youth organization. In each Dongria village there is a dormitory for the unmarried girls which is called *Adasbetta*. It is at this place that the unmarried girls of the village sleep and spend time in dancing and singing with the unmarried boys visiting them from their affinal villages. There may be more than one dormitory in a village.

Political Organization

A Dongria Khond village is a cohesive unit socially as well as politically. The *Jani* is a magico-religious specialist and functions as the formal sacred head of the village. He presides over the village council which is attended by all village elders. There is a village messenger called *Barika* who belong to the Domb community. He is an important person in the sense that he is the real spokesman of the village and establishes liaison between the village and outside agencies including government officials. The highest secular headman is called *Mandal* who functions as the head of confederacy of a group of villages. Important matters concerning boundary disputes, witchcraft, and adultery are referred to the *Mandal* for arbitration. The official working as assistant to the *Mandal* as well as to the *Jani* is called *Bis Majhi*. He is the custodian of village funds and collects subscription from the people as and when necessary.

Life-Cycle

BIRTH

The birth of a child in a Dongria Khond house is believed to be the birth of one of their ancestors and the blessings of supernatural powers. The striking aspect of the birth rites is that the mother after giving birth to the child performs her works at home as usual. She does not observe any restrictions. She cooks the food for the family and serves them as usual. She also performs all economic activities both indoor and outdoor. However, the midwife takes care of the baby for the first four days. The restrictions which are observed are in respect of ritual matters.

The period of prohibition lasts for 21 days. During this period the family does not take part in any common social and religious functions of the village. The people of other households do not come in physical contact with any member of this family and no member of the household takes any non-vegetarian diet. The male members of the household do not cut their hair, shave their beards and pare their nails. All these restrictions are lifted after the purificatory rituals are performed on the 21st day.

MARRIAGE

Adult marriage is most common among the Dongria Khonds. The minimum age of a boy would be 22 and in the case of the girl it should be more than 16 years. The marriage takes place at the groom's house. The *Jani* of the village performs the marriage rituals and the groom's father gives a grand feast on this occasion. One peculiarity of the Dongria marriage is that the younger brother of the groom is permitted as a matter of custom to stay with the couple in the same room where they spend the first night together. However, the real honeymoon is observed not at home but in natural surrounding somewhere in the hills. Secondly the payment of the bride price prevails among the Dongria Khonds. The bride price consists of Rs. 500 to Rs. 800 in cash, two cows and about 40 kg of rice and 5 tins of liquor.

DEATH

As soon as the death occurs in a family the near and dear one's and the relatives who gather at the deceased family rent the air with loud lamentation until the dead body is removed from the house not by any member of the deceased clan but by the people of other clans. Among the Dongria Khonds the dead body is placed in a pit and the pyre containing logs of wood is placed on the dead body. The pyre is set on fire and when the entire body is burnt, water is poured to put the fire out. The Dongria Khonds observe death prohibition for two days.

The village *Jani* performs the purificatory rites in the house of the deceased and through these rituals calls the departed soul to come and live united with the souls of other ancestral spirits in the house.

Religion and magic

Dharanipenu is believed to be the supreme deity of the Dongria Khond. She is installed in a hut called *Kudi* in the middle of the village street. She is worshipped during *Meriah* or *Kedu* festival (Buffalo sacrifice). All rituals observed by the Dongrias start with the worship of *Dharanipenu*. Next to *Dharanipenu* in importance is the *Kotebalipenu*, a male deity which is believed to be the husband of the *Dharanipenu*. Next to *Kotebali* in importance is *Jatra Kudipenu*, another male deity which is installed at the outskirt of the village. The village *shaman* worships him every month. Besides these important deities there are many other deities which find their abode in water, air, trees and forest.

Of all the rituals those connected with buffalo sacrifice (*Kedu* festival) is most important. It is the biggest festival observed in Dongria Khond villages. It is observed in the month of *Magh* and lasts for eight days. All works are suspended at least for a month prior to the performance of this ritual in order to make necessary preparations for the festival. On the 4th day of the ritual the buffalo is sacrificed. Blows after blows are given on the animal with sharp axes and the animal is hacked to death. It is believed that the more the animal is tortured the more *Dharanipenu* is satisfied. The flesh of the animal is distributed among the relatives and friends and it is believed that the performance of the ritual enhances the fertility of the soil and the people get a bumper crop and hence become healthy and happy.

THE JUANG

Setting and Settlements

The Juang is one of the primitive tribes of Orissa. They used to wear leaves of sal trees and it was from his original costume that the tribe had obtained from their neighbours the name *Patua* (the people of leaf dress). They are found only in Orissa confined exclusively to Keonjhar district and Dhenkanal district. Out of the 30875 total Juang population as per 1981 census the population enumerated in Keonjhar was 15467 and in Dhenkanal was 14573 and of the remaining 835 population 765 Juang population was found in Cuttack district.

The Juangs of Keonjhar district represent the primitive section and those living in Dhenkanal district represent the acculturized section of the tribe. The territory inhabited by the Juangs in Keonjhar district is called *Juangpirh.* The ethnographic account which is presented here is related to the primitive section of the tribe of the Juangpirh.

Settlement Pattern and House Types

The Juang villages are generally located in the hill-slopes, at the upper reaches of the valleys. They are located in places where there is a good supply of water and plenty of forests in the hill-slope suitable for shifting cultivation. Besides these two conditions the omens must be favourable for habitation of a chosen site. Conspicuous in every Juang village is the bachelor's dormitory which is called *Mandaghar* in Keonjhar and *Majang* in Dhenkanal district. It is the largest hut built in the centre of the village. A wooden platform is raised in the enclosed part adjacent to the back wall and on this platform seeds of various crops grown by the Juangs in shifting cultivation are kept in straw beans and leaf packets. A number of flat drums of the type of tambourine called *Changu* are kept hanging from deer horns which are fixed to the walls of the dormitory. The roof is supported by massive wooden pillars with beautiful carving of animals and geometric designs on them. The *Mandaghar* is built by all people and is kept in good condition.

The *Mandaghar* is an institution of great importance. It is here that the unmarried boys of the village sleep at night around the smouldering fire which is kept alight day and night throughout the year. The men of the village assemble at the *Mandaghar* to discuss every important event in their corporate life. It is here that they settle distribution of swidden plots for shifting cultivation among themselves. The guests and visitors are entertained at that place. The open space in front of the *Mandaghar* is the place where the boys and girls dance together at night. In short, the *Mandaghar* functions as a recreation centre, village assembly house, school of dancing and music, arts and crafts centre and a rest shed.

HOUSE

The Juang house is rectangular in ground plan. It is about 15' long and 12' wide. A door is provided in front which serves as both entrance and exit and there is no window in any house. The walls are made of wooden poles plastered with mud and the roof is thatched with thatching grass. A small narrow verandah runs in front of the house.

Inside the house on one side is the kitchen and the raised earthen platform for keeping water pots. The central portion is used for sleeping and entertaining visitors and at the doorway a mortar is fixed to the ground. It is here that the grains are husked by means of a pestle. The house has a courtyard in front with a scaffold enclosing it.

ECONOMIC LIFE

It is necessary to give a detailed account of the techniques of collecting food and their survival requirements because on this factor depends a realistic planning for their development. For generations, the Juangs have been depending upon their surrounding forests for their all types of requirements including food. Not long ago their dietary habits were based entirely on forest collection and not much on shifting cultivation. In fact, the nineteenth century ethnographic reports of Samuells (1856), Dalton (1872), and Hunter (1877) have mentioned in their books that the Juangs were not shifting cultivators and that chase was their primary source of food supply. The older Juangs say that they had seen in their childhood that shifting cultivation was practised sporadically and that they were very happy roaming about in the forest and collecting plenty of nutritious roots, tubers, fruits and leaves to take care of food. Honey was available in plenty in the forest and a palmful of honey mixed in water made one forget the pang of hunger for about 10 to 12 hours.

Things have now changed. Shifting cultivation has taken the place of a pivot around which the activities of life revolve. With the increase in population there has been considerable increase of pressure on available forest resources, resulting in over exploitation and large scale depletion of natural resources.

Today three cropping systems are generally observed in the Juangpirh.

1. *Kitchen garden* : The lands around the homestead are used for growing seasonal and vegetable crops. These are pumpkin, ash gourd, bottle gourd, taro, yam ginger, turmeric, papaya, banana and many other different vegetables.
2. *Unirrigated land* : Under unirrigated land comes the different types in which different crops are grown, such crops constitutes one of maize, mustard and horsegram.
3. The irrigated low lands on the bank of hill streams. These lands are mainly used for rice and wheat cultivation.

SWIDDEN CULTIVATION

Besides these lands near village and valley bottom, the Juangs grow crops in the hill slopes which are under swidden cultivation. In this case two plots are used every year for growing crops. The principal crop grown in the first year of swidden cultivation is *Ramtila* (*Guizotia abyssinica*). It is sown in the month of June-July and harvested in the month of November-December.

This crop may be grown single in a separate land and also along with other crops in the following pattern:

1. In the first year, along the border of a new swidden plot, the *Ramtila* is sown and in its middle either *Suturi* (*Vigna umbellata*) or another variety of *Suturi* (*Vigna mungo*) is sown.
2. In the ditches near this swidden plot where Juangs throw litters, ash and decomposed plant parts, the *Gadiri* (*Colocasia esculenta*) is planted.
3. Sweet potato (*Ipomoea batatas*) is occasionally planted near the niger field.

In the second year of swidden cultivation varieties of crops are grown in the following pattern:

1. In the middle of the patch paddy (*Oryza sativa*) and *Sennai* (*Cajanas cajan*) are sown during the month of May-June.
2. In the middle of the same patch some other crops are also grown. These are *Kengza* (*Cucumis sativus*) and *Uti* (*Cucumis melo var momordica*).
3. In the border of the plot the following crops are grown: (i) *Kudu* (*Eleusine coracana*); (ii) *Akayang* (*Setaria italica*); (iii) *Gingari* (*Sorghum Spp.*); (iv) *Sulur* (*Phaseolus mungo*); (v) *Kesadha* (*Pennisetum typhoides*); (vi) *Kalar* (*Vigna unguiculata*); (vii) *Suturi* (*Vigna umbellata*).

Again along the border the Juangs follow a definite pattern of cropping as discussed below:

1. In the border of the field the *Eleusine coracana* is sown. Inner to it the *Ragi* (*Vigna unguiculata*) is planted. Inner-most lining in the boundary is occupied by the *Sorghum Spp.* So, *Vigna*

Sp. lies in between two millets i.e. *Eleusine Sp.* and *Sorghum Sp.*

Maturation period of the *Sorghum Sp.* and *Vigna unguiculata* is almost equal. *Vigna Sp.,* twines over the *Sorghum* plant. The most important symbiotic contribution of the *Vigna* is that it fixes atmospheric nitrogen for above cited millets.

2. Similarly, sometime *Mara sulur* (*Phaseolus mungo*) is sown in between millets in the ridges of the field.
3. *Pennisetum typhoides* is also sown along the border.
4. *Jali* (*Panicum miliaceum*) and *Jatia* (*Panicum miliare*) are sown in a separate patch near the paddy crop because these are free tillering bushy millets.
5. *Juani* (*Zea mays*) is sown sporadically. The maize grows luxuriantly in the soil of anthills (termite). So, it is preferred to put the seeds near the soil of termite colony. Usually, two varieties of maize are grown by the Juangs.
   (i) One variety is grown in the second year of swidden cultivation. It is sown in the month of June and harvested in the month of August-September.
   (ii) Other variety is grown near the village, the sowing and harvesting period being the same as above.

In this short account of the tribe, due to lack of space, it is not possible to discuss the technicalities of crop diversity and reasons for mixed cropping but it will suffice to say that the crops grown in the plots are harvested in different times helping the people to tide over food scarcity. Moreover the crop diversity helps to protect the crops against pest attacks.

3rd Year Swidden Cultivation

In the plot used in the 3rd year of swidden cultivation *Guizotia abyssinica* is grown. This is the final year of cultivation in a particular *taila* land (swidden plots). Then the land is left fallow for about 5-7 years to recuperate. By the time the Juangs leave the lands under shifting cultivation, it is much in the devastated state due to complete destruction of the vegetation, soil erosion, land slide and due to depletion of natural forests.

WETLAND FARMING

The irrigated land along the bank of the stream is best suited for the cultivation of rice. But such lands are very much limited and in short supply. However, the tribe has adopted the hybrid variety of rice in the block.

The main occupation of the Juangs is slash and burn method of cultivation which they call *Bringa* and *Kaman* or *Taila chasa*. This method involves the clearing of a patch of forest in the hill-slope by cutting the trees and clearing the bushes and burning them into ashes. The cleared patch is tilled by means of either a hand hoe or cattle drawn plough. Seeds of various types of crops mixed together are sown apart. Sometimes seeds of some pulses are dibbled in holes dug by means of a digging stick. When the crops ripen they are harvested one after another.

A Juang takes up two plots under shifting cultivation every year. Of them one is cultivated a year before and as such it is known as the second year *taila* land while the another one is cleared in the current year for cultivation and hence known as first year *taila* land. Oil seeds are grown in the first year *taila* and paddy and minor millets are grown in the second year *taila* lands.

There are mango and jackfruit trees with which the Juang villages abound all over the Juangpirh. The Juangs live on these fruits throughout the summer season when they ripe and are available in plenty. The trees of date palm are found in large number in the Juang country and the Juangs tap the palm juice and drink it in the femented form.

Social Organization

The smallest social unit among the Juang is the family which is invariably of nuclear type. It comprises parents and unmarried children. Sometimes old parents who cannot live alone are found living in the family of one of their sons.

The next higher unit is *Sept* or *Bak* as it is called in the Juang language. The social system of the Juangs is so confusing that every village gives a different list of *Septs,* the reason being that it has imitated the neighbouring Hindu castes. In fact, the Juangs observe village exogamy rather than *Sept* exogamy. Out of this practice has emerged two different sets of villages namely *Kutumba* villages or agnatic villages and *Bandhu* villages or cognatic villages. No marriage can take place among persons belonging to *Kutumba* or consanguinal villages. They can establish marriage relationship with those of their *Bandhu* villages.

The Juangs have a language of their own which goes by the name of the tribe. The people of the tribe identify themselves as the Juang and do not marry outside their group. The myths and legends reinforce their self-identity by supporting their views and values in the matter of their origin from a common ancestor and keeping themselves as a distinct cultural group.

Youth Organization

The most distinctive aspect of the Juang culture is the bachelor's dormitory and the youth organization which is associated with it. Every unmarried boy is the member of the *Mandaghar*. He ceases to be a member after his marriage. The male members are called *Kangerki*. In order to be a full-fledged *Kangar,* that is, an unmarried boy of marriageable age group, he must be a formal member of the bachelor's dormitory and has to undergo an initiation rite on the day of *Amba Nua* (first mango eating) ceremony which is observed in the months of February-March.

Even though there is no full-fledged spinsters' dormitory, the unmarried girls sleep together in the house of a widow where some accommodation is available for this purpose. The unmarried girls are called *Selanki*. In order to be a recognized *Selanki* of the village she asks the elder *Selanki*s to give her a share of the gifts given to them by the *Kangerki*s. On getting a share and using them by herself she attains the status of a full-fledged *Selanki* and is now entitled to offer gifts along with other elder *Selanki*s to their beloved *Kangerki*s. She is also permitted to accompany other *Selanki*s of her village when they go out on dancing visits to their *Bandhu* villages to dance with the *Kangerki*s of such villages. It may be mentioned that since village exogamy is practised among the Juangs, the *Kangerki*s and *Selanki*s of the same village are related to one another as brothers and sisters and therefore do not dance together. In such a system the *Kangerkis* visit their *Bandhu* villages to dance with *Selankis* of these villages and vice versa. Among the Juangs, dancing is considered a love-affair and culminates in match-making. This explains why avoidance is observed in the matter of *Kangerkis* and *Selankis* of the same village dancing together.

Political Organization

The Juang country or the Juangpirh as it is called is divided into six sub-*pirhs* each having a number of villages. Each sub-*pirh* has a headman called *Sardar* with a village headman called *Pradhan* in each of its villages.

There are many officials at the village level. The topmost official is the *Pradhan* who is the headman of the village. He is in-charge of secular matters of the village. The religious headman is called *Buita* or *Dehuri* who is as important as the *Pradhan*. He officiates all ritual performances and is in charge of propitiating the gods and goddesses. Whenever the village meeting is held, both the *Pradhan* and *Buita* have to be present. The *Pradhan* presides over the meeting, leads discussions, and with *Buita* and others takes decisions on all matters unanimously.

Next to the *Pradhan* in secular matters is the *Karji*. As an assistant headman his post is as important as that of the *Pradhan*. *Dangua* is the messenger-cum-watchman and sometimes serves as assistant headman. The village elders who are called *Barabai* occupy very high position in the political system of the village and attend the village meetings and assist the headman in taking decisions on matters which are discussed in the meeting. It is the village meeting which takes decisions in the matter of distribution of *taila* lands among the villagers for shifting cultivation. *Dehuri* is the first to cut the tree by his axe in a swidden plot and sets fire to the dried matter in the swidden. Then all others follow suit.

Life-Cycle

BIRTH

During pregnancy a Juang woman observes many restrictions in the matters of food, movement and work. All precautions are taken so that she is kept free from the influence of evil eye and evil spirits and there is no miscarriage and the child is delivered smoothly. No midwife is employed during delivery and the birth takes place in the hut and the child is delivered in a squatting posture. If it is a girl the cord is cut by means of a knife and if it is a boy child it is cut by means of an arrowhead. The placenta is buried at the back of the house or at the place of delivery. When the umbilical stump falls it is wrapped in a leaf and tucked in the thatch uttering blessings and wishes as "May many more children be born."

Birth prohibition is observed for a week. During this period the mother is kept on a strict diet and is segregated. On the 7th day she takes bath early morning and fills in the pit dug at the back where she was bathing, throws away old and used pots and shaves the baby's hair. But a relative cuts the hair of the child's father. The child is given a name. When a child is born it is believed that one of the ancestors has been reborn and accordingly the name of that ancestor who is believed to have been reborn is given to the child.

MARRIAGE

Marriages are performed after harvest and before rains set in. The negotiations start around the time of *Pus Punai* which is celebrated in the month of January.

Various types of marriages are common among the Juangs. Of all types, arranged marriage is considered most prestigious. In this case the bride is brought to the groom's house where the marriage takes place and payment of bride price is in vogue among the Juang.

The other forms of marriage are the *Digar Kania* (marriage by capture), *Mana Mani* (love marriage), *Ghar Jamai* (a man marrying the daughter of man having no son and staying in his house and inheriting his property as the son does). Besides these marriage types, there are cases of *Wadi Kania* (child marriage), *Burha Kania* (widow marriage), and *Daki Kania* (marriage between a man and a divorced woman).

DEATH

As soon as the death occurs the relatives apply turmeric paste and oil on the dead body. A pyre is raised under a tree. The body is carried by the elders to the cremation ground. The pyre is set on fire and when it is in full blaze the dead body is thrown into the fire, after which the pall bearers run back home without looking back. They throw away the used pots and pans from the house of the deceased and clean the house. A feast is arranged on the following day at the same hour when the person expired. A few village elders make an image of the deceased person in the ashes and insert a piece of charred bone into it and after worshipping it they throw it in a nearby hill stream. After bathing they return to the house of deceased. One of them cuts the hair of the male members of the bereaved family and sprinkles cow dung water on them for purification. They then put some *arua* rice and copper coin in an earthen pot and place it at the doorway of the deceased's house. After sacrificing a chicken they call the soul of the deceased back home. Then they keep the pot inside the house to be used by the inmates for domestic purpose after a week or so.

Religion and Magic

The supreme god of the Juangs is the *Dharm Deota,* the Sun god. Next in order of importance is the *Gram Siri,* village Mother Goddess, who is installed by the side of the *Mandaghar* in the centre of the village. *Rusi* and *Rusani* which are supposed to be their ancestors are remembered in every activity of the daily life. Besides these principal deities, they believe in many other supernatural beings which pervade everywhere in their habitat in the forest, in water, in trees, in stones and in any other objects. These deities are worshipped on all festive occasions and particularly before commencing any agricultural operations, construction of houses and marriage ceremonies. When any fruits like mango and jackfruit ripen and when any crops are harvested, the concerned deities, ancestral spirits and mother goddess are worshipped by offering such fruits and crops first to them. Unless that is done no one can eat them. Any violation of such traditions and customs brings misfortune and mishap to them.

Development and Change

The Juangpirh is a part of the Keonjhar Integrated Tribal Development Agency (ITDA). A special project called Juang Development Agency under the category of a Micro Project is in operation in the Juangpirh. The main problem of this area is the practice of shifting cultivation which is responsible for denudation of forests and soil erosion. Some *Podu* prevention programmes such as Sisal, Sabai grass and pineapple plantation and water harvesting structure have been implemented. In spite of all efforts the practice is going on as usual. But there appears to be a change in the mind of the people towards taking up wet paddy cultivation in lands lying in valleys. The Juangs are aware that the population is increasing and as a result of repeated cutting and burning the hill-slopes have become almost barren and unfertile. The productivity has been seriously affected and therefore the yield has diminished. In such a situation the Juangs are keen to adopt any other types of crop husbandry as alternative to shifting cultivation.

The most feasible alternative is the cultivation of valley bottom lands and plantation of fruit trees in the lower hill-slopes immediately above the valleys and reforestation of hill-tops with trees of economic value. Pasture development can be taken up in the hill-slope between the area under horticulture and that under reforestation. Kitchen garden can be developed in the backyards and the uplands close to the homestead lands can be utilized for growing oil seeds such as niger and mustard.

THE HILL KHARIA

Setting

The Kharia tribe is divided into three groups namely, the Pahadi Kharias or Hill Kharias, the Dhelki Kharias and the Dudh Kharias. Of these three sections of the tribe the Hill Kharia section is identified as the primitive section of the tribe. This tribe, which recorded a population of 1,44,174 in Orissa as per the 1981 census, is found in large concentration in three districts of the State namely Sundergarh (pop. 89,294), Sambalpur (pop. 31,090) and Mayurbhanj (pop. 14,985). The majority of the Hill Kharias is found in the Mayurbhanj district particularly in and around the Simlipal hills of the district. The other two sections of the tribe are distributed in the other two districts. Earlier scholars like Russel and Hiralal have mentioned that the term Kharia has been derived from Kharkharia which means a palanquin or litter. The Kharia legend indicates that the Kharia and another community namely, the Puran were the autochthons (natives) of Mayurbhanj. The Kharias trace their origin from a pea-fowl's egg. They assert that the Bhanj royal family of Mayurbhanj came out from the yolk, the Puranas from the white and Kharias from the shell of the pea-fowl's egg.

Kharia Village

The Kharia villages are situated in the forests or in place close to the forests. The settlement conforms largely to a shapeless cluster in which the houses are scattered within a small area. In some cases the villages conforming to a linear pattern having huts built close to each other on either side of the narrow village street are also met with.

Before a village is set-up in a particular place the Kharias test the omen to find out whether or not the place is suitable for habitation. What they do is that the religious head of the village called *Dehuri* and a few others visit the tentatively selected sites. The *Dehuri* digs a pit and fix a post in it. He places some white rice near the post and also an arecanut and marks the post with vermilion. After having done this they leave the place and return the next morning to examine whether the grains are intact and not distributed. If they find that the materials are in original position and not displaced it is taken as a good sign and the site is finally selected for building houses.

Generally the Hill Kharia villages are small in size with households varying from 10 to 30 families. In some places there are also much smaller villages having five to ten households. The Hill Kharia villages which are located in the forest are homogeneous, whereas those situated in the plains are heterogeneous in composition. Although they live with other communities in a village they have a separate hamlet of their own.

House Types

The site thus selected is cleared and levelled. The layout of each house is marked on the ground by its owner. The longer side of the house are laid in the east-west direction and the shorter side in the north-south direction. The north-western corner of the foundation is given more importance and therefore this side is made little longer.

The first pole which is fixed on the ground is called *Murdhana Khunta* and it is fixed in the middle on the eastern side of the foundation. The pit in which the pole is fixed is filled with earth not with hand but with his head. For this purpose the owner of the house lies down on the ground with face downward and pushes the earth with his head into the pit. After this post is fixed, the other posts are fixed on the ground in their respective places. The space between the pillars is filled by the wooden poles erected close to one another in the foundation. Then the saplings of certain trees are set in the narrow gap between the wooden poles. The wattle structure which makes the wall on all sides of the house is kept in position by tying them with thin branches of the trees. After the wattle work on the wall is finished, the pillars of the verandah and those on the middle line of the house are set erect on the ground in their respective places. On the whole 15 pillars of *sal* wood are required in the construction of a house.

All houses are single roomed and the roof divided into two sloped. Rafters of *sal* trees make the slopes of the roof. The roof is thatched by means of a kind of grass which is locally available in the forest.

The wattle wall is plastered with mud on both sides. No colour washing is given to the walls as is done by the neighbouring Mundari tribes. The house is built on a plinth which is raised by 2 ft above the ground. A verandah is provided in front of the house. The house has only one door which is fixed in the front wall of the house.

A mortar is fixed to the floor about a foot off from the door. It is in this mortar that the grains are pounded with the help of a pestle. A small semi-circular raised platform is provided in the corner of the house near the mortar for the fowls to sit on their eggs. The hearth is provided in another corner of the house. Three pieces of stone placed in a triangular fashion on the ground make the oven where food is cooked. Offerings of food and drink are given to the ancestors in another corner of the house near the hearth. By the side of this sacred corner a loft is provided to keep the household articles on it. A goat pen is built outside, close to the house. The house will have a fence in front and space between the fence and the house is used as the kitchen garden where chilli, cucumber, bean, etc., are grown in season.

Economic Life

The Hill Kharias entirely depend upon the forest for their livelihood. They regard forest as their nourishing mother which provides them food, shelter and enriches their folklore. They collect minor forest products of many kinds. Some of these produces are *Genduli* gum, *Bahada* gum, *Charseeds, sal* seeds and leaves, *Kendu* fruits, *Mahua* flowers and seeds, Myrobalans, *Kusum* fruits, honey and bees wax, datepalm leaves, tasar cocoons, hydes and horns, lac, tamarind, tapioca, resin, broomsticks, *Karanj* seeds and sticks. Most of these forest products find market for sale but lacking in cooperative organization, they do not get a fair price for these things. The local traders, petty money lenders and the *Sahukars* (traders) who live in the area exploit them in business transactions related to marketing of forest produce.

The noteworthy aspect of the forest life of the Hill Kharias is their skill in collection of honey and preparation of *Palua* (arrowroot), a product extracted from tubers. The Hill Kharias from Simlipal hills are able climbers. They are expert collectors of honey and bee wax. The steep precipice of lofty mountains of the Simlipal hills are studded with bee-hives. The Kharias with the help of ropes descend down to the precipitous places to tap these hives. These precipitous sites having innumerable bee-hives cannot be reached on foot. Therefore, a ladder, made of two ropes of twisted fibres of Siali creeper, with bars made of bamboo rods fixed to the ropes is fastened to the top end to some tree or heavy stone and is hung down so as to reach a little lower than the level of the hive. Two more ropes of Siali creeper are let down, one with an ignited bamboo torch emitting smoke and another with leaf basket or an empty tin canister placed in a hammock like swing attached to it. The ropes are held first at the top end by men. A Kharia slides down the rope ladder, picks up the torch and moves it around the hive gently so as to scare away the bees. The hanging basket is kept in position at the bottom of the hive and held fast there. Then the Kharia pokes at the hive by means of a stick and breaks it so that the honey and the pieces of the hive fall into the basket. After the whole hive is broken and placed in the basket he shouts at the man at the top to pull up the rope to which the basket is tied. The process is so risky that a slight slip can lead to disaster.

The Hill Kharias are engaged in the collection of forest produce round the year except the monsoon season when the activities slow down. They camp outside in the dense forest for several days till the collection is over. Most of the collections are individually owned except the collection of honey which is a group endeavour and the honey which is collected is shared among the households who join in the pursuit.

Another expertise shown by the Hill Kharias is in respect of collection of *Palua* or arrowroots. It is the work of the men to collect tubers and extract arrowroot out of them. They dig out the tubers and remove the stems which they leave at the spot to grow and yield tubers next year. Roots and soil are removed and these clean tubers are kept under water in hill streams for a day or two. Then these are rubbed against a stone and the paste that is formed flows down into the stone packed hole dug nearby for this purpose. The paste is collected from the hole and kept in an earthen pot. It is washed and filtered several times and is finally converted into lumps which when dry make *Palua* ready for sale.

The real gatherers of arrowroot are known as *Badia*. These *Badias* form into small groups, each group having one or two influential, intelligent, and outspoken leaders. The local traders have contact with these leaders. The pay advance to these leaders and through them procure arrowroot from the *Badia*s. In this process the leaders and the traders get more benefit and the real gatherers are always at a loss.

The Hill Kharias are knowledgeable about many herbal medicines. The Simlipal hills are full of various types of medicinal herbs and the Kharias are very much acquainted with these herbs. Being far away from urban centres and having very little touch with the outside world they make use of the herbal medicines to cure their ailments. The roots, leaves, tubers, herbs, insects and animals constitute their food items. Barks and seeds of a number of trees like *Ashok, Sunari, Arjun, Sal,* etc., are collected in large quantity by them and sold to local businessmen. Different kinds of birds, squirrels and other animals which are in demand in the bordering villages are caught by them and sold to private persons. Various recent restrictions imposed by the Forest Department in the collection of forest produce have restricted the Hill Kharia in their habit of foraging, thereby creating hardship in the life of these people.

Social Organization

Family is the smallest social unit among the Hill Kharias and it is the nuclear type of family which is the most common among them. A family comprises parents and unmarried children. The size of a family on an average is 4 to 5 in number. No clan organization is found among the Hill Kharias. Lineage regulates marriage. They consider themselves equal to the Mundas and Santals, but no martial relationship is established with them nor they have any commensal relationship with them.

Political Organization

Every Hill Kharia village has its traditional *panchayat* and village headman and other leaders. The village headman is called *Pradhan* who presides over the village meeting and decides inter-personal disputes, cases of breaches of social customs and customary laws. At the time of epidemics and other serious happenings he raises funds to meet the expenses on ritual performances and other preventive measures.

Besides the village, there is a confederacy called *Parha* or *Birha* which is composed of a group of neighbouring villages. This inter-village council is a sort of *Kutumb Sabha* or council of agnates related to one another by blood. The headman of the *Birha* is known as *Dhira* and *Dandia* who is the eldest, wisest and most influential *Pradhan* of the constituent villages. Matters and cases which cannot be settled at the level of the village council are referred to the *Birha* confederacy for final settlements. Particularly cases of ex-communication are referred to the inter-village council for the re-admittance of the guilty person into the society.

Life-Cycle and Rituals

BIRTH

Birth takes place in the house and the birth prohibition is observed for nine days. On the last day the mother takes purificatory bath and bathes the child also. The child is given a name on this day. The ear piercing ceremony is observed when the child becomes 5 to 6 years old.

MARRIAGE

Arranged marriage is most common among the Hill Kharias. The groom's father pays the bride price which includes Rs. 60 in cash, six pieces of clothes, one mound of paddy, two barrels of liquor, one goat and some other things which are required for the wedding feast. Marriage by elopement and capture is also prevalent. Widow re-marriage is allowed and divorce is permitted. Adult marriage is common. But cases of pre-pubertal marriage in the case of girls are also met with.

DEATH

The Hill Kharias follow the custom of burial of the dead bodies and observe ritual prohibition for a period of 20 days.

Religion

The Hill Kharias believe in many gods and goddesses. *Thakurani* or the Earth Goddess is considered the supreme deity of the Hill Kharias. They worship *Dharani Devata* and also the Sun. The Hill Kharias are very particular about the worship of the spirits residing in the forests. No Kharias will venture to go out into the forest for collection of honey and wax without propitiating the forest deities. Similarly every activity connected with hunting and food-gathering is proceeded by ritual observances and propitiation.

THE KUTIA KHOND

Setting

Around Belghar, a place about 70 km away to the south-west of Baliguda town in Phulbani district of Orissa live the Kutia Khonds in the remote hills of the Eastern Ghats. This area forms part of the Tumudibandh block and Kotagarh block. An all weather road meandering through these hill ranges connects Belghar with Tumudibandh. This road·continues westwards up to Ambadola on the Vijaynagaram-Raipur Rail-way.

The survey undertaken by the Kutia Khond Development Agency (KKDA) in the year 1990 shows that the Kutia population in 68 inhabited villages situated around Belghar was 4090 and the number of households was 1025. The average size of a household according to this survey comes to 4 persons. The sex ratio is recorded at 1092 females per 1000 males. The level of literacy was at 2.9 per cent in 1980 but it has increased to 7.92 per cent. The Kutias speak Kui dialect. They are able to understand Oriya but cannot speak.

Kutia Villages and Houses

The Kutia villages are situated in the foot-hills or in the valleys surrounded by densely forested high hills. A village has two rows of houses flanked by a narrow village street. The village conforms to the east-west setting of the rows of houses in a linear pattern. The houses of one row faces towards north and those of the other row towards south. Conspicuous in the village are the youth dormitories for young men and women which are built at the end of the rows of houses. Cattlesheds are built separately at the back of the houses.

The Kutia Khonds build their houses on a rectangular ground plan. A Kutia house consists of a single room partitioned inside into two parts, one part set apart as kitchen room and the other part used as a living room. In some cases it is partitioned into three parts. The walls are made of *Sal* saplings plastered with mud on both sides. The roof is thatched with locally made tiles. The floor of the house is about 2 ft below the level of the village road and this low lying floor of the house is called *Kutti* which has given the name to the tribe as Kutia Khond. Each house have a verandah in front which is used as a sitting place. In recent developments it is seen that the verandah has been divided into two parts. One of its part is used as guest-room while the other part opposite to the first is used as a sitting place.

The house is provided with two doors one in front and the other at the back of the house. The mortar in which the rice is pounded is fixed into the floor at the middle of the living room. The Kutia Khond pound rice and other grains in the mortar by means of pestle.

There is an extra room built for the women-folk to retire during the menstrual cycle. In some villages there may be four to five such rooms available for common use. Many women enjoy the facility of such common accommodation even though they have provision in their own houses. These rooms when free are used by the household as goatshed or pig sty.

At the middle of the village is installed the *Dharani Penu* and *Karumunda*. It is the tradition that the *Dharani Penu* and *Karumunda* should be placed almost at the middle of the village and therefore any extension of the village on either end is not allowed because it will distort the seat of the deity.

The space at the back of the house is used for kitchen garden and the sheds of domestic animals are also constructed there. Most of the Kutia villages have jackfruit trees which are considered auspicious. *Salap* trees (*Caryota urens*) are also found in the area of settlement.

In every village there are one or two families of Domb or Pana community. The members of this community tend cattle of the Kutia Khond. Their houses are located at a little distance from the main village. At the extreme end of the village is the place for depositing garbages. Sometimes compost pits are found at such places.

Each Kutia Khond village was formerly composed of a single clan. But it has now become multi-clan in composition. Traditionally the people with Jani surname used to live in one row and the people bearing the Majhi surname lived on the other row. But in the present times the people of both surnames are living together in the same rows.

Dress

A Kutia Khond male wears a loincloth of one and a half cubits long and less than a foot broad. This loincloth covers only the lower private part of the body. He keeps the upper part of the body uncovered. The clothes used by the Kutia Khond women consists of three pieces, one piece covering the upper part of the body like an apron hanging in front up to the thigh, the second piece is a piece of loincloth worn between the thighs and tugged at the back to the waist string, and the third piece is a plain skirt worn to cover loin.

The traditional customs of the Kutia Khonds have undergone many changes. The young boys and even many adult persons have adopted modern dress like pants, trousers and shirts, etc. Similarly the young girls have replaced the upper aprons with towels. In many cases they are found wearing printed sarees and blouses. The Kutia Khonds are very fond of wearing ornaments which are made of silver, brass, aluminium and transparent plastics. The women wear ear and nose rings, necklaces, finger rings, anklets and toe rings. Their hair is arranged into a bun adorned by coloured ribbons and forest flowers. The men used to have long hairs arranged into a knot at the back of the head but this has changed.

Economic Life

Both men and women in the Kutia society wake early morning, when the cock crows. As soon as they get up from bed the male members go straight to the *Salap* trees to have a drink of toddy or do some work in the kitchen garden. In rainy season when they are not able to go out they keep themselves engaged in some indoor activities such as repairing of houses, mending agricultural implements or spending time in gossiping and smoking. In the meantime the women do the pounding of the foodgrains by means of mortar and pestle and go out to fetch water and start cooking the morning meal.

As the sun rises, after taking their food the men proceed to the fields to work in swidden patches. The women also join them in the fieldwork. Both work till midday and then take their lunch and rest for sometime. They resume their work again in the afternoon. Before sunset they leave the field and come back home. On their way back, they carry with them some firewood and take bath in the nearby hill stream and go straight to the *Salap* trees to have a drink. At home, in the early part of the night, they relax and spend time gossiping among themselves. By 7 o' clock they finish their dinner and after a few hours they go to sleep. This routine varies from season to season.

The main source of their livelihood is shifting cultivation. They cultivate a number of crops in the swidden plots. Some of them have lands in the plain in which they cultivate paddy. Not all crops grown in the swidden plots are meant for consumption at home. Some crops are sold in the market for money with which they buy their clothes, ornaments and their daily necessities like kerosine, salt, tobacco, match-box, etc. All types of minor millets that are grown are used as foodstuff and never sold in the market. Similarly, all vegetables grown in the kitchen garden are consumed at home. But oilseeds like mustard and *til* are sold in the market for cash.

The Kutia Khonds are not able to produce sufficient amount of food crops. They face scarcity of food in months between summer and rainy seasons. During this lean period they do not get two square meals a day. They subsist on millets, gruels, mango stones and sago palm pith.

In addition to cultivation of crops they practice hunting and collect minor forest produce which they sell in the market. When they suffer the acute crisis or scarcity they even dispose of some livestocks like poultry, goats, etc., for cash with which they buy foodstuffs.

Amongst the Kutia Khonds live the Panos, a scheduled caste community of traders and businessmen. The Panos are more intelligent and educated than the Kutia Khonds who are very backward. The Panos act as the co-ordinator between the Kutia Khonds and other non-tribal traders. The Panos are well versed in both Kui and Oriya languages and therefore serve the Kutias as their spokesmen and mediators.

The Panos carry on their trading with the Kutia Khonds round the year. The articles which they sell to the Kutia Khonds are salt, dry fish, some readymade food items, match-box, country sugar and biscuits. They also supply liquor to the Kutia Khonds and their cattle. They have expanded their business by selling some modern articles such as cosmetics, ornaments, silk and nylon garments.

Bartar system is still in vogue in the Kutia society. For a bottle of liquor the Pano merchant charges 1 kg of paddy in exchange, a price which is three times more than the money value of a bottle of liquor. There are several other ways by which the Kutias are similarly exploited by the Panos and other local money-lenders and merchants. During the lean period when the Kutias face the scarcity of food, they borrow money from the Panos giving them word to pay back the loan in crops after the harvest. The traders purchase the crops at very low prices and when the Kutias fails to clear the debt they have to work as a bonded labour.

However, many changes have been taking place among the Kutias. The development programmes sponsored by both the Central and State Governments are contributing significantly to the transformation in the socio economic condition of the Kutia Khonds. At Belghar there are several institutions such as Police Outpost, the Micro project of the Kutia Khond Development Agency, Agricultural Extension Officer's Office, Veterinary Hospital, Post Office, Health centre and weekly market complex. There is also LAMPS and a Gramya Bank. The Kutia Khonds of the neighbourhood have interaction with these agencies and are being benefited from the services rendered by these agencies. But the impact of these agencies on the Kutia Khonds have not been very much spectacular. The Kutias still continue to live in an unhygienic condition and suffer from certain diseases like malaria, sickle-cell anemia, leprosy and stomach trouble. There has been no change in their cultivation of crops in the swiddens. The practice of shifting cultivation still goes on as usual causing colossal destruction of vegetation of forest resources. Educationally the Kutia Khonds are very backwards. The exploitation of the local merchants and *Sahukars* (traders) goes on unabated.

Social Organization

FAMILY

Family is the smallest social unit among the Kutia Khonds. Most of the families are of nuclear type. Parents and unmarried children constitute a nuclear family. Father is the authority and all decisions are taken by him. As soon as the sons get married and bring their wives, it becomes difficult to accommodate them in the same house. Therefore, they build their own houses and live with their wives separately. However, any residential separation does not break the relationship which exists between the parents and the sons. As soon as the daughter is married, she leaves the house of her parents and goes to settle in the house of her parents-in-law. In this sense, the system of residence is patrilocal. In some cases the boy goes to live in the house of his would be father-in-law and when time comes he marries his daughter and stays as a *Gharjamai* with the parents of his wife.

CLAN

The next higher social group is clan. Each clan has a myth of its own, indicating its origin. Most of the clans are totemic. Some of the clans are listed below:

1. *Andanja*, 2. *Bandanaka*, 3. *Dulaka*, 4. *Gunjika*, 5. *Mindanja*, 6. *Nondruka*, 7. *Prepanja*, 8. *Rodimika*, 9. *Sakudaka*, 10. *Oblaka*.

There are many such clans existing in the Kutia society. Each clan believes to have descended from a common ancestor and is exogamous.

The tribe is divided into two lineage groups, one belonging to the *Majhi* lineage and the other to the *Jani* lineage. In a village having two rows of houses, one row is occupied by the households of the *Jani* lineage and the other row to those of the *Majhi* lineage. A boy of one row can marry a girl of the other row but not in his own row. It is the tradition among the Kutia Khonds that after marriage the girl goes to live in the house of her husband. The married woman adopts the lineage of her husband. In this case, the tribe follows the patrilineal system of succession. Since one lineage consists of many clans which are exogamous, there has been considerable admixture through marriage. Thus, cases of marriages between *Majhi* and *Jani* lineages, *Jani* and *Jani* lineages and *Majhi* and *Majhi* lineages are met with in the Kutia society.

Life-Cycle

BIRTH

The birth of a child in a Kutia family is a matter of great happiness, no matter whether it is a boy or a girl. It is believed that some ancestor has taken birth and it is symbolic of their relationship with ancestral spirits. As soon as the labour pain starts, the woman is taken to the backside of the house. Sometimes delivery also takes place in the house which is used commonly by the village women during their menstruation period. An old woman having experience in delivery attends the woman and helps her to deliver the child. The lady attendant cuts the umbilical cord with a knife and gives it to the father of the child who along with the placenta buries these in a deep hole in the backyard. The smoke of resin helps the mother and child to take rest without being biiten by mosquitoes. The room is also kept warm. The umbilical cord falls down and the baby is given a warm water bath in which *neem* leaves are boiled. Turmeric paste is also anointed over the body of the baby at the time of bath.

The mother is confined in segregation for a month because she is considered impure. A ritual is performed as a part of the process of purification. The house deity is offered with liquor and food and a feast is arranged which is enjoyed by each and every household in the village. On this occasion a leaf cup full of cooked rice is given to each household.

A name is given to the child when it attains three years of age. The village priest by means of divination finds out which ancestor has taken rebirth and accordingly the name of the ancestor is given to the child.

MARRIAGE

Marriage is a very significant event in the life of a person. Various types of marriages are in vogue among the Kutia Khonds. These include marriage by elopement, capture, sorrorate marriage and arranged marriages. Of all the types, the marriage by negotiation is most prestigious. In this case the family members of the groom visits the house of the bride with rice and liquor and give them to the father of the girl. If the rice and liquor are accepted by him it is indicative of his approval of this marriage proposal. During the period between the negotiation and the actual marriage, the payment of the bride price is made by instalments. When the entire amount of the bride price is paid then the date of the marriage is decided by the two families.

On the day of marriage the bridegroom accompanied by his friends and villagers proceed to the village of the girl. The guests are offered *mahua* liquor first and later they are invited to have food which is cooked in the house of the bride. On this occasion both buffalo meat and goat meat are cooked. The old people and the father of the boy as well as the girl sit at one place and eat the buffalo meat. It is believed by them that the buffalo meat establishes the affinal relationship, which is termed as *Samudhi*, between the girl's father and the boy's father. After this relationship, the boys and the girls present on the occasion at the girl's house sing and dance.

Then arrangements are made for the bride to leave her house and proceed to the village of the groom. At the time of departure the *Jani* of the village gives blessings to the bride near the shrine of *Dharani Penu*. The girl is given a bath and clothed with a new saree and adorned with ornaments. At the outskirts of the village, as per the custom of the tribe, the bride is made to cling to a *Sal* pole and the women of her village encircle her. The women of the bridegroom's village try to pull out the bride from the *Sal* stump. This involves a lot of pulling and pushing in accompaniment of singing and dancing. Finally when the women of the groom's village pulls out the bride they all proceed to the groom's village. A feast is arranged by the father of the groom to entertain the visiting guests and relatives.

On the eighth day the parents of the girl and their friends come to the groom's house to take her back to her village. The visiting guests, relatives and the parents of the girl are entertained by the parents of the groom. When the time for the girl to depart approaches, the *Jani* of the villages gives his blessings to the bride. Many people go halfway to bid farewell to her and tell her to comeback soon. A buffalo is given by the parents of the groom to be used for a common feast at the girl's village. When the girl is with her parents, her husband visits her often. In course of time the girl becomes pregnant and once she is pregnant, she no longer stays with her parents and comes back to her husband's house and the couple lead a normal life as usual.

DEATH

As soon as a death occurs in a household the news is sent to the relatives. The dead body is kept covered with a piece of cloth for sometime so that the assembled relatives will have their last look at deceased. The body is carried to the cremation ground by means of a cot. If it is a natural death it is cremated and if it is a pregnant woman it is buried. The assembled relatives are fed not by the family of the deceased but by the villagers. Similarly, the members of the bereaved family are fed by the villagers during the whole period of ritual probihition which lasts for three days. The *Jani* offers food everyday to the departed soul during the probihition period. On the last day a feast is cooked in new earthen pots with millets contributed by the relatives and villagers and every-body present in this occasion participate in the feast. *Mahua* liquor is also served to them.

Political Organization

In the past the entire area which forms the present Belghar and its neighbouring regions was divided into several territorial divisions called *Muttah.* It was a revenue unit with a *Muttah Majhi* as its administrative head. A *Muttah* was composed of a group of adjacent villages with a *Pat Majhi* as the secular head in each village. To assist him in discharging his duties there were some assistants such as *Bis Majhi* and *Chhatia.* The *Muttah Majhi* otherwise called *Patra* was from a *Paik* caste whereas the *Pat Majhi* were from the Kutia Khonds and the Chhatia Pano community.

The *Muttah Majhi* used to collect revenue from the villages which were under his jurisdiction. The *Pat Majhi* and the *Bis Majhi* helped him in his work and controlled the village. He used to preside over the village council and give decisions relating to monetary matters, social customs and cultural traditions, inter-personal conflicts, monthly routine of ritual festivals and agricultural operations. The *Chhatia* who acted as the messenger used to call villagers to the village assembly and also played the role of a mediator in business transactions.

Presently there is a magico-religious head called the *Jani* who presides over festivals and rituals performed individually and collectively in the village. He attends the village council and participates in all deliberations. He is very much respected and occupies a high position in the Kutia society.

The modern statutory *panchayat* system has not brought much change in the traditional political system. In many cases the *Bis Majhi* has become a ward member representing his village in the *Gram Panchayat* system and plays a dual role as the head of the traditional village council and as the elected representative of the village working in the modern statutory *Gram Panchayat* system.

Dance and Music

The Kutia Khonds are fond of dancing and singing. Their songs differ according to the occasion and are related to the origin of the world and its constituent materials on the one hand and to the changes which are taking place in the world and human society in course of time, on the other. Love and affection, happiness and sorrow, are all expressed through songs. Dancing and singing accompanied by the music of drums, bells and flutes, are an integral part of their life.

Religious Beliefs and Practices

The Kutia pantheon is full of numberless supernatural beings. They have priests, *Shamans* and sorcerers to propitiate them and invoke them on different occasions. Some of them are benevolent and many others are malevolent. All the animate and inanimate matters existing around them in the universe possess life substance and are part of the spirit world. The common term used for these deities and spirits is *Penu*. The *Penus* are of various forms, and are believed to be omnipresent. Not only do they reside in earth, air, water, forests, trees, sky, hills and villages and also at home, even they appear in dreams and express their desires and wants, and demand offerings and sacrifices. Many festivals are observed by the Kutia Khonds round the year. During these festivals different *Penus* are propitiated for different purposes.

THE LODHA

Setting

The Lodha stands separate from all other tribal groups because unlike others they pursue various criminal activities and are very much aggressive in nature. In fact, the Lodha was labelled as criminal tribe till the revocation of the Criminal Tribes Act, 1962. The tribe is included in the list as one of the Primitive Tribes of Orissa. It is a small tribe having a total population of 5,088 and their main concentration is in the Suliapada and Morada blocks of Mayurbhanj district.

The Lodhas were forest dwellers. Their primary occupation was rearing the tusser silkworm in the host trees of *Sal* (*Shorea robusta*) and Asan (*Terminalia tomentosa*). Relentless march of deforestation threw the Lodhas out of their traditional source of livelihood and dislodged them from their sylvan surrounding. Having no alternative of their choice and skill to fall back upon, they resorted to stealing and burglary against their will to satisfy their hunger. The process of displacement is discussed in detail in the chapter dealing with economic life.

The district of Mayurbhanj is between $21^0$17' and $22^0$34' north latitude and between $85^0$40' and $87^0$10' east longitude. It is bounded on north by the Singhbhum district of Bihar and the Midnapur district of West Bengal; on the south by the districts of Balasore and Kendujhar, on the east by the districts of Midnapur and Balasore and on the west by the districts of Kendujhar and Singhbhum. Suliapada P.S. and Muruda P.S. which lie to the extreme east of the district are contiguous with Midnapur district and it is in this area that these two police stations are located and also the Midnapur district where the Lodhas live. The area under these two police stations come under the eastern division of the district and is characterized by a land which is moderately wooded and sloping from the foot of the hills towards the sea. The Lodhas are found living in separate hamlets of multi-caste villages. But it is a common-sight to see that most of the Lodha villages are situated inside the dense forests which are difficult of access. The origin of the Lodha tribe has been lost in antiquity. They claim to have migrated from Madhya Pradesh sometimes in the eighteenth century to the Mayurbhanj and Balasore districts of Orissa. The adjoining areas in West Bengal and Bihar show a large concentration of Lodhas particularly in the Midnapore and Singhbhum districts, where their number is more than 26,000.

The Lodhas claim that they were descendants of *Jarasabara* who used to worship the Lord Jagannatha. Based on this belief they regard themselves superior in social status than any other tribes and therefore refrain themselves from dining in the houses of other communities and they identify themselves as *Lodhasabar*.

The Lodhas belong to the North Munda group speaking *Mundari* as their mother tongue. By virtue of their long association and contact with their Hindu neighbours, they have forgotten their *Mundari* speech and now speak a dialect composed of distorted Bengali, Oriya and Mundari.

Settlement and Houses

The Lodhas live in villages which are in many cases exclusively theirs. Sometimes they live with other communities in villages which are heterogeneous in caste composition. In such cases they have their own hamlets far apart from the main village which is occupied by the Hindu caste. In a Lodha village the houses are scattered here and there and the village approaches a pattern of shapeless cluster. The houses are single roomed, straw thatched and mud walled. A portion of the house is used to keep the goats and cattle. Sometimes these animals are kept on the side verandah. In one corner of the house on a raised platform near the hearth, the seat of the ancestral spirits is located. Some well to do Lodha families have multi-roomed houses with spacious courtyards and kitchen gardens fenced with bamboo poles and twigs.

Economic Life

Most of the Lodhas are in pre-agricultural level of technology pursuing hunting, food gathering, collection of minor forest produce and tusser cultivation in the forests. Apart from the collection of fruits, roots and tubers for their own consumption, they collect *Kendu* leaves to make country cigarettes, *Sal* and *Siali* leaves to make leaf cups and plates, *Sabai* grass to make ropes. They also collect honey, lac, resin, *Sal* seeds, *Mahua* flowers, firewood which they sell in the market to earn a livelihood.

The Lodhas present a pathetic picture in respect of their economic life. As said earlier, in early days they used to rear the tusser silkworm in the forests having *Asan* and *Sal* tree in abundance. These two forest species are the best feed plants for rearing silkworms. With the opening up of these forest regions many outsiders including the forest contractors penetrated into these areas and cut down these trees for commercial purposes. With rapid deforestation and prohibitory forest laws the Lodhas have been thrown out of forest-based subsistence. Having no knowledge in other pursuits to fall back upon and being ignorant of agricultural technology, the Lodhas were forced to take up unfair means and looting and stealing activities just for their survival. Many Lodhas have turned into regular criminals and some of them thrive on wages earned through agricultural labour and construction works. Since they are dreaded for their criminal activities, the common peasants of the locality do not dare to engage them in their farms and household activities. Cases of burglary and molestation of women by the Lodhas have terrified the common people of the locality who keep the Lodhas always at bay. All these situations have made the Lodhas very much aggressive and the harassments to which they are subjected by the police, public and government officials have rather worsened the situation instead of improving the inter-community relationship.

Social Organization

Family is the smallest social unit in the Lodha society. Majority of the Lodha families are of nuclear type comprising the parents and their unmarried children. Some cases of joint and extended families are also met with. Polygyny is prevalent in the Lodha society. The father being the seniormost male member is regarded as the head of the family and the family property is inherited along the male line. After marriage a daughter leaves her parental house and joins the family of her parents-in-laws. These customs show that Lodhas family is patriarchal, patrilineal and patrilocal.

The Lodha social system includes clan organization. There are nine different clan groups namely: 1. *Bugta* (a kind of tuber) 2. *Malik* (Shark), 3. *Kotal* (grasshopper), 4. *Naak* (Sal fish), 5. *Digar*, (Porpoise), 6. *Parmanik* (a bird named *Manik*), 7. *Dandapat* or *Bag* (Tiger) 8. *Ahari* (Chandafish), 9. *Bhuya* (Sal fish). Each clan is of totemic origin and also exogamous. Taboos are observed by the clan members in respect of their respective totemic objects. In the case of women clan identity changes after marriage but it is not so in the case of a man who belongs to the clan of his birth throughout his life. After clan comes the tribe which is the largest social unit and is endogamous.

Political Organization

Every Lodha village has its own traditional village *panchayat* called *Desh*. All adult male persons are members of the village *panchayat*. The village headman called *Mukhi* or *Sardar* presides over the village *panchayat* and decides cases relating to breach of social customs, norms and taboos in consultation with the village elders. The *Mukhia* gives his verdict over the cases which is obeyed by one and all. There is a village messenger called *Dakua* who assists the village headman. The *Dakua* of the village hails from *Kotal* clan.

In every village there is a village priest called *Talia* or *Chharidar* who presides over all ritual performances and worships deities. There is a functionary called *Hantakar* who sacrifices animals on ritual occasions. The Lodha villages have one or two medicine men and *Shamans* who are known as *Gunni* and *Byakra* respectively.

Life-Cycle

BIRTH

A pregnant woman observes certain taboos in respect of diet, sexual intercourse and movement. Goat and fowl are sacrificed and offered to the local deities to ensure smooth delivery and well-being of the mother and the child. As soon as the labour pain starts, an old woman of the village is called for to serve as the midwife. Birth prohibitions is observed for 21 days and during this period the mother and the baby remain confined to the house and certain precautionary taboos are observed. The baby is breast fed by the mother up to the age of six months. After six months two ceremonies namely the hair cutting and rice feeding are observed.

MARRIAGE

Marriage is an important social event in the life of a person. Adult marriage is common among the Lodhas. The most common mode of marriage is marriage by negotiation. A mediator is engaged by both the sides to carry on negotiation and settle the bride price. Cases of child marriage, love marriage, marriage by service, and marriages by exchange of sisters are also met with in the Lodha society. Besides these types, the Lodhas follow the custom of levirate and sorrorate types of marriages. Widow re-marriage is prevalent among them and divorce is allowed.

DEATH

The dead body is either buried or cremated. Death prohibitions lasts for 10 days. Purificatory rituals are performed on the 10th day as well as on the 11th day. On the day of purification, the agnates and cognates and also the co-villagers are entertained with a feast arranged by the members of the family of the deceased.

Religion

Lodhas believe in many gods and goddesses. Among them the *Dharam Devta* who is regarded as the supreme being is benevolent. The next in importance is *Basumata* who represents the mother earth. There is deity called *Sitala* who is regarded as the goddess of epidemics. The forest is believed to be the abode of many spirits. Among them *Baram* is considered most important. The Lodhas observe a number of magico-religious festivals and rituals round the year. The important festivals are *Sitala puja* and *Chandi puja* observed to propitiate the spirits so that no calamities take place in the village and no ghosts and spirits attack them. Every year ancestor worship which is called *Natun Hanri* is observed in the month of *Chaitra*. It is a sort of annual *Shradha* ceremony during which food and drink are offered to the ancestors.

THE PAUDI BHUINYA

Setting

The Bhuinya is one of the most widespread tribes of Orissa. Of the total population of 2,07,792 as per 1981 census, 1,99,400 Bhuinyas are found distributed in four districts namely, Sundergarh (Pop. 67552), Kendujhar (Pop. 64.273), Mayurbhanj (Pop. 41,580) and Sambalpur (Pop. 26.025). There are many sections of the tribe like: Rajkoli and Paraja Bhuinyas who are agriculturists, Paik Bhuinyas who represent the militia Khandayats, Ghatwar Bhuinyas who are land holders and Paudi Bhuinyas who are primarily shifting cultivators. This Paudi Bhuinya section has been identified as one of the primitive tribes of Orissa and it is with this section that the present ethnographic text deals.

The Paudi Bhuinyas are found in largest concentration in four adjacent areas namely, Banspal block of Kendujhar district, Pallahara block of Dhenkanal district, Koira block of Sundergarh district, Deoghar block of Sambalpur district.

The Bhuinyas have no language of their own. Oriya has been their mother tongue. Unlike the plains' Bhuinyas who are able to speak Oriya fluently, the Paudi Bhuinyas pronounce Oriya in a peculiar way. There is no peculiarity in the dress of both men and women. The men wear *dhotis*, *banyan*, shirt as the Oriyas of the neighbourhood do. Similarly the women wear sarees like the Oriya women. There is no difference in ornaments used by both Bhuinya women and Oriya women.

Settlement Pattern

The hilly terrain and valley region form the homeland of the Paudi Bhuinyas. Many villages are situated in open table lands uphills and most of the villages are difficult to access and are fairly isolated and lie hidden in the thick *Sal* forests. The villages are located in such places where sufficient hill slopes are available for shifting cultivation and thick forests for hunting and food gathering. Presence of a good perennial stream is a necessary condition for the location of a settlement. Besides these factors, the place must have spiritual sanction for human habitation. Construction of houses does not conform to any regular pattern. In some cases they are built either on both sides of the main village path or are dispersed on all sides. Each household has a courtyard around which the huts are built. The number of huts which a family has around the courtyard depends upon the family size and economic condition. The cowshed forms a separate hut and is built on one side of the courtyard. Every family has kitchen garden at the back of the house where chillies, tobacco and vegetables are grown. The lands immediately around the village are used for growing thatching grass, maize and mustard. Most conspicuous in a Bhuinya village are jackfruit and mango trees which are grown around the village. These groves indicate from a distance the presence of a Bhuinya village. In every Bhuinya village there may be a few milk-men families who live in a separate ward.

The most attractive and commodious hut built in the centre of the village is the bachelor's dormitory which is called *Mandaghar* in Kendujhar and *Durbarghar* in Sundergarh. This hut not only serves as a dormitory of the unmarried boys who sleep there at night but it is used for many other purposes. It serves as a guest-house in the sense that any visiting guests, relatives and officials are accommodated there during their night halt. It is the meeting place of the village council where the village headman, priest and elders of the village meet and deliberate on multifarious village affairs. The seeds of various crops grown by the Paudi Bhuinyas in lands under shifting cultivation are stored there. In this sense it is used as a granary of the village. The *changus* or the circular single membrane drums played by men at the time of dancing are kept suspended by means of strings from deer antlers fixed to the walls. On a raised wooden platform, in the inner portion of the hut, are kept straw packed bundles containing stocks of grains of the village youths.

The size of a Bhuinya village varies from a few houses to a very large number of houses. There may be villages as small as five to ten houses and there may be very big villages having more than 50 houses. In big villages there may be many wards each inhabited by families which are related to one another by blood.

BHUINYA HUT

The construction of a new house is always begun either on Friday or on Wednesday. The sacred pillar is fixed first on the ground. The head of the household does so after observing the specific rituals and sanctity. In fact, the sacred pillar which is fixed in central position forms one of the pillars of the sacred inner chamber. After the house is constructed, another ritual is performed in which the ancestral spirits are properly installed in the inner chamber and food and drink are offered to them.

A Bhuinya hut is rectangular in shape with a two sloped roof thatched with grass. The walls are made of logs of wood which are fixed vertically to the ground close to one another and are plastered with mud and cowdung. The rafters and beams are also made of logs of wood. The houses are provided with doors which are made of split bamboos plastered with mud and cowdung. An earthen verandah is built around the house or only in front for sitting purpose. No window is provided in the house.

A Bhuinya house has mainly three portions. The innermost portion is used for storing foodgrains on a raised platform. A part of the middle portion is set apart for the kitchen. From the hearth runs a narrow passage leading to a small and secluded space called *Bhitar* where the ancestral spirits are worshipped. The remaining part of the middle portion is used as sleeping apartment. The kitchen-cum-sleeping portion is kept separate from the third outermost portion by means of a partition wall to which a door is fixed facilitating entry into the kitchen and store portions of the house. The mortar is fixed in the floor of the middle portion of the house where foodgrains are husked by means of a pestle. Close to the walls near the kitchen are kept waterpots on a raised earthen platform. The chickens and goats take their shelter under the wooden platform in the store room.

It may be mentioned here that a family may have a *Bhitar* chamber in one of the huts under its possession. This hut is called *Mulaghar* (main house) while other huts are known as *Melaghar* (outer house). No entry of outsiders into the *Mulaghar* is allowed because the kitchen and the *Bhitar* section of the hut is held most sacred. In some villages, a group of families belonging to a single lineage may have a common *Bhitar* or *Mulaghar* as they all have a set of common ancestral spirits. A Bhuinya family have a shed separately built to serve as the lying-in room. The parturient woman spends one or two months after delivery in this shed and it is only after the purificatory rites that she is allowed to enter the *Mulaghar*.

Household Appliances, Dress and Ornaments

The household articles of a Paudi Bhuinya family are only a few which consist of some earthen vessels, gourd containers, broom sticks, bamboo baskets, mortar and pestle, grinding stone, palm- leaf mats, leaf-made raincoat, hoe, axe, plough, some digging sticks, bow and arrows, straw made grain bins and some aluminium utensils.

Both traditional and modern types of utensils are seen in a Bhuinya house. For water storage, both earthen pitcher and metal pitcher of aluminium or brass are used. The most common water container (or carrier) in a Bhuinya house is *tumba* which is a dried shell of bitter-gourd fruit. *Tumba* is too dear to a Bhuinya because it keeps water cool for a considerable period of time. So, while working in the fields during summer, *tumba* water is a great reliever of thrust. Large size *tumba*s are kept at home for domestic use of water.

The cooking utensils include modern metal articles such as vessel (*dekchi*), bowl (*bela*), small bowl (*gina*), ladle (*danka*), etc. However, the most striking feature of traditional use is the leaf cups and leaf plates used for dining purpose. Leaf plates are mostly used in community feasts where rice is served on it.

There is nothing special in the dress of the Bhuinya men and women. Men wear *dhoti, banian,* shirt, etc., and women wear sarees and use ornaments of the type which are used by the Oriya women.

Food

Rice is the staple food of the Paudi Bhuinya. Paddy is grown by them in their land, but it is not sufficient to go the year round. Therefore, they exchange their products which they get from shifting cultivation such as black gram (*biri*), niger, mustard, and maize for paddy. Besides, such crops as *ragi, suan, gulchi, kangu* and some other minor millets and cereals which are grown in the lands of the shifting cultivation supplement their rice diet. They take various types of green leaves, vegetables, mushrooms, tubers, etc., as additional dishes.

The groves of jackfruits and mango trees abound the Bhuinya villages. These fruits ripen in summer season and so the Bhuinyas depend upon these fruits throughout the summer months. The Bhuinyas take both unripe and ripe jackfruits and mangoes. The unripe jackfruits make good curry which they relish very much. The seeds of the ripe jackfruits are also eaten by cooking with other vegetables. Unripe mangoes make pickles and the ripe mangoes give sweet pulp which they enjoy eating. They also make mango jelly which they eat as well as sell in the weekly *hat*. The kernel of the mango stone is also eaten by them. The mango stones are dried and the kernels taken out of them are dried and pulverized. Cakes are made of the powdered kernels by baking.

The forests used to be the food bank of the Paudi Bhuinyas. It used to give them tubers, rhizomes, leaves and shoots, various types of fruits, flowers, seeds, grains, which are of great nutritious value. Besides food gathering, they used to carry on hunting in the forests to supplement their food with non-vegetarian diet. Consequent upon deforestation, the wild plants and animals have become rare resulting in considerable nutritional deficiency. Since water sources are scarce, fishing is not an important activity. Festivals and rituals which are observed round the year are the only occasions when fowls and goats are sacrificed to propitiate several deities and these sacrificial meat meets the much needed protein diet to some extent. Certain berries and seeds like those of *Bahunia vahili* which are rich in protein, but unknown to the people, are eaten in season. Certain flowers like those of which contain honey are found in the locality. While going to the field a person breaks a branch of this tree with full of flowers and goes on sucking the honey from the flowers one after another. On market days they get a chance to get sweets of different types and enjoy the time in company of others of the fellow age-group.

Usually the adults eat twice or thrice and the children many times a day. The meal is prepared by women, by boiling method. On festive occasions the women prepare *ragi* or rice cakes and porridge. Milk and milk products are purchased occasionally from the milkmen as they do not milch their cows.

The Paudi Bhuinyas drink various types of liquor such as *Mahua* liquor, rice beer, toddy extracted from datepalm juice. The Bhuinyas drink liquor as a substitute for food, and to get relief from fatigue after strenuous fieldwork. Liquor is offered to their deities and ancestral spirits to appease them. Guests and relatives are entertained with drinks during marriage ceremonies and festivities and other rituals associated with agricultural cycle. The Paudis get *Mahua* liquor from the vendors in exchange of agricultural produce, whereas rice beer is prepared at home for the simple reason that they do not accept it from the hands of other castes or tribes.

Life-Cycle

Mainly there are three events in the life-cycle: birth, marriage and death.

BIRTH

Birth of a child in a Bhuinya family is a matter of great rejoice. A woman who is barren is looked down upon and occupies a lower position in society than a woman who has many children. Although a male child is desired more than a female child, but the children of both the sexes are an asset to the family. Being patrilocal, the sons continue to live with their parents throughout their life whereas daughters leave their parents after their marriage and go to live with their husbands in their respective villages. But so long as they are unmarried the daughters contribute their labour as much as the sons do to support their parents. Moreover, each daughter fetches a bride price for her parents in marriage.

A shed is constructed as lying-in room. As soon as the labour pain starts she is removed to this room. A mid-wife is immediately called in. It does not matter whether she belongs to the Bhuinya tribe or to any other caste and tribe. She takes care of the baby for which she is paid some cash including a piece of new cloth and foodstuff. If it is not a normal delivery, the head of the family prays the ancestral spirits at the *Bhitar* with a pot full of water. After the worship is over, some water is sprinkled on the woman and some is given to her to drink. In spite of this if the labour pain continues a witch doctor is consulted. He reads omens and finds out the spirit which has obstructed the delivery and takes step to remove the difficulties for the delivery of the child without pain.

On the 7th day both the baby and the mother take their first purificatory bath. The mother ties around her neck a piece of new thread soaked in turmeric water. A similar piece of thread is also tied round the neck of the baby. From this day, the members of the family may take water from her hands, but she is not allowed to enter the kitchen and cook the meals.

MARRIAGE

No Bhuinya marries outside the tribe because the tribe is endogamous.

Similarly, marrying within own clan is prohibited because it is exogamous. Previously all the households of a village belonged to a single *Khilli* or clan. Therefore, no one married within the village. But later the Bhuinyas belonging to the same clan were found living in different villages. Therefore, the villages inhabited by the same clan formed a non-marrying group called *Kutumba* villages which means all the households belonging to *Kutumba* villages are related to one another by blood. These villages may have marital relationship with villages other than the *Kutumba* and these villages form a cognatic group of villages which are called *Bandhu* villages. Nowadays the composition of the villages has become heterogeneous. Therefore, cases of marriage within the village are met with. Since the tribe is patrilineal, the daughters after their marriage leave the house of their parents and go to live with their husbands in other villages. Generally the marriage is monogamous but if the first wife dies or does not bear any child he may take a second wife. Widow re-marriage is not common, but cases of such marriage are met with in some villages. Cross-cousin marriage is not common and the cases or sorrorate or levirate marriages are very rare. Similarly, marriage by exchange is a rare occurrence.

Various forms of marriage are met with among the Bhuinyas. These are: marriage by negotiation (*mangibibha),* love marriage with arrangement (*Cadalesara*), marriage by capture (*Phulkhusi*), marriage by elopement (*Chicha*), and widow remarriage (*Dharipala*).

Marriage by elopement and marriage by capture are common forms of marriage but marriage by arrangements or negotiation is a recent phenomenon. In the case of arranged marriage a brahmin is invited to perform the ceremony and the bridegroom is dressed with crowns placed onto his head (*mukuta*). But *mukuta baha* marriage is most uncommon. The marriage by arrangement is very much elaborate and also expensive.

Among the Paudi Bhuinyas the custom of payment of bride wealth is prevalent. The items and the amount of bride price are same for all types of marriage. The items which constitute the bride wealth are as follows:

1. One bullock for the bride's father.
2. One bullock for her father's younger brother.
3. One bullock for her mother's brother.
4. Some cash and some rice for the middle men.
5. Sufficient quantity of rice for the preparation of gruel.
6. One rupee and a saree for the bride's mother.
7. Sufficient rice and goat for the feast at the bride's village.

DEATH RITES

When a person dies, his kinsmen and near relatives start wailing loudly till the dead body is carried to the burial ground. Both the cognates and the agnates of the deceased carry the dead body to the burial ground. A pit of sufficient length and breadth is dug and the corpse is laid down with head facing north. The eldest son puts the soil first on the corpse and others standing nearby fill up the pit with soil. The pollution period lasts for three days. During the pollution period all the *Kutumba* families as well as the *Bandhu* families throw away the used earthen vessels. The clothes are properly washed. Similarly mats and other household materials are all washed in water. On the final day of purification all the *Kutumba* male members clip their hair and shave their beard and both men and women pare their nails.

The Paudi Bhuinya believe that life does not come to an end with death. The soul lives in the form of a spirit. The spirit finally comes back home and settles down in the sacred *Bhitar* as an ancestral spirit. Not all spirits become the ancestral spirits and find place in the *Bhitar* to stay and to be worshipped by the survivors.

Social Organization

FAMILY

Family is the smallest social unit. The nuclear type of the family is common. It comprises parents and unmarried children. Among the Paudi Bhuinyas the family is partilineal. Property is always inherited by the sons after the death of the father and it is equally distributed among all the sons. After marriage a daughter leaves her parents and goes to her husband and stays with him in his village. In this case the residence among the Bhuinyas is patrilocal. The eldest male member of the family is considered as the family head. He is usually the father in a nuclear and extended family or the eldest brother in a joint family where the father is dead. The father exercises considerable authority over all the members of the family and all others are expected to obey him. The father owns the property and it is not divided among his sons during his lifetime. In this sense the family is patriarchal.

LINEAGE

The next bigger social unit is the lineage or *Kutumba* formed by a group of families related to one another by blood. The relationship between the lineage groups is based on the mutual help and co-operation. Exchange of labour at the time of construction of house and agricultural operations, exchange of food during festivals and organization of joint functions and observance of birth and death prohibitions jointly, are some of the striking features which govern the activities of the lineage members.

Several *Kutumbas* form an exogamous unit called *Khilli* (clan). All the members of *Khilli* believe to have descended from a common ancestor. The next bigger unit is the village which may comprise members of one *Khilli* or several *Khillis*. In the past the Bhuinya villages were homogeneous and all the households in a village were related to one another by blood and therefore intra-village marriage was forbidden. Broadly, the Bhuinya villages are divided into two groups — *Bandhu* villages (cognatic) where marriage is possible and *Kutumba* villages (agnatic) where marriage is not possible. Recently due to the in-and-out migration, the composition of villages has undergone change. Now, villages with both cognatic and agnatic groups are not rare.

YOUTH ORGANIZATION

The indigenous youth organization of the types of bachelor's dormitory which were in existence in many tribal communities are in the present time in the process of disintegration but in some cases such organizations have withstood the onslaught of modern forces and have survived till today. The youth organization have altogether disappeared among the Bhuinyas who are living in the plains but such organizations are present among the Paudi Bhuinyas of interior areas like Koira region of Bonai and Bhuinyapirh of Kendujhar district. Even in these areas the spinsters' dormitory is present. The bachelor's dormitory is called *Mandaghar* in Kendujhar and *Durbarghar* in Bonai of Sundergarh district. The unmarried boys above 14 years become members of the dormitory. Although the girls' dormitory has disappeared, unmarried girls above 12 years of age form a group and sleep in the house of a widow of the village or in different houses wherever extra accommodation is available. For all other purposes their activities are associated with the bachelors' dormitory of the village. The boys take care of thatching and repairing of the dormitory whereas the girls do the cleaning and plastering of the walls and the floor and sweeping of the place where the dancing of the boys and the girls is held.

The unmarried boys who are called *Dhangada*s and the unmarried girls who are called *Dhangdi*s have specific duties and responsibilities in respect of the maintenance and upkeep of the dormitory. The boys bring logs of wood from the forest for the sacred fire which is kept lit during the day and night throughout the year. Whenever a marriage takes place in any family it is the boys who fetch firewood for cooking foods for the feast and also supply water. They also do the cooking of the marriage feast and are required to accompany the bride to the groom's village playing the *changu* on the way. When any communal feast is arranged on any social and religious occasion the boys supply firewood and water for cooking the foods. Whenever the girls of their *bandhu* villages come on a visit to their villages, the boys raise contributions and collect grains and other food materials to feed the girls during their stay in the village. The unmarried boys and the girls are sometimes hired by any villager to work on his field on payment of cash or kind. In some villages it is found that the girls and the boys cultivate a patch of land jointly and utilize the yield for common purpose.

As regards the girls they also perform certain duties and are in-charge of certain other responsibilities. It is the work of the girls to plaster the dormitory and keep the place clean. Whenever any distinguished visitor happens to come on a visit to the village the girls keep the dormitory clean and supply leaf cups and plates for him to take meals. They supply sleeping mats woven in date palm leaves to the boys and in return the boys supply them with firewood for their sleeping apartment. In marriage the girls accompany the bride to the groom's village and sing marriage songs throughout the journey. Whenever the boys of a Bandhu village come on a visit it is the duty of the girls of the village to look after them and arrange their food.

The association between the boys and the girls continues so long as they are unmarried and enjoy the membership in the dormitory but this association ceases to exist when the membership in the dormitory is terminated with their marriage. Before a member of the dormitory is married, he or she is entertained with a farewell feast arranged by the members of the dormitory. On this occasion the departing boy offers puffed rice, sweets, combs, mirrors and tobacco to his dormitory. The farewell ceremony observed on the occasion of departing companionship means only termination of their companionship at the dormitory level but it gives lease for a new life in other stages of their life-cycle.

Political Organization

In every Paudi village there is a traditional village *panchayat* and there are secular and religious leaders to take care of social and religious matters. Generally the Paudi villages are free from inter-personal conflicts and disruptive forces of party politics and majority vote. Everyone participates in the decision-making process and all decision are reached by unanimity. The village headman, *Padhan,* presides over the *panchayat.* A group of villages form a confederacy called *Pirha.* The *panchayat* at this level is called *Pirha Panchayat* and the secular headman who presides over it is called *Sardar.*

In a Bhuinya village, the governance is carried out by leaders such as the *Dehuri, Padhan* and *Naika.* However, certain posts such as the *Naika* has become defunct in the modern context. According to the Bhuinyas, *Naika* and *Padhan* do have the same role to play — that of justice dispensation. To maintain the post of the *Naika* villagers used to pay some annual remuneration. In recent times such remunerations have become burdensome for the Bhuinyas and hence, they have done away with post.

In the changed traditional leadership set-up the following functionaries take care of the day-to-day affairs in a village.

PADHAN

He is the secular head of the village and looks after the problems within the village and between villages (along with the *Padhan* of other villages). He is assisted by the *Dehuri* or the religious head. Unlike among the Juangs, *Padhan* is the most important village leader in a Bhuinya village and although the *Dehuri* assists him in justice dispensation, he is mostly confined to ritual duties.

DEHURI

Even though the *Dehuri* is regarded as ritual functionary, nonetheless he draws highest respect from the villagers, because he is the link between the mortals and the supernatural beings. His views carry weight which the villagers value.

DAKUA

He is the assistant for the above two leaders and maintains link between the functionaries and the villagers. All decisions and proceedings of the village council are intimated to the villagers through the *Dakua*.

MEMBER

After the statutory *panchayat* was instituted by the government, the "member" post was created at the village level to involve the government in day-to-day affairs of the village. Although the prime function of the member is to see the village development works, he is also involved in the intra-village and inter-village disputes.

In dispensation of justice and dispute settlements which mainly result from land and forest use, the traditional council has been playing pivotal role since generations and has maintained peace and tranquillity in the Bhuinyapirh. Punishment for violation of traditional norms and laws range between a *mana* and a *Khandi* of paddy grains. Forest offences are penalized according to the nature of the offence. For instance, the size of a tree felled determines the amount of grain to be paid in fine to the village council.

The primary functions of the village *panchayat* are to decide partition to property among brothers, distribute land for shifting cultivation, organize religious ceremonies and maintain peace and order in the village. In the earlier dispensation *Padhan* and *Sardar* were very powerful and men of authority. They used to collect land revenue from the ryots and maintain law and order in their respective areas of operation. After Independence and abolition of intermediary system and merger of feudatory states with Orissa these traditional political organizations have been weakened. The introduction of statutory *panchayat* has further weakened the old political order and *Pirha* organization.

Economic Life

AGRICULTURE

The economic life of the Bhuinyas mainly centres around shifting cultivation which is the primary source of their livelihood. To a large extent it is supplemented by collection of minor forest produce and to some extent by wet and dry cultivation and by hunting, fishing and wage earning. Other than those mentioned above, some of them particularly those living in the plains have taken to petty trade and commerce and industrial employment. Rope making is the recreational activity of the Bhuinya women. The Bhuinya follow sex-division of labour for certain activities. Generally heavier works such as cutting trees, ploughing, sowing, hunting and fishing fall on the shoulders of men, while lighter works such as cooking and other domestic works are the monopoly of women and thatching houses and climbing trees are taboo for them. Works like forest clearing, weeding, transplanting, harvesting, threshing, collection of minor forest produce are attended by both men and women.

The land under valley bottom (*Bila*) are put to permanent cultivation where paddy is the only crop grown. As water is available in the valley throughout the year, these lands are suitable for paddy cultivation. Such a favourable condition has induced them to apply chemical fertilizer in their wet lands for better production. In addition to these lands they have plain lands at elevated place (*Nala*) which are used for growing niger, pulses and minor millets. The kitchen garden (*Eakadi*) is meant for growing vegetables, tobacco, maize and mustard. The *Bila, Nala* and *Bakadi* lands are privately owned while the lands under shifting cultivation are communally held. Both sowing and transplanting are practised in growing paddy in wet land while only sowing is practised in growing crops in *Nala* and *Bakadi* lands. Except *Bakadi* land and wet land no other types of land are manured and the use of bullock driven ploughs for tilling all types of land is common in the village.

Cultivation is a family affair in which all able bodied adult members of the family co-operate. Whenever any extra labour is required it is commissioned not by hire but by exchange basis. Outside labour is required only for weeding and harvesting. A man having no draught animals may take the help of another having such animals. In such cases he has to till the land of the owner of the animals for the same number of days he used the animals in his land.

The Bhuinya domesticate various animals like cow, bullock, buffalo, goat, sheep and fowl. The main object for keeping cows is not for milk but for cultivation and breeding. Cowdung is used as manure.

The Bhuinyas are in the habit of collecting minor forest produce extensively for their own consumption and also for sale as a secondary source of income. The important items of forests collection include *mahua* flower, *mahua* seed, mango, jackfruit, tamarind, *harida, anala, sal* seed, *kusum*, various types of green leaves, mushrooms, edible roots and tubers. They also collect firewood, thatching grass, fibres for rope making and different types of herbs and shrubs of medicinal value.

The Bhuinya practise shifting cultivation extensively which goes by the term *Taila chasa*. They generally cultivate a patch of forest land for three consecutive years after which it is left abandoned. The patch under first year of cultivation is known as *Biringa,* the second year as *Kaman* and the third as *Guda*. These patches are located on flat hill slopes stretching up to the foot-hills. The hills in this area are generally flat topped and without much stone boulders and the gradient is gentle. The lands under shifting cultivation are confined 5^0 to 12^0 slope. After cultivating a patch of land for three years they leave it fallow for a period of 5 to 7 years for recuperation. Previously the fallow period was 12 to 15 years. But the main cause for its reduction is the population pressure and shortage of land for paddy cultivation. The land under shifting cultivation belong to the village and a patch of swidden after distribution by the village committee remain in cultivating possession of a man as long as he continues to cultivate it.

The first year of shifting cultivation (*Biringa*) involves several stages such as the selection of hill slopes in December-January by the village committee headed by *Padhan*, tree felling and bush clearing (*Guchhakata*) from February to April, piling of felled trees and firing (*Anapuda*) in April-May, bush clearing (*Patikata*) in May, sowing (*Buna*) in July, ploughing and hoeing (*Bhuinyange*) in July, immediately after hoeing, weeding and debushing (*Judabachha*) in September-October after *Ashiaripuja*, watching the crops in November-December and finally harvesting from December onwards. The crops grown in the swidden during the first year are *kolatha, birhi, rasi,* and various types of vegetables, pulses and creeper plants.

During the second year of shifting cultivation (*Kaman*) the main crop grown is a short duration paddy along with *Jawar* (*Gangei*). The former is sown in the middle of the plot and the latter on the borders of the plot. Besides, they grow *kodo, mandia, kangu* and various types of vegetables in the second year.

In the third year of shifting cultivation (*Guda*) only niger is grown. If a patch fetches good harvest in the second year then it is cultivated for the third year. The same patch can be brought under fourth year cultivation if there is a good harvest in the third year.

HUNTING AND FOOD GATHERING

The Paudi Bhuinyas go out for hunting and food gathering in the nearby forests to supplement their income from agricultural sources. Food gathering is done in all the seasons and by both men and women. Their collection includes such items as wild tubers, fruits, and flowers, green leaves, mushrooms honey, *mahua* flowers. Some forest products are available in plenty in summer season and some in winter and rainy season. Mango trees are in great abundance in the Bhuinya country. Basket full of mangoes are collected in this season. Both green and ripe mangoes are a great favourite of the Bhuinyas. Minor forest products like lac, fibres, resin, myrobalans, oil yielding seeds, medicinal herbs, firewood, and timbers are a great source of income of the Bhuinyas. With the gradual deforestation of the forest the income from this source is on the decline.

ANIMAL HUSBANDRY

The Bhuinyas are not so skilled in animal husbandry as they are in agriculture. They keep cows, bullocks, buffaloes, goats, sheep and poultry. The cattle are used for ploughing the lambs, and the goats and chickens are sacrificed on ritual occasions to appease the deities and on ceremonial occasions to entertain guests and relatives. Cowdung is the source of manure which they apply in the *Bakadi* lands and kitchen gardens. They are not habituated to drinking milk and therefore they do not milk the cows. Some Bhuinya families sell buffalo milk and milk products for cash. The cattle and goats are let loose in the forest to graze under the supervision of a cowherd. Stalk feeding is not practised. The buffaloes are herded separately and boys of milkman community or even a Paudi Bhuinya takes care of buffaloes of the village throughout the year. For this, all the households of a village pay a fix amount which is settled with the herdsman at the beginning of the year.

OTHER SOURCES OF INCOME

The Bhuinya country is no longer inaccessible. Roads have been built and the movement of people has increased. With the opening up of the territory, many developmental projects have been implemented in these areas. Mining operations have started to extract minerals. Plantation of trees and social forestry programmes are under way in many places. These activities have provided opportunities to the Bhuinyas to work as wage earners in their leisure time and improve their economic condition and their outlook.

Religious Universe

The Bhuinya believe in the existence of three spheres, namely *sarga* (heaven), *bhuin* (earth) and *patal* (earth's crust). For them, all human beings when alive are on earth only, but after their death they either move to the heaven or hover around in space over the earth. *Patal,* the underground, is believed to be the abode for the unknown spirits. Their belief in "rebirth" makes them feel that after death the soul enters another body and takes birth in the form of an animal. An individual with all his desires fulfilled may not have rebirth after his death, but a person having premature death may keep coming to trouble not only his family members, but other people in the village as well.

To cope with such situations and also all other events believed to be caused by the supernaturals, the Bhuinyas take recourse to propitiation of a number of deities, spirits and ghosts in different ways. The religious headman called *dehuri* propitiates the deities on festive occasion. The spirits commonly known are as follows.

BHUINYA PANTHEON

At the top of the pantheon are the Bhuinya's high deities, *Dharam Devta* and *Basumata.* All the deities both benevolent and malevolent spirits are known collectively as *devta*s while ghosts are called as *bhuta*s.

High Deities

Dharam Devta is the sun god giving life to all human beings and keeping a watchful eye on everybody. He is the husband of *Basumata* — the mother earth who provides food to every human being. Like the Juangs, the Bhuinyas utter names of these deities on every ritual occasion. They protect the Bhuinyas from all evil elements. They are entirely benevolent and do not harm anyone under any circumstances. The village priest *Dehuri* start every ritual with the utterance of these two names simply because they are so vital and indispensable to Bhuinya survival.

Supreme Ancestors

Of no less importance are the procreators — *Bodam budha* and *Bodam budhi* — of the Bhuinyas. Every Bhuinya family worships the supreme ancestors on every ritual performed at home. They are also worshipped on all the communal ritual occasions. The abode of *Bodam Budha* is in the *Medha* or *Sala* (sacred grove) at the outskirts of a village. Very close to him is the abode of *Bodam Budhi* in the same sacred grove. Some pieces of stone represent both the deities.

Village Deity

Pat is the village goddess and everybody is afraid of her wrath and therefore the ritual observances connected with her are strictly followed, lest she may prove fatal to human life and livestock. The village goddess has different names in different villages. For example, in Saharpur she is known as *Bharali pat*, while in Pada Kesada, she is *Maa pat*. Her stone emblem, located at the centre of the village in a hut close to the *darbar* (dormitory and community centre), is given a ceremonial bath on a ritual occasion called *Devta gadha* in the month of *Magsira*. She is benevolent as long as there is no default in her propitiation. In Saharpur, there are three deities in the pit hut. The other two deities are the *Maha pat* (goddess) and *Duarchuni* (goddess).

Other Deities in the Sacred Grove

Besides *Bodam*, there are two more gods in the *medha*. They are *Gainseri* and *Jhankara* in case of Saharpur and *Gainseri* and *Asar Basar* in case of Sapkanta. In the village visited, it has been found that *Bodam* and *Gainseri* are two common deities, while the third deity has a local name. All of them are in stone emblems.

It is interesting to know that the deities in the sacred grove are worshipped by different religious functionaries. While *Bodam* and *Gainseri* are worshipped by the *Dehuri*, the *Padhan* (secular head in a village) worships the third deity — *Jhankara* — in case of Saharpur. The names of these deities are taken on all communal ritual occasions which are observed at the sacred grove. It is a taboo to urinate or defecate in the sacred grove. Anyone doing so is believed to meet premature death. Utmost care is taken to keep the premises of the sacred grove clean and pure. Like *Bodam*, the other two deities are benevolent *devtas*, but may cause damage to life and property, if neglected or overlooked in worship.

Next in rank are the *devtas* having their abode in different parts of the village such as forest, stream, hill, etc. They are generally malevolent in nature. They have different names in different villages.

Baitarani Pat

Like the Juangs, the Bhuinyas worship the river Baitarani as a powerful goddess. But while in case of the Juangs the goddess's abode included the hill from which the river has originated, here among the Bhuinyas, the abode of the goddess is the river itself.

Khandianali

It is a malevolent spirit residing in the agricultural fields. Before starting agricultural activities, all the Bhuinyas having agricultural land propitiate the spirit by offering rice, vermilion, turmeric, flower and incense.

Kumbhanali

This malevolent spirit resides in a small pool of water at a hilltop. People generally do not go near this pool out of fear of attack by the spirit.

Chuapani

It is a malevolent spirit residing in a stream on the hill-slope. The Bhuinyas used to carry out shifting cultivation all along the hill slopes. However, the patch of swidden where the spirit resides never yielded good crops. Believing that the spirit is causing all the damage, the villagers stopped swidden cultivation on the patch, after a series of propitiation attempts failed to reverse the trend. The patch, therefore, gives a green look, with many trees standing tall. This is a good case of religion being helpful in conservation of forest.

RITUALS AND FESTIVALS

The festivals observed by the Paudi Bhuinyas in a calendar year are mentioned in the list given in Table 2.7.

Table 2.7 : Rituals and Festivals observed by the Paudi Bhuinyas in a calendar year

Sl. No.	*Name of the Rituals/ Festivals*	*Month in which observed*	*Purpose of observance*
1.	*Devta gadha*	November-December	Purification of the village
2.	*Maghapudi*	December-January	Bidding farewell to the bygone year and welcoming a new agricultural year.
3.	*Badam Jatera*	March-April	Observed in honour of the ancestors
4.	*Sian Puja*	March-April	To worship the river Baitarani and drive away the evil spirits from village.
5.	*Melani*	March-April	To propitiate all deities and spirits to keep the livestock free from diseases.
6.	*Jutala*	April-May	Observed to keep off the children from the evil spirits.
7.	*Pachchda*	May-June	Observed for marking first sowing of paddy.
8.	*Tertia*	May-June	Observed on the occasion of sowing paddy.
9.	*Asadi or Bihida*	August	Observed to ensure better agriculture

Sl. No.	*Name of the Rituals/ Festivals*	*Month in which observed*	*Purpose of observance*
10.	*Dhana Nua*	September-October	To mark eating of new rice
11.	*Karama*	November-December	To worship the Karma Devta for a good harvest

THE SAORA (LANJIA SAORA)

Habitat

The Saora is a great tribe which is distributed throughout Orissa and adjacent Andhra Pradesh. They are divided into many sub-tribes bearing names according to their economic pursuits. The tribe is called by various terms such as Saora, Savar, Saura, Sabara, Sahara and noted for its mythic relationship with the Jagannatha cult. The Saora is believed to be the descendants of the Sabaras mentioned in the *Ramayana* and the *Mahabharata*. This tribe was referred to as Swari by Pliny and Sabari by Plotemy. J.V. Sitapati, a great linguist, was of the opinion that the name of the tribe should be written as Sora according to the tribal dialect. But the term Saora which is used in the ethnographic literatures is used in this text.

According to the 1981 census, the Saora population in Orissa was 3,70,061. A similar community enumerated separately under the term Shabar Lodha was as numerous as the Saoras. It recorded a population of 3,29,207 in the same 1981 census. Taken together these two groups become the second largest tribe in the State next to the Kondh tribe whose numerical strength was 9,89,342 in the same census period. The Saora tribe is distributed in all the undivided 13 districts of Orissa. Whenever the district is mentioned in this text, it refers to one of the original 13 undivided districts. Their main concentration is in five districts, namely, Sambalpur (pop.1,07,697), Koraput (pop. 45,941), Ganjam (pop. 69,201), Bolangir (pop. 46,587) and Puri (pop. 45,418).

There are several sub-divisions of the Saora tribe based on occupation, social status and food habits. Some of the important sub-divisions are (1) Arsi Saora (weavers), (2) Kindal Saora (basket makers), (3) Kumbi Saora (pot makers), (4) Laura Saora (iron workers), (5) Mulla Saora (inhabitants of hilly tracts), (6) Jati Saora (Saoras living in the plains), and (7) Lanjia Saora (the most primitive section of the Saora tribe). The text gives a description of the Lanjia Saoras who are found in large concentration in Gumma block of the Parlakimidi sub-division in Ganjam district and Gunpur block of the Gunpur sub-divison in Koraput district. These areas are full of high hill ranges clothed with thick forests. On the way from Gunpur to Puttasingi comes a village called *Jaltar* which is situated at a distance of 10 km away from Gunpur. From this place one has to climb hill ranges, rising to about 3000 ft above the sea level, for a distance of another 10 km to reach Puttasingi village, a central non-Saora village inhabited by the local traders, money-lenders and merchants. Extending from Puttasingi to Gumma and beyond up to Seranga, the entire landscape dotted with Saora villages is full of scenic valleys with terraced paddy fields and swidden patches. With the Lanjia Saoras live the Dombs and the Panos, a Christianized Scheduled Caste community, in separate settlements of which Puttasingi, Gumma and Serangi are most important. These are the main business centres where the itinerant traders belonging to the Pano community are found in large concentration.

The Village

In the Saora country the hills are considered units of settlement. The place which is selected for human settlements must have hills and water resources. The hills are very important for carrying on shifting cultivation in the hill slopes. Another characteristic of the Saora settlements is the terraces which are built from the foot-hills right upto the hill-tops. These terraced fields with stone packed walls and contour bounding exhibit great engineering skill of the Lanjia Saoras. It is in these terraces that paddy is grown under irrigated conditions. The nearby hill streams are diverted very skillfully towards the terraces for irrigation purposes.

The Saora settlements do not conform to any preplanned architectural design. Some settlements conform to a linear pattern and others to a shapeless cluster. Most of the Saora villages are located in the hill-slopes close to the foot-hills. Since sufficient plain lands are not available, the place has to be levelled for the construction of the houses. The levelling takes the form of terrace on which individual houses are built. A village may have several rows of houses on terraces one upon the other. Where the land is of irregular shape with ups and downs, it becomes difficult to make regular long terraces and in such a situation the houses are built here and there and therefore the settlement pattern conforms to a shapeless cluster of houses. Generally, the families who are related to one another by blood, making a lineage or a *Birinda* as it is called, live together in a terrace. Where sufficient space is not available in the same row, the additional related families go to the next step in terraces and build houses there to settle down. Thus in some cases, houses belonging to one *Birinda* are found living in a long row in a terrace and in other cases *Birinda* members are scattered in different clusters. The village path runs up and down the terraces between the rows of houses.

Generally, the Saora houses are small and are built on rectangular ground plan. The walls are either stone packed plastered with mud or mud walled. The plinth of the house is raised high to allow free drainage. The verandah in front is wide enough for the members of the household to sit and spend time gossiping and doing some household works such as husking grains, making mats and ropes. Some of the agricultural implements, like plough, are kept on the verandah. In some cases, a pig sty is provided in the space below the elevated verandah. Similarly, a fowl pen is also provided at one end below the front verandah.

The main room which is used for sleeping serves as a passage from front to the back of the house. A partition wall on the inner side separates the portion used for cooking meals and storing water. A loft made of wooden planks is provided in the kitchen portion. The hearth is under the loft where the housewife cooks the meals for the family members.

The mortar in which grains are pounded is fixed in the floor of the main house near the front door. In one corner of the house near the hearth is the place for the family deities placed in earthen pots.

Many household articles like bows and arrows, sickle, knife, hand axe, etc., are struck to the roof.

Economic Life

The Saoras depend primarily on agriculture for their livelihood. They also collect forest produce and hunt animals which supplement their income from cultivation. The Saoras practise three types of cultivation — the first being the kitchen gardening in lands near the houses; the second type, which is a major one, is the shifting cultivation in the hill-slopes; and the third type is the paddy cultivation in terraced fields under irrigated conditions. Shifting cultivation is extensively practised by the Saoras. The period of cultivation in a swidden patch is generally two years and the period of fallow varies from four to six years. Of all the mixed crops grown in the swidden, the pulses mostly *Cajanas cajan* and turmeric are the two important crops. Besides these major crops, minor millets of various types are also grown in the swiddens.

Paddy is cultivated in the terraced fields in the lower reaches of the hills and cereals mostly *ragi* (*Elusine corocana*), Horse gram (*Olichos biflorus*) and black gram (*Phaseolus aurcus*) are grown in the uplands.

The Saoras are very laborious and have extended vast labour in terracing the hill-slopes to make paddy fields. The terraces are built right on the beds of hill-streams and extend to a long distance, from the depth of the valleys to the hill-slopes and some running almost to the hill-top. The platform of the terraces are flat throughout and the fall of the terraces is stone packed. The construction of the terrace is so ingeniously and skillfully made that very little soil is carried down with the water that flows from the higher terraces to the lower. In fact, the Saoras are very careful cultivators skilled in revetment, terracing and water management. It is interesting to note that the flow of water from the higher terraces to the lower terraces is very skillfully engineered. It is controlled by the channels and water-ways which are provided in the ridges of the terraces.

There is another way of facilitating the flow of water from the higher terraces to the lower ones. Two or three pits are dug at the lower side of an upper terrace and these pits are packed with boulders. The water flows to these pits and from there through the boulders trickles to the terraces down below.

The highlands of the Saora country is characterized by typical topography and climatic conditions which are most congenial for horticultural plantations particularly orange and other citrous plants. High altitude, good drainage, and cool climate have favoured the growth of orange plants in the hill-slopes replacing in many places the shifting cultivation. Lacking in co-operative organization and improved knowledge in horticulture, the Saoras are not able to get the profit to the extent that could have been generated had there not been any organizational constraints and limitations.

The Co-operative Labour System, which is called *Ansir*, is in vogue among the Saoras. *Ansir* is a kind of labour system in which different families help each other by working on the fields during agricultural season. The team is given food and drink by the person in whose land they work and there is no labour charges in cash. There is another type of labour system in which a man or a woman works in the field of another person without expecting payment. This is a voluntary labour system for mutual help. The members of *Birinda* help each other at the time of need. A kind of mutual help is also prevalent in the case of cattle tending. In this case, all families living in a village provide one person from each family by turn to tend cattle of the villagers.

Bartar system is also prevalent in Saora economic life. The Pano women move from village to village with the usable goods of daily necessities like matchbox, salt, tobacco, dry fish, biscuits, chocolates, etc., and sell these things in exchange for grains.

Social Organization

Family is the smallest social unit of the Saora society. The nuclear family type is most common and also the most numerous. A family comprises parents and unmarried children. There may be old grand parents or widow sisters in the family. Among the Saoras, the family is male dominated. The senior- most male member of the family is the head. It is, therefore, patriarchal.

The Saoras have no exogamous totemic clans, no phratries and no moieties. The main exogamous unit is the extended family, the members of which believe to have descended from a common ancestor. This unit is called *Birinda* which is based on patrilineage. A woman does not change her *Birinda* membership even after marriage. A person's mother's *Birinda* plays an important part in his or her affairs. There is no clear rule of post marital residence. Married sisters are found living in the same village with their seminal brothers and the bond between the seminal sisters is very close and intimate. But normally the sisters after marriage leave their parents and go to live with their parents-in-law in other villages. In this case the Saora society is patrilocal.

The ownership of property always goes to the male members on a hereditary basis. Though women play a great role in managing the property, they are not given any right to own any property of their parents. In the matter of property inheritance, the sons enjoy greater rights than the daughters. After the husband's death, if the wife does not have son then she is not entitled to get the property of her husband. The property goes to the nearest *Birinda* member who gives the widow's daughter to marriage and provide the former livelihood till death. The assets of a woman which she has brought from her father's house on her marriage are recognized as her own belongings and her husband has no right over her property.

Political Organization

Every Saora village has well established political organization. Each village, politically speaking, is autonomous and locally self-supporting like Mundari tribes of central India. The Saoras have no indigenous centralized political authority or political confederacies. Among them each village has a secular headman called *Gomang* who is a man of high prestige. Equally important is the village religious headman who is known as the *Buyya*. The offices of secular and religious headmen are hereditary and the rule of primogeniture regulates succession. In addition to these offices which are indigenous, there is in some villages an astrologer called *Disari* and this post is achieved not ascribed like the religious and secular headmanship. In many villages there are village *shamans* (sorcerers). There are diviner — *shamans* and doctor — *shamans* and they are of either sex. In most villages there is a post called *Barika* who acts as the village messenger. Invariably he belongs to either Domb or Pano community.

Allotment of land on the hill-slopes among the villagers for shifting cultivation is made in a common village meeting attended by all adult male members. This custom is now rarely followed since the swidden patches do not change hands and the villagers continue to carry on shifting cultivation year after year in the patches which were allotted to them long ago. Even though no one has any legal right of ownership over the swidden patches but every cultivator feels to have ownership rights notionally over the patches which are in his possession for years.

Annual cycle of festivals and days and times of holding them are decided unanimously in village meetings. Cases relating to the partition of property, sale and mortgage of lands, cases of divorce and many social matters are decided in the village meetings. Over every village meetings the village *Gomango* had to preside, initiate discussions, and make public the unanimously arrived decisions.

The relationship in the Saora community is multiplex and it acts like an organism in which every individual acts in accordance with the wishes of others of the community because of social harmony and face to face relationship. All decisions whether social or political are arrived at not by the majority vote but by consensus. Real political democracy is at work in Saora villages. The implementation of statutory gram *panchayat* in the Saora villages serves nothing but creates conflict between the indigenous political institution and the emerging new leadership.

Religious Beliefs and Practices

Of all the tribes of Orissa, the Saoras are most religious. They live in the world of the spirits and supernatural beings which are believed to influence the course of nature and human life. As a result, they devote most of their time, energy and money to propitiate these spirits and deities. They worship these deities with great devotion and with a sense of gratitude. They appease the wrath of the malignant spirits with customary offerings and sacrifices and keep them in good temper. They also worship the indifferent natural spirits to seek relief from evil spirits. The Saoras believe that every part of the world and every object is possessed by a spirit. The hills, trees, streams, lands, marketplaces, villages, houses, hearths, pots and pans, water, air and in fact every nook and corner of the Saora inhabit are possessed by different spirits. Even though the Saora cosmology is very much elaborate, confusing and complicated, but certain broad principles of their religion can be deciphered. These principles are as follows :

1. Every human being is believed to have two souls, the *Sudapuradan,* or big soul and *Sannapuradan* or little soul. The big soul can have an independent existence and is immortal whereas the little one does not outlast the destruction of its physical body.
2. When the soul leaves the body after death it becomes a shadow which is changed into an ancestor by observing the *Guar* ceremony.
3. The Saora pantheon comprises numberless gods and spirits which can be broadly classified into the following categories.
   (i) *Sonunanji,* referring to sky gods and some local deities and malevolent deities, cause human tragedy, mishap and pain.

(ii) *Kitunganji,* represented by a collective form of deity called *Kittungsum,* is believed to be the creator of the world and all living beings.

(iii) *Kulbanji,* stands for the shadows and human souls not admitted to the world of ancestors and not the object of worship.

4. A few gods and spirits are regularly worshipped and no god has anything of the type of shrine except the icons or the ritual paintings on the walls representing particular deities and spirits which are invoked at the time of crisis. Different spirits and deities exist everywhere in the Saora world and no social, domestic and economic and other aspects of life exists without being influenced by the deities and the spirits.

The deities differ from one another in nature, function, character and activities. Some are benevolent, some neutral and others malevolent. The spirits are very much vigilant and if they find that someone has not observed the rituals properly, he is subjected to the wrath of the spirit. He falls ill and some mishap happens to his family and his crop is destroyed and he is attacked by wild animals.

The Saoras observe many rituals and ceremonies which can be classified in two categories, those observed at the individual family level and those observed by community at the village level. The rites and rituals which are connected with life-cycle (birth, marriage and death) come under the first category and those related to different agricultural operations and community biennial or triennial rituals fall into the second category. Some of the important agricultural festivals observed by the Saoras are related to crops grown such as millet, sweet potato, corn and redgrams. Certain other rituals are related to fruits such as mango fruits. These rituals are observed on a community basis. Similarly, the biennial and triennial *Gāur* festival in which stone slabs are erected in memory of the deceased are observed by the village community.

Saora Icons

One great speciality of the Saoras is their wall paintings known as icons. These icons are drawn on the walls inside the house. These paintings consist of various sketches of human beings, horses, elephants, gunmen, sun, moon, snakes, trees, and various objects of nature. These paintings are of great religious significance representing a unidimensional shrine dedicated to a particular deity in order to please it so that it may spare the members of the household from their invidious attention. The icons which were previously drawn for certain purposes are erased by smearing the walls with a solution mixed with red soil and a new icon is drawn to serve some other purpose. In this way at frequent intervals icons are drawn as and when the occasions arise.

There are various types of icons such as icons drawn for averting a mishap in the family, curing illness, improving fertility of the soil and increasing the yield of the crops, ensuring a smooth and easy delivery of a child, etc. The constituent sketches of the icon differ according to the purpose. The icon meant for improving the fertility of the soil depicts a pregnant women and persons carrying paddy bundles or bunches of banana.

DETAILS OF SOME TYPES OF ICONS

Icons designed to promote or preserve the fertility of the crops

These types of icons depict agricultural operations such as ploughing and hoeing, sowing and harvesting. In some icons the pictures of pregnant women, women carrying seeds, a potter laden with pots, gods seated on elephants and such other fertility symbols are depicted. The fertility icons are dedicated to the *labosum* or earth-god and to the ancestors whose interests in the harvests and prosperity of the Saoras are emphasized.

A standard picture of a fertility icon may have the following composition and form. In a square outline there may be figures of a ploughman with a cigar or pipe in his mouth and his son ploughing; a cow followed by its calf; a pregnant woman carrying seeds on her head, a potter and his wife laden with pots to cook the bumper crops which are expected, an elephant with some gods or spirits sitting on it and more particularly the *Jemra* killing and *Sidibirdi* which are associated with the rite of consecration of seeds called *Jammolpur*. In short, the fertility icons are *Jammolpur* icons dedicated to *Labosum*.

Icons dedicated to gods to avert disease

In some of the sacrifices offered to the gods for the sake of getting well and recovering from illness, the *shaman* prescribes painting of an icon. Such pictures consists of drawings of servants, pets, guards, dancing girls, elephants, horses with clerks riding on them, potters with loads of pots and bundles of grass carried by men, snakes, monkeys depicted at the upper border of the icon. The idea is to show what a splendid house the god has and how many servants, bodyguards and others are there in his house and what important people call on him, the sole purpose being to flatter the god for the sake of which the icon has been made.

An instance may be given to show the type of icon made for dedicating to a god for the purpose of averting any accident and illness. At the time of the harvest of red gram, the Saoras celebrate the festival of *Gadalpur*, at which sacrifice is made to *Gadalsum*. It is strictly taboo to cut grass before *Gadalpur*. The custom is that the priest cuts the grass first and then others follow him. Any breach of the custom results in serious consequences, and in order to satisfy the god which is offended by such breach of the custom, a suitable icon is drawn. In one such icon a person, representing one who has broken the taboo, is shown with a load of grass upon a strong tiger who is shown springing. In two sets of icons drawn one for *Gadalsum* (deity in charge of grass) and another for *Berusum* (deity of the hills), several people are depicted representing the grass cutters, tutelars are shown sitting or watching the scene in which the *Gadalsum* and *Barusum* are riding elephants, and other gods either riding or standing. Then there are figures of birds and monkeys signalling the presence of a snake or a tiger in the neighbourhood.

The icons are drawn representing the marriage ceremony of the gods. In such icons there may be a palace representing the palace of the god and figures of people in dancing posture around palace, pictures of trees and monkeys on them in joyful mood, figures of the mother, sisters, brothers of the concerned god, dancing, drawings of sun, moon, stars shining down on the scene, gods coming on elephant back to attend the marriage, potters coming with loads of pots for rice-beer, important people coming with goats for feast, men bringing in a *sambhar* killed by the god's servants, unwanted guests being attacked by the god's dog. The obvious intention of all these is to depict what an important god he is; how many servants he has; what powerful people, friends and relatives he can command; and what an expensive wedding he can afford.

Icons made to assist child birth

The icons drawn to assist childbirth contain a pregnancy or delivery motif and generally dedicated to *Gadejangboi* who is notorious for interfering at the time of delivery. In such icons a woman who is to deliver the child is depicted with *Gadejangboi* holding her. Another god called *Darammaboi* may be drawn and she would be shown with her hand on the mother's belly ready to remove the child from the womb. There may be the picture of a girl (supposed to be the daughter of *Darammaboi*) holding a pot of water to bathe the mother and child after delivery.

Icons which represent shrines and hills

The icons in most cases stands for the house of a spirit. Shrine-icons are made when there is a demand from a spirit to have a place for him to rest. Hill-icons may be drawn if one has offended a hill-god by cutting a clearing on his hill or by collecting herbs or picking leaves without offering sacrifices. The icon of this type represents a hill-god's house dedicated generally to *Barongsum* — an old Saora word for mountain god.

If the Saoras of a village fall ill when they go to make a clearing on a hill, they believe that the illness is due to the dissatisfaction of the hill-gods such as *Labosum, Myungboi* or *Myungsum,* the Sun god and *Tangarbasum*. The icon drawn to please these gods may have pictures of concentric circles with sketches of shrines representing the house of *Myungsum,* figures of hills and of elephants with *Labosum* and other gods riding on. There may also be the pictures of wild animals like tiger. *Tangarsum*'s house may be represented by squares within squares drawn in lines with figures of human being all around and those of monkeys at the top of the squares and a potter with a load of pots standing nearby.

In one such pictures Verrier Elwin has shown a man on a bicycle representing a Forest Guard who was obstructing the Saoras in their work of clearing the hill-slopes for cultivation. The idea of including the Guard who was treated as one of the hill-gods in the icon was that he would be pleased and leave them alone undisturbed.

Icon made in honour of tutelars

Icons are made to solemnize marriage between a *Shaman* and his tutelar or a *Shamenin* and her tutelar. Such icons are also drawn at the instance when the tutelars feel that their relations are neglected. These icons are rather elaborate because many figures of human beings and tutelars who are related to one another are depicted with drawings of birds and animals and plants to beautify the picture.

Icons made in honour of the dead

The ancestors, according to the Saoras, need constantly the attention and care of the living because they lead a wretched life in the underworld. They demand food and drink and comfort from their living children and grandchildren and are very much satisfied when icons are drawn in their favour and sacrifices are offered to them.

The icons which are made in their honour depict comfortable houses with large number of rooms full of wives and servants, food and drink. The icons also depict important and wealthy friends and relations visiting them and there are houses, elephants and bicycles (now cars and aeroplanes added to pictures) for them to ride about.

In brief, the chief characteristic features of the Saora icon are that they are made for ritual purposes rather than for decoration and display. Often they are drawn in the darkest part of the house not easily accessible by visitors and outsiders. The elaborations shown in the icons apart from the central theme are not for beauty but for flattery which the gods like and appreciate most.

The icons vary in style, shape, size and elaboration depending upon the economic condition of the villages. The icons found in Pottasingi area of the Gunpur sub-division, which is situated in a fertile valley and where the Saoras are prosperous, are large in size, complicated, much elaborate and timely drawn. The icons found in the villages around Seranga in Parlakemidi sub-division where the Saora lead a very simple life under modest economic condition near the level of poverty are not so much complicated and detailed as the Pottasingi icons are.

The pictures drawn in the icons are conventional, and on the whole realistic and rarely symbolized in any case. The drawings of figures whether they are of human beings, animals, plants, material objects and heavenly bodies are in full and never in parts. But certain drawings of hills and houses are symbolically depicted in the various geometric designs.

The icons are invariably graphic messages directed towards the gods and spirits. They depict a story and recite a prayer of praise and flattery and in most cases may be taken as a piece of architecture in the sense that they are drawn to serve as earthly unidimensional homes meant for the gods and spirits to reside. The theological belief of the Saoras is personified in the icons which also serve as record of their dreams, hopes, fears and aspirations. It is not the instinct of secular art of the beauty and decoration but the cult and the myth associated with the supernatural world which have inspired the Saoras to give vent to their ritually motivated artistic expressions through the icons.

The *Shaman* or medicine man draws the icons and performs necessary rites connected with them. The religious functionaries who perform the rites and rituals are mainly from the categories of *Buyya* and *Kudan*. The *Buyya* presides over all agricultural festivals and *Kudan*, who is the *Shaman*, combines the function of a priest, prophet and medicine man. The position of the *Buyya* is handed down from the father to son whereas the position of a *Kudan* is not hereditary. It is achieved on the basis of merits and knowledge of a person about the prestigious priestly services and science of indigenous medicine and skill in drawing icons.

There are male *Shamans* called *Kudan* and female *Shamans* called *Kudanboi*. A male *Shaman* has a female tutelary and a female *Shaman* or *Shamanin* has a male tutelary. The relationship between the two sets of pairs is the same as that of husband and wife. Both the *Shaman* and the *Shamanin* are equally skilled diviners and medicine persons. They can establish direct communication with their respective tutelaries and prevail upon them to provide clues for curing illness and controlling evil sprits.

Life-Cycle

BIRTH

As soon as the labour pain starts the woman is confined to a corner of the house. An experienced elderly woman is immediately called for to help her in delivery. The umbilical cord is cut by the midwife by a sharp arrowhead. The placenta is buried in a pit in one corner of the house. The mother and the baby are given bath in tepid water. The period of prohibition lasts for seven days. On the last day the woman takes bath and cooks food which is shared by the other members of the family. After a few days a name is given to the baby. For this purpose the name of an ancestor is chosen for naming the child.

MARRIAGE

Various types of marriages are in vogue among the Saoras, the most common being the arranged marriage. In the case of marriage by arrangements it is the parents of the groom who take the initiative. The bride price varies from Rs. 60 to Rs. 100 and 8 to 10 pots of country liquor. Before marriage the groom's father accompanied by relatives and kinsmen visit the bride's house more than once with pots of liquor. On one occasion an arrow is taken and the engagement is finalized. On another occasion the amount of bride price is fixed and paid before the day of bethrotal. On the day of bethrotal, the groom's party visits the girl's house with several pots of wine. On this occasion they are entertained with sumptuous food and drink. One year thereafter the bride is sent to the groom's house and this day is celebrated by dancing and drinking and from this day the groom and the bride are recognized as husband and wife. The Saoras practise both sorrorate and levirate types of marriage. If a man has many swidden patches he has to have more than one wife so that each of them can clear a patch of land thereby growing more crops and getting more produce from the fields.

DEATH

The Saoras cremate the dead body in case of normal death but if it is a death by accident, by cholera and small pox, the practice of burial is followed. The corpse is carried to the cremation ground accompanied by musical band and the body is placed on the pyre and burnt. Next day the family members of the deceased visit the cremation ground to examine the ashes and to find out the signs of the cause of death. In the evening a fowl is killed in the cremation ground and cooked with rice and neem leaves which is shared by the mourners.

After a year or so the *Gaur* ceremony is observed. On this occasion menhirs are erected on the ground and a large buffalo is sacrificed. This is followed by three successive *Karja* ceremony in every second or third year to commemorate and honour the dead. This ceremony is observed in the month of March or April when the people are generally free from agricultural operations.

As pointed out above, with death rites two great rituals are associated, these are *Gaur* and *Karja*.

Gaur Ceremony

The *Gaur* is performed in two families — one in which she had taken birth and the another is the family of her husband. The brother of the deceased, accompanied by the *Kudan* and *Kudanboi* and her blood kins, goes to the cremation ground to collect bones from the burning pyre. The charred bones are kept at home or in the cremation ground. It may be mentioned that in the event of death of a woman, her parent's family takes major interest in the performance of the *Gaur*.

On the appointed day the dead person's kinsmen go out in a procession accompanied by the music party to the nearby hill and fetch a long flat stone and keep in the place called *Genuar* (place where menhirs are erected in memory of the dead persons). The *Kudan* and the *Kudanboi* perform necessary rituals and the assembled kin members place the slab erect in the hole dug for this purpose in the *Genuar*.

A buffalo is sacrificed and a great feast is arranged. The meat of the sacrificial animal is cooked and with rice, red gram and other cooked items served to the members of the family of the deceased and all the guests and relatives attending the ritual.

Karja Ceremony

The *Karja* ceremony is the greatest festival of the Saoras. It is collectively observed by all households. This ceremony is a sort of commemoration festival observed in memory of all the spirits of the dead persons who died during the last three years. The kins of all the dead persons take initiative and organize the commemoration festival every year in the month of March. The spirit of the dead is commemorated three times, once in each of the three consecutive years and all the spirits of the dead persons who died in the last three years in the village are commemorated collectively in a joint ceremony by all the concerned households. The main objective of the *Karja* ceremony is to express gratitude and gratefulness to the dead, who during their life span on the earth laboured in the paddy fields and swidden patches and died. *Karja* is also observed with the idea that the family members of the deceased can live in plenty and happiness. Through this ceremony the needs of the spirits are provided for its happy and peaceful life in other world. On the whole the *Karja* ceremony marks the end of a death ritual cycle.

The *Karja* ceremony lasts for three days. During these three days the *Shaman* is kept busy in the spirit hunt. On the first day a ladder made of bamboo is fixed into the mortar hole in the living room. The spirits are invited and the buffaloes which are contributed by the kins and relatives of the persons who died in the last three years are sacrificed at one end of the village and the spirits are worshipped by offering the blood of the buffaloes. By evening of the third day all rituals are finished and all the assembled guests and relatives and kin members of the dead persons enjoy the feast cooked for this purpose. After having finished eating the food, all people assembled on this occasion lead the *Shaman*s to their respective houses in accompaniment of traditional music and thereafter all people leave for their respective villages.

Part II
Tribal Development

3

Strategies of Tribal Development in Retrospect

THE diversities of India, be it economic, political, social, cultural, historical or any other, has continually remained the core issue in the development approach of the plans and policies of the country. This approach is imperative because the structure of the society and the milieu prevailing across India is widely diverse and complexly heterogeneous.

So far as the social diversity is concerned, the tribals alone, who constitute 7.8 per cent of the total population in the country, have as many as 250 communities, 105 languages and 225 subsidiary languages, and are scattered along the length and breadth of the country. Even amongst them, there are groups as large as about 5 millions and as small as a few hundreds only. Each community, irrespective of its demography, has come to occupy a place of its own in national life, retaining its own identity and culture. They have their own special ways of both working and living because they follow such occupations which their geographic surroundings, cultural background and their degree of progress give them the utmost satisfaction and greatest chance of survival. Therefore the Kukis of Manipur are quite different from the Kolams of Maharashtra and the Kondhs of Orissa have differences as compared with the Bhils of central India.

So far as the demography of the tribals are concerned, they are concentrated in some areas while in some other areas they are sparse or dispersed and in some places there are no tribals at all. The tribals have been concentrated mostly in central India across the States of Orissa, Bihar, Madhya Pradesh, Andhra Pradesh, Maharastra, Gujarat and Rajasthan. In all these States put together, their population is 80.44 per cent (1991 census) of the total tribal population in India; maximum percentage being 23.73 per cent in Madhya Pradesh. However, there are some smaller States in the north-east where their percentage is very high out of the State's total population, but their total number is not large. The States such as Nagaland, Arunachal Pradesh, Mizoram and Meghalaya are included in this category having tribals more than 80 per cent of the total population in each of these States.

The diversity and the existing heterogeneity of the tribals were taken into consideration when the approach for development of scheduled tribes was first laid down by the first prime minister of India, Late Pandit Jawaharlal Nehru in his "Tribal Panchsheel." The Panchsheel which was later ratified by the Dhebar Commission and Shilu Ao Committee, stated specifically that the development of tribals should be along the lines of their own genius and that there should be no imposition on them. It also provided for integration of tribals with the rest of the society in a manner that their traditions and cultures remain unaffected and there was no loss of their identity. It was also emphasized to safeguard their rights over land and forest, and, to prepare and train them to take care of their administration and development.

During the British rule the task of tribal development suffered much due to their policy of isolation and indifferent attitude towards them. As a result, the tribals remained under-developed while the non-tribals had achieved considerable development and therefore a hiatus was created between the tribals and non-tribals.

It is only after Independence that the needs and the problems of the tribals were recognized and systematically addressed. To this end, the Constitution of India has enunciated several provisions by which it empowers the state to redress their problems and to take actions necessary for their development. Article 46 of the Constitution enjoins the State to promote with special care the educational and economic interests of the weaker sections of the people and, in particular, of the Scheduled Castes and the Scheduled Tribes. It also requires the State to protect them from social injustice and exploitation. Other constitutional provisions such as Article 244, 339 (2), 275, 15, 16 and 19 can be referred to this end. The report of the Study Team on Social Welfare and Welfare of Backward Classes (Renuka Ray report, 1959), the Report of the Scheduled Areas and Scheduled Tribes Commission (Dhebar Commmission, 1960-61), the Report of the Study Team on Tribal Development Programmes, All-India (P. Shilu Ao Committee, 1969), and the Report of the Expert Committee (1972) under the chairmanship of S.C. Dube, focused on different aspects of tribal development in the country. Majority of them have recommended integrated approach towards tribal development. Therefore since the Fifth Five-Year Plan onwards, the strategy for integrated development became the main thrust of the tribal development planning and it led to the launching of the Tribal Sub-Plan concept.

Tribal Sub-Plan (TSP)

The development experience and the weaknesses in policies and programmes of tribal development, following up to the end of the Fourth Plan, were taken into consideration while formulating the Tribal Sub-Plan during the Fifth Plan period.

The weaknesses in policies and programmes are the following :

(a) Financial and physical resource crunch for executing multi-sectoral programmes.

(b) There was failure to comprehend distinctive characteristics of the tribal areas and the Scheduled Tribes.

(c) The policies and programmes as well as the administrative machinery were not sufficiently moulded to the tribal needs.

A detailed and comprehensive review of the tribal problem was also taken into account when the concept of Tribal Sub-Plan strategy was evolved. The problem was broadly divided into (i) areas of tribal socio-economic development, (ii) building inner strength of the tribal communities, and (iii) area development with focus on development of the tribal communities.

The objectives of Tribal Sub-Plan strategy are two-fold which have been formulated on the basis of these problems. These objectives are:

(a) Socio-economic development of the Scheduled Tribes, and

(b) Protection of the Scheduled Tribes against exploitation.

However, three basic parameters of the tribal situation in the country were recognized in the evolution of the Tribal Sub-Plan concept. First, that there is diversity in the social, political, economic and cultural milieu of different tribal communities. Second, that the demographic pattern of these communities is such that they are concentrated in parts of some States and dispersed in others. Third, that the primitive tribal communities live in secluded regions. Therefore, the broad strategy has had to be related to their level of development and pattern of distribution.

In order to implement the Tribal Sub-Plan strategy effectively, areas of concentration of tribal population have been identified and separate administrative units have been established in 20 States and union territories. Annexure 1 gives information regarding the Tribal Sub-Plan States, total population, Scheduled Tribe (ST) population and percentage of Scheduled Tribe population to total population according to 1991 census.

So far as financing is concerned, there are no clear guidelines on quantification under Tribal Sub-Plan. The Tribal Sub-Plan being a plan within the State plan, draws outlays from different sectors. Each department of the government has a responsibility to provide funds for the development of the Scheduled Tribes.

Most of the time, financing by the State plan is found to be inadequate. Therefore, the requisite resources are pooled from other sources, viz., (i) Investment by Central Ministries, (ii) Special Central Assistance (SCA) by the Central Government, and (iii) Institutional Finance.

During successive plan periods since the Fifth Five-Year Plan, the strategy of Tribal Sub-Plan has adopted various approaches and prepared many programmes accordingly for the development of the Scheduled Tribes in India. The concept of the Integrated Tribal Development Project (ITDP) was conceived as the lowest unit of integrated development approach of the Tribal Sub-Plan during the Fifth Plan and they have been continuing since then. At the time of review of the tribal development programmes in the same plan period, it was decided to set-up Micro Projects for the extremely backward groups known as Primitive Tribes. During the Sixth Plan, the Modified Area Development Approach (MADA) was adopted to cover smaller areas of tribal concentration and during the Seventh Plan, the Tribal Sub-Plan strategy was extended to all the Scheduled Tribes in the country, including the dispersed Scheduled Tribes. The approaches are mentioned below in brief.

Integrated Tribal Development Projects (ITDPs)

Since the strategy of Tribal Sub-Plan is to prepare programmes for the specific needs of the area and the people, planning has to begin from the lowest unit, i.e., Integrated Tribal Development Project. One Integrated Tribal Development project covers an area of a Tehsil or a Block or more in which the Scheduled Tribe population is 50 per cent of the total population or more. Apart from some states such as Assam, West Bengal, Karnataka, in all other Tribal Sub-Plan States/ Union Territories, the Integrated Tribal Development Projects are generally contiguous areas. There are 194 Integrated Tribal Development Projects in 20 Tribal Sub-Plan States/Union Territories and each Integrated Tribal Development Project is headed by a Project

Officer. The Project Officers are designated as Administrators or Project Directors in some States. The staff structure and delegation of power in the Integrated Tribal Development Projects vary from State to State. In Andhra Pradesh and Orissa, the Agency model has been adopted and there the Integrated Tribal Development Projects are known as Integrated Tribal Development Agencies (ITDAs). The Integrated Tribal Development Agency is an agency registered under the Societies Registration Act. The Integrated Development Agencies, therefore, enjoy certain autonomous decision-making powers than the Integrated Tribal Development Projects which are under the direct administrative control of the government. Many a time, in development planning for the Scheduled Tribes, the Integrated Tribal Development Project functions as an intermediary or co-ordinating agency between the Block at the lower level and the State at the upper level.

Modified Area Development Approach (MADA) Pockets

During the Sixth Plan, the Tribal Sub-Plan approach was extended to identify pockets of concentration of Scheduled Tribe population containing 50 per cent or more Scheduled Tribe population within a total population of 10,000. These pockets are known as Modified Area Development Approach Pockets. There are about 250 Modified Area Development Approach pockets in 20 Tribal Sub-Plan States/Union Territories. The developmental programmes in these pockets are implemented by the line departments of the State Governments/ Union Territories administration and there is no separate administrative structure for such pockets.

Clusters

Clusters are identified pockets of tribal concentration containing 50 per cent or more Scheduled Tribe population within a total population of about 5,000. There are 77 clusters in India. The process of programme implementation and the administrative structure are same in case of Cluster approach as they are in Modified Area Development Approach Pockets.

Till the end of the Sixth Plan, 74 per cent of the total Scheduled Tribe population had been covered under the Integrated Tribal Development Projects, Modified Area Development Approach Pockets and Clusters in all the Tribal Sub-Plan States/Union Territories. Immediately after the Sixth Plan, the States were instructed to cover the dispersed Scheduled Tribe population under the Tribal Sub-Plan.

Primitive Tribes and Micro Projects

It was mentioned earlier that the Micro Project approach was initiated during the Fifth Plan specially for the Primitive Tribes. The Primitive Tribes were identified as the most backward tribes among all the tribes in the Dhebar Commission Report. The Commission divided the Scheduled Tribes into four categories : (1) those living in the remotest corners and for that reason almost in the primitive stage, (2) those in the shifting cultivation stage, (3) those who are regular agriculture practitioners, and (4) those who have already been assimilated. This classification can be referred to different stages of socio-economic development and integration.

75 Scheduled Tribes have been identified as Primitive Tribal Groups (PTGs) in 15 out of 20 Tribal Sub-Plan States/Union Territories. Annexure 2 gives State/Union Territory-wise list of these Primitive Tribal Groups. The Primitive Tribal Groups are characterized by :

(a) Pre-agricultural level of technology, and

(b) Extremely low level of literacy.

The Primitive Tribal Groups use pre-agricultural technology for hunting, food gathering and shifting cultivation. These are the ways in which they earn their livelihood. For hunting animals they use bows, arrows, snares, traps, etc., and for shifting cultivation and food gathering they use crude implements such as digging stick, bill hook, hoe and axe, etc.

Besides the above-said characteristics, many others are also observed among the Primitive Tribal Groups. Some of these characteristics are given below :

(c) Diminishing or stagnant population.

(d) Live in inaccessible and difficult terrain.

(e) Material belongings being few and very simple.

(f) Prevalence of communal ownership of land.

(g) Authority vested on village headman and all ritual functions performed by a religious headman.

(h) No written laws present except tradition-bound customary laws.

(i) Slow in adaptation of change and development.

(j) Very little economic diversification.

(k) Strong belief in super-naturalism, sorcery, black magic and witchcraft.

On the whole the Primitive Tribal Groups have such attributes as distinctiveness, smallness, homogeneity, all providing self-sufficiency. These attributes are found in different degrees in different Primitive Tribal Groups.

The Primitive Tribal Groups may be residing either within or outside the Integrated Tribal Development Projects/Modified Area Development Approach Pockets/Clusters. As the Tribal Sub-Plan approach gives special attention to the development of Primitive Tribal Groups, certain States have set-up Micro Projects within and outside the Integrated Tribal Development Projects to this end.

The Micro Projects are financed by the funds provided by the Government of India under the provision of Special Central

Assistance. This assistance has been conceived to be in the nature of an additive to the State plan funds. In areas where the State plan provisions are not forthcoming due to shortage of funds in a particular sector or for any other reason, the Special Central Assistance is provided as a gap filler. As per the data available, a total amount of Rs. 4.88 crore had been released to the States on a year to year basis during the Fifth Plan. This amount has increased to Rs. 330 crore and Rs. 329.61 crore in 1996-97 and 1997-98 respectively. Rs. 22.93 crore had been given to the States under Special Central Assistance for the development of the Primitive Tribal Groups by the end of the Sixth Plan. During the first four years of the Seventh Plan, another Rs. 21 crore have been given by the Government of India to States for these groups.

The project reports are generally modified, and changes are incorporated in the successive development strategy and approach, according to the recommendations of the Working Groups set-up by the Government of India on a time to time basis. The Working Group while reviewing the development of the Primitive Tribal Groups felt that not much have been done for the development of these tribes. Some of the important views and the recommendations of different Working Groups are discussed below to have an assessment of the Micro Projects and the development of the Primitive Tribes.

- The setting-up of Micro Projects for the Primitive Tribes as a separate administrative structure has been corroborated by the Working Group on Tribal Development during the Sixth Plan (1980-85). The report of the Working Group says that 250 different tribal communities require 250 different blue-prints for the development of each of them. But during the Sixth Plan period, the administration was considered to be not equipped for such an exercise. But according to the said report, in so far as the Primitive Tribal Groups are concerned, since they require sensitive and delicate handling, separate project reports for each of the primitive communities identified, should be prepared. The reports also said that the project reports should give adequate attention to their special problems and a separate administrative structure is necessary for their development.

- The Working Group has reiterated the guidelines of the Ministry of Home Affairs in which it is stated that the Primitive Tribal Groups have to be distinguished from the poors and that a Primitive Tribal Group need not necessarily be poor. It is clarified that in some cases the concept of poverty may not even be known to them. But the people may have deprivation which is different from poverty and to eliminate deprivation, the guidelines have suggested that programmes can be taken up as a part of the general developmental effort of the area.

Other important recommendations of the concerned Working Group are the following :

(a) The programmes must specially take into consideration the eco-system.

(b) The first phase of development should focus on conservation as well as reorganization of the traditional skills of the groups and the second phase should spell out the development programme.

The Working Group on the development of Scheduled Tribes during the Seventh Plan (1985-90) has also emphasized on the worth of aforesaid recommendations in its report. The Working Group has warned that the imposition of stereotyped economic development schemes on the Primitive Tribal Groups will do more harm than good of the people. Therefore it laid stress on the need for sensitive handling of such schemes.

The report has also mentioned about eliminating the apathy of concerned people towards change and advancement. Entry points should be opened up to offer development access to these groups. It has cited one instance in which it has been shown that how the Juangs of Orissa have favourably been disposed towards receiving medical facilities in view of ailments that afflict them. In another instance it has been demonstrated that the entry point has been opened by the establishment of the co-operative societies called Large-Size Multipurpose Co-operative Society (LAMPS) through which the Saoras of Orissa, exploited through manipulations by intermediaries, would very much like to sell their minor forest produce and transact other businesses. In the long run, however, the report has stated that the planning process has to comprehend a multi-sectoral approach, though the thrust will have to be on the aspects which are of particular relevance in the context of a particular group.

The declining population trend of some Primitive Tribal Groups was also of considerable concern to the Working Group. The Group has emphasized on the need of finding out causative factors for such declining trend. It has also suggested for taking necessary steps to free the members of these groups from general or specific illness and for promoting the level of their health. The Working Group has given a few more recommendations in addition to the above-said suggestions. They are discussed below:

(a) Saturation approach towards the economic development of each Primitive Tribal Group should be adopted. In saturation approach, all the families of the group are covered under the developmental schemes. Family-wise economic development plans and programmes of infrastructure necessary for such plans should be formulated while adopting a holistic approach to their development.

(b) The project reports for the Primitive Tribes should include special measures to be taken for improving education, health, nutrition, drinking water supply, transport and communication. Adult education both for men and women was also given enormous importance by the Working Group.

(c) Staff are to be provided with 100 per cent basic pay, special allowance, residential and vehicular facilities, etc., to encourage them to work in the areas of the Primitive Tribals Groups.

(d) Voluntary organizations should be induced to work among the Primitive Tribal Groups and share the responsibility of the care and nursing of them along with the governmental agencies.

(e) Special attention should be paid to protective and non-exploitative measures and a complete ban on purchase and settlement of land and other property, etc., by outsiders in the area should be imposed.

(f) At the formulation, implementation, field visit and review stages of all programmes for these groups, the leaders and functionaries of the traditional tribal institutions must be actively involved.

(g) Programmes of immunization against infant mortality as well as morbidity and programmes related to restoration of resources in these areas should be given top priority.

All the aforesaid suggestions and recommendations have been backed by the Working Group on Development and Welfare of Scheduled Tribes during the Eighth Plan in its report (1990-95). Added to these suggestions and recommendations, a few others have been proposed by the above-said Working Group which are given below :

(a) The programmes for the development of Primitive Tribal Groups which are taken up under Special Central Assistance, should be supplemented by the State plan funds. The feedback received regarding the results of such programmes should be adequate.

(b) The provision of social service or infrastructure should not be delayed or avoided even if the per capita cost is high on account of low population density or difficult topography.

(c) High subsidy must be provided to the members of the Primitive Tribal Groups in family-oriented income generating schemes.

(d) The Working Group is of the view that the suitable personnel, those who are competent and empathetic, should be employed to work among these groups. These personnel should be willing to work for the development of the Primitive Tribal Groups. Monetary and non-monetary incentives should be given to the personnels posted to work in areas inhabited by Primitive Tribal Groups. The Working Group even recommended the institution of national awards for such personnel for excellence in their work.

Now the question is, to what extent the governments both Central and State have been able to deliver to these people and what is the economic impact of the developmental schemes on the people which are undertaken by the governments through various Micro Projects. Whether the governments have taken steps according to the recommendations and suggestions given by various Working Groups or have failed to do so due to certain impediments, are needed to be analysed. Other aspects such as change in the attitude, aspiration, awareness, lifeways, consumption and production pattern of people and their adaptability to eco-cultural changes should also be inquired into.

Annexure I : Scheduled Tribe Population of Tribal Sub-Plan States

Sl. No.	TSP State/U.T.	Total Population	Sch. Tribe Population	% of ST toTotal Population
1.	Andhra Pradesh	66,508,008	4,199,481	6.31
2.	Assam	22,414,322	2,874,441	12.82
3.	Bihar	86,374,465	6,616,914	7.66
4.	Gujarat	41,309,582	6,161,775	14.91
5.	Himachal Pradesh	5,170,877	218,349	4.22
6.	Jammu & Kashmir	7,718,700	—	—
7.	Karnataka	44,977,201	1,915,691	4.25
8.	Kerala	29,098,518	320,967	1.10
9.	Madhya Pradesh	66,181,170	15,399,034	23.26
10.	Maharashtra 78,937,187	7,318,281	9.27	
11.	Manipur	1,837,149	632,173	34.41
12.	Orissa	31,659,736	7,032,214	22.21
13.	Rajasthan	44,005,990	5,474,881	12.44
14.	Sikkim	406,457	90,901	22.36
15.	Tamil Nadu	55,858,946	574,194	1.02
16.	Tripura	2,757,205	853,345	30.94
17.	Uttar Pradesh	139,112,287	287,901	0.20
18.	West Bengal	68,077,965	3,808,760	5.59
19.	Andaman & Nicobar Islands	280,661	26,770	9.53
20.	Daman & Diu	101,586	11,724	11.54
Total 20	—	**785,069,312**	**63,817,796**	**8.12**

Note : - The Total is estimated exclusing the Jammu and Kashmir because the ST population of the state is not available.

Source *:- Census of India, 1991,* and *Annual Report, 1994-95, Ministry of Welfare, Government of India.*

Annexure II : List of Approved Primitive Tribal Groups

Sl.No.	State/U.T.	Name of the Primitive Tribal Groups
1.	Andhra pradesh	1. Gutob Gadaba
		2. Bodo Gadaba Poroja
		3. Bondo Poroja
		4. Khond Poroja
		5. Parengi Poroja Khond
		6. Kutia Khond
		7. Dongaria Khond
		8. Konda Savaras
		9. Thoti
		10. Chenchu
		11. Konda Reddy
		12. Kolam
2.	Bihar	13. Asur
		14. Birhor
		15. Birjia
		16. Korwa
		17. Malpaharia
		18. Pahariya
		19. Savar
		20. Sauria Paharia
		21. Hill Kharia
3.	Gujarat	22. Kathodi
		23. Kolgha
		24. Padhar
		25. Kotwalia
		26. Siddi
4.	Karnataka	27. Jenu Kuruba
		28. Koraga
5.	Kerala	29. Cholanaikayan
		30. Kurumba
		31. Kadar
		32. Kattunayakan
		33. Koraga

6.	Madhya Pradesh	34.	Abujh Maria
		35.	Baiga
		36.	Bharia
		37.	Hill Koba
		38.	Kamar
		39.	Saharia
		40.	Birhor
7.	Maharashtra	41.	Katkaria (Kathodia)
		42.	Kolam
		43.	Maria Gond
8.	Manipur	44.	Marram.
9.	Orissa	45.	Didayi
		46.	Mankiridia
		47.	Lodha
		48.	Kharia
		49.	Bondo
		50.	Dongria Kondh
		51.	Juang
		52.	Kutia Kondh
		53.	Lanjia Saora
		54.	Paudi Bhuinya
		55.	Saora
		56.	Birhor
		57.	Chuktia Bhunjia
10.	Rajasthan	58.	Seharia
11.	Tamil Nadu	59.	Kattu Naickan
		60.	Kotas
		61.	Kurumbas
		62.	Irulas
		63.	Paniyans
		64.	Todas
12.	Tripura	65.	Reangs
13.	Uttar Pradesh	66.	Buxas
		67.	Rajis
14.	West Bengal	68.	Totos
		69.	Birhor
		70.	Lodhas

15.	Andaman & Nicobar Islands	71.	Shompens
		72.	Onges
		73.	Great Andamanese
		74.	Jarwas
		75.	Sentenelese

Source :- *Fourth Report, Rashtriya Anusuchit Jati Tatha Anusuchit Janajati Ayog, 1996-97 & 1997-98.*

4

Developmental Strategies for Primitive Tribes

THE census of 1991 shows that Orissa covers a geographical area of 1,55,707 sq km and the total population of the state is 3,16,59,736. There are as many as 62 Scheduled Tribes in Orissa, the total population of which is 70,32,214. This population is about 22.21 per cent of the State population.

21 Integrated Tribal Development Agencies have been established in Orissa, all of which cover a total area of 63,896 sq km and a total population of 87.28 lakh. The Integrated Tribal Development Agencies have covered 67.53 per cent of the Scheduled Tribe population of Orissa. The Scheduled Tribe population within the Integrated Tribal Development Agencies is 54.41 per cent of the total population. 46 Modified Area Development Approach Pockets and 14 Clusters have also been identified in Orissa. The Modified Area Development Approach Pockets cover 8.06 per cent and the Clusters cover 0.75 per cent of the state Scheduled Tribe population. However, the Integrated Tribal Development Agencies, the Modified Area Development Approach Pockets and the Clusters in total cover about 76.35 per cent of the State Scheduled Tribe population.

As far as the development of the Primitive Tribal Groups are concerned, 13 out of total 62 tribal communities have been identified as such tribes on the basis of three criteria which are in line with the yardsticks maintained by the Government of India. According to these yardsticks a Primitive Tribal Group has the following characteristics:

1. Pre-agricultural technology.
2. Low level of literacy.
3. Stagnant or diminishing population.

The names of the Primitive Tribal Groups and their locations are given in Table 4.1.

Table 4.1 : The Primitive Tribal Groups of Orissa and Their Locations

Sl. No.	*Name of the Primitive Tribal Group*	*Name of the Location (Districts)*
1.	Bondo	Malkanagiri
2.	Didayi	Malkanagiri
3.	Dongria Kondh	Rayagada
4.	Lanjia Saora	Rayagada and Gajapati
5.	Saora	Ganjam and Gajapati
6.	Kutia Kondh	Kandhamal & Kalahandi
7.	Juang	Keonjhar
8.	Paudi Bhuinya	Angul, Sundargarh and Deogarh
9.	Lodha	Mayurbhanj
10.	Hill Khadia	Mayurbhanj
11.	Mankidia	Mayurbhanj
12.	Birhor	Mayurbhanj and Sundargarh
13.	Chuktia Bhunjia	Nawapara

Source : *Action Plan for the Development of Primitive Tribal Groups during Eighth Plan (1993-97)* and *Annual Plan (1993-94)*, Tribal Welfare Department, Government of Orissa.

Micro Projects for the development of the Primitive Tribal Groups, were constituted in 1979-80 under the Societies Registration Act, 1860. The governing Body of this project is generally headed by the collector of the concerned district or the Project Administrator of the concerned Integrated Tribal Development Agency. There are 17 Micro Projects established in different primitive tribal pockets of

Orissa. Table 4.2 gives the name of the Micro Projects, Delivery Centres, Primitive Tribal Groups and the districts.

Table 4.2 : The Micro Projects of Orissa and their locations

Sl. No.	*Name of the Micro Projects*	*Delivery Centre*	*Name of the Primitive Tribal Group*	*Name of the District*
1.	Bondo Development Agency	Mudulipada	Bondo	Malkanagiri
2.	Didayi Development Agency	Bayapada (Kudumul-guma)	Didayi	Malkangiri
3.	Dongria Kondh Dev. Agency	Chatikona	Dongria Khond	Rayagada
4.	Dongria Kondh Dev. Agency	Parasali	Dongria Khond	Rayagada
5.	Lanjia Saora Dev. Agency	Puttasingi	Lanjia Saora	Rayagada
6.	Lanjia Saora Dev. Agency	Seranga	Lanjia Saora	Gajapati
7.	Saora Dev. Agency	Chandragiri	Saora	Gajapati
8.	Thumba Dev. Agency	Patrapur (Thumba)	Saora	Ganjam
9.	Kutia Kondh Dev. Agency	Belghar	Kutia Kondh	Kandhamal
10.	Kutia Kondh Dev. Agency	Lanjiagarh	Kutia Kondh	Kalahandi
11.	Juang Dev. Agency	Gonasika	Juang	Keonjhar
12.	Paudi Bhuinya Dev. Agency	Khuntgaon	Paudi Bhuinya	Sundargarh
13.	Paudi Bhuinya Dev. Agency	Jamardiha	Paudi Bhuinya	Angul
14.	Paudi Bhuinya Dev. Agency	Barkote	Paudi Bhuinya	Debagarh

Sl. No.	*Name of the Micro Projects*	*Delivery Centre*	*Name of the Primitive Tribal Group*	*Name of the District*
15.	Hill Khadia & Mankidia Dev. Agency.	Jashipur	Hill Khadia & Mankidia	Mayurbhanj
16.	Lodha Dev. Agency.	Morada	Lodha	Mayurbhanj
17.	Chuktia-Bhunjia Dev. Agency	Komna	Chuktia Bhunjia	Nuapada

Source : *Action Plan for the Development of Primitive Tribal Groups during Eighth Plan (1993-97)* and *Annual Plan (1993-94)*, Tribal Welfare Department, Government of Orissa

The locations of the Micro projects identified in small circles in the map of Orissa, are given on page no. 212.

Among all the Micro Projects the Bondo Development Agency was the first project which was set-up in the former district of Koraput (presently known as Malkanagiri district) in 1977. In the following year seven Micro Projects were set-up in different parts of the State. In 1979 one more Micro Project was established and by the end of the Fifth Plan, there were nine such projects in Orissa. Only one Micro Project was established during the Sixth Plan period. But during the Seventh Plan, five Projects were set-up in different primitive tribal areas. However, during the Eighth Plan, two more Micro Projects were set-up, i.e., one for the development of the Paudi Bhuinyas in the Barkote area of the Deogarh district and one for the Chuktia Bhunjias in the Komna area of the Nawapara district.

13 projects out of 17, are located within the Tribal Sub-Plan area and the rest four are outside the Tribal Sub-Plan area. The Micro Projects located outside the Tribal Sub-Plan are:

1. Paudi Bhuinya Development Agency, Jamardihi, Angul district.

2. Paudi Bhuinya Development Agency, Barkote, Deogarh district.
3. Thumba Development Agency, Thumba, Ganjam district.
4. Chuktia Bhunjia Development Agency, Komna, Nawapara district.

According to the data available up to 1995-96, 17 Micro Projects cover 537 villages. The total tribal population covered under these projects is 61,240. Among all the projects, the Kutia Kondh Development Agency of Kandhamal district has the largest number of villages, i.e., 69 under its operation, followed by the Dongria Kondh Development Agency of the Rayagada district which covers 63 villages. The Lodha Development Agency of the Mayurbhanj district has the lowest number of villages, i.e., eight. The Didayi Development Agency of the Malkanagiri district has the largest coverage of population, i.e., 5,990 and the Chuktia-Bhunjia Development Agency of the Nawapara district, having a population of 1,579 has the lowest coverage. So far as literacy is concerned, the Paudi Bhuinya Development Agency of the Sundargarh district has the highest literacy rate, i.e., 70.02 per cent while the literacy rate of the Bondo Development Agency of the Malkanagiri district is the lowest among all, i.e., 4.79 per cent. Table 4.3 gives projectwise information about no. of villages, literacy rate and population, etc.

Table 4.3 : Detailed information about the Micro Projects of Orissa

Sl. No.	*Name of Micro Project*	*District*	*Part of Blocks Covered*
1.	Bondo Development Agency, Mudulipada	Malkanagiri	Khairput
2.	Didayi Development Agency, Bayapada	Malkanagiri	Kudumulguma, Khairput
3.	Dongria Kondh Development Agency, Chatikona	Rayagada	Bissam-Cuttack and Muniguda
4.	Dongria Kondh Development Agency, Parasali	Rayagada	K.Singhpur

Sl. No.	*Name of Micro Project*	*District*	*Part of Blocks Covered*
5.	Lanjia Saora Development Agency, Puttasinghi	Rayagada	Gunupur
6.	Lanjia Saora Development Agency, Seranga	Gajapati	Gumma
7.	Saora Development Agency, Chandragiri	Gajapati	Mohana
8.	Thumba Development Agency Thumba	Ganjam	Patrapur
9.	Kutia Kondh Development Agency, Belghar	Kandhamal	Tumudibandha
10.	Kutia Kondh Development Agency, Lanjigarh	Kalahandi	Lanjigarh
11.	Juang Development Agency, Gonasika	Keonjhar	Bansapal
12.	Paudi Bhuinya Development Agency, Khuntagaon	Sundergarh	Lahunipada
13.	Paudi Bhuinya Development Agency, Jamardihi	Angul	Pallahara
14.	Paudi Bhuinya Development Agency, Rugudakudar	Deogarh	Barkote
15.	Hill-Kharia and Mankidia Development Agency, Gudugudia	Mayurbhanj	Jashipur and Karanjia
16.	Lodha Development Agency, Moroda	Mayurbhanj	Suliapada and Moroda
17.	Chuktia-Bhunjia Development Agency, Sunabeda	Nawapara	Komna

Sl. No.	*Establishment year of Micro Project*	*Number of Villages*	*Primitive Tribal Population as per 1991 Census*	*Literacy Rate (In %)*	*Percentage of Primitive Tribal Population to Total Primitive Tribal Population of all Micro Projects.*
01	1976-77	35	5,050	4.79	8.25
02	1986-87	38	5,990	39.93	9.78
03	1978-79	63	5.181	29.11	8.46
04	1987-88	49	2,485	7.32	4.06
05	1984-85	19	3,544	33.86	5.79
06	1978-79	21	4,043	9.42	6.60
07	1978-79	26	3,420	13.86	5.58
08	1978-79	55	3,057	26.79	4.99
09	1978-79	69	4,578	18.00	7.48
10	1986-87	17	1,901	27.72	3.10
11	1978-79	32	5,774	12.24	9.43
12	1978-79	27	5,433	70.02	8.87
13	1978-79	21	3.026	16.36	4.94
14	1993-94	19	2.467	14.07	4.03
15	1986-87	21	1,660	27.71	2.71
16	1985-86	8	2,052	22.66	3.35
17	1994-95	17	1,579	8.11	2.58
	Total	**537**	**61,240**	**24.20**	**100.00**

Sourcc : *Annual Administration Report of Scheduled Castes and Scheduled Tribes Development Department for the year 1995-96, Government of Orissa.*

The Socio-economic indicators such as population growth rate, percentage of households practising shifting cultivation and percentage of households above poverty line, etc., imply the development perspective of the Primitive Tribal Groups and the impact of the Micro Projects on them. Information regarding these indicators of the Micro Projects are given in Table 4.4.

MAP OF ORISSA SHOWING LOCATIONS OF EXISTING MICRO PROJECTS

1. Bondo Development Agency, Mudulipada.
2. Didayi Development Agency, Kudumulguma.
3. Dongria Kondh Development Agency, Chatikona.
4. Dongria Kondh Development Agency, Parasali.
5. Lanjia Saora Development Agency, Puttasingi.
6. Lanjia Saora Development Agency, Seranga.
7. Saora Development Agency, Chandragiri.
8. Kutia Kondh Development Agency, Belghar.
9. Thumba Development Agency, Thumba.
10. Kutia Kondh Development Agency, Lanjigarh.
11. Juang Development Agency, Gonasika.
12. Paudi Bhuinya Development Agency, Jamardiha.
13. Paudi Bhuinya Development Agency, Khuntgaon.
14. Paudi Bhuinya Development Agency, Barkote.
15. Hill Kharia and Mankidia Development Agency, Jashipur.
16. Lodha Development Agency, Morada.
17. Chukti-Bhunjia Development Agency, Komna.

Table 4.4 : Information about various Socio-Economic indicators of different Micro Projects in Orissa

Sl. No.	*Name of the Project*	*Annual growth rate of Population (In %)*	*Households Practising Shifting Cultivation (In %)*	*H.H. Above Poverty Line (in %)*
1.	Bondo Development Agency, Mudulipada	1.04	100	-
2.	Didayi Development Agency, Kudmulguma	0.86	73	-
3.	Dongria Kondh Development Agency, Chatikona	0.92	66.18	42.92
4.	Dongria Kondh Development Agency, Parasali	0.88	100	-
5.	Lanjia Saora Development Agency, Puttasinghi	-	-	17.33
6.	Lanjia Saora Development Agency, Seranga	0.62	-	8.91
7.	Saora Development Agency, Chandragiri	1.01	-	-
8.	Thumba Development Agency, Thumba	0.72	-	29.30
9.	Kutia Kondh Development Agency, Belghar	1.36	100	-
10.	Kutia Kondh Development Agency, Lanjigarh	-	-	-
11.	Juang Development Agency, Gonasika	2.66	-	-

Sl. No.	*Name of the Project*	*Annual growth rate of Population (In %)*	*Households Practising Shifting Cultivation (In %)*	*H.H. Above Poverty Line (in %)*
12.	Paudi Bhuinya Development Agency, Khuntgaon	1.6	-	24.31
13.	Paudi Bhuinya Development Agency, Jamardihi	2.8	10	15.27
14.	Paudi Bhuinya Development Agency, Barkote	-	15.88	-
15.	Hill Kharia and Mankidia Development Agency, Jashipur	1	-	1.2
16.	Lodha Development Agency, Morada	-	-	-
17.	Chuktia-Bhunjia Development Agency, Komna	-	-	-

Source : *Action Plan for the Development of Primitive Tribal Groups during Eighth Plan (1993-97)* and *Annual Plan (1993-94),* Tribal Welfare Department, Government of Orissa.

The data in the table above, show that the annual population growth rate is low in all the project areas. The growth rate is negative (0.86 per cent) in the Didayi Development Agency. Data regarding the households practising shifting cultivation are available for only seven agencies. Such data indicate the backwardness of the various Primitive Tribal Groups. In all these agencies, except two Paudi Bhuinya Development Agencies at Khuntgaon and Jamardiha, the practice of shifting cultivation is high among the people.

The practice of such cultivation by 100 per cent is seen in three agencies, i.e., Bondo Development Agency, Mudulipada, Dongria

Kondh Development Agency, Parasali and Kutia Kondh Development Agency, Belghar.

Data regarding percentage of the households above the poverty line are available for seven agencies. Dongria Kondh Development Agency at Chatikona has the highest percentage of households above the poverty line, i.e., 42.92 per cent. Among all the agencies, poverty is most prevalent in the Hill Kharia and Mankidia Development Agency where only 1.2 per cent of the total households are above the poverty line.

Data about the total funds allocated to each Micro Project up to 1998-99 since their inception and the total funds utilized are given in Table 4.5.

Table 4.5 : Allocation of Funds to the Micro Projects in Orissa

Sl. No.	*Name of the Micro Project*	*Year of inception*	*Total funds allocated till 1998-99 (In Rs.)*	*Total funds utilized (In Rs.)*
1.	Bondo Development Agency, Mudulipada	1977	22,773,562	22,900,938
2.	Didayi Development Agency, Kudmulguma	1986	17,005.000	15,804,828
3.	Dongria Kondh Development Agency, Chatikona	1978	21.208,000	20,453,792
4.	Dongria Kondh Development Agency, Parasali	1987	10,530,800	10,303,444
5.	Lanjia Saora Development Agency, Puttasinghi	1984	14,812,000	15,382,538
6.	Lanjia Saora Development Agency, Seranga	1979	19,025,610	18,267,244
7.	Saora Development Agency, Chandragiri	1978	17,163,053	17,549,219

Sl. No.	*Name of the Micro Project*	*Year of inception*	*Total funds allocated till 1998-99 (In Rs.)*	*Total funds utilized (In Rs.)*
8.	Thumba Development Agency, Thumba	1978	15,174,859	17,087,601
9.	Kutia Kondh Development Agency, Belghar	1978	16,383,901	15,604,143
10.	Kutia Kondh Development Agency, Lanjigarh	1986	8,779,000	8,740,706
11.	Juang Development Agency, Gonasika	1978	19,690,470	19,246,183
12.	Paudi Bhuinya Development Agency, Khuntgaon	1978	15,876,970	16,134,792
13.	Paudi Bhuinya Development Agency, Jamardihi	1978	18,709,000	16,888,672
14.	Paudi Bhuinya Development Agency, Barkote	1993	-	
15.	Hill Kharia and Mankidia Development Agency, Jashipur	1987	14,654,893	14,521,869
16.	Lodha Development Agency, Morada	1986	9,258,007	6,042,121
17.	Chuktia-Bhunjia Development Agency, Komna	1994	3,384,000	2,366,579
	Total		**244,429,125**	**237,294,669**

Source : *Action Plan for the Development of Primitive Tribal Groups during Eighth Plan (1993-97)* and *Annual Plan (1993-94)*, Tribal Welfare Department and Monitoring Cell, Scheduled Castes and Scheduled Tribes Development Department, Government of Orissa.

The average annual per capita investment for beneficiaries in each project area has been estimated from the data available from 1993-94 to 1998-99. Table 4.6 gives information regarding the total amount of funds utilized, total number beneficiaries covered, and average annual per capita investment under beneficiaries during 1993-94 and 1998-99.

Table 4.6 : Annual per Capita Expenditure for the Beneficiaries of Different Micro Projects of Orissa During 1993-99

Sl. No.	*Name of the Project*	*Total Amount of Funds Utilized (In Rs.)*	*Number of Beneficiaries Covered*	*Average Annual per Capita Investment (In Rs.)*
1.	Bondo Development Agency, Mudulipada	93,19,071	14,040	663.75
2.	Didayi Development Agency, Kudmulguma	78,36,639	8,312	942.81
3.	Dongria Kondh Development Agency, Chatikona	-	-	-
4.	Dongria Kondh Development Agency, Parasali	50,92,115	1,826	2788.67
5.	Lanjia Saora Development Agency, Puttasinghi	-	-	-
6.	Lanjia Saora Development Agency, Seranga	82,43,032	4,424	1863.25
7.	Saora Development Agency, Chandragiri	75,93,916	3,772	2013.23
8.	Thumba Development Agency, Thumba	87,26,123	3,282	2658.78
9.	Kutia Kondh Development Agency, Belghar	-	-	-

Sl. No.	Name of the Project	Total Amount of Funds Utilized (In Rs.)	Number of Beneficiaries Covered	Average Annual per Capita Investment (In Rs.)
10.	Kutia Kondh Development Agency, Lanjigarh	48,24,033	1,260	3828.60
11.	Juang Development Agency, Gonasika	-	-	-
12.	Paudi Bhuinya Development Agency, Khuntgaon	65,51,577	3,507	1925.17
13.	Paudi Bhuinya Development Agency, Jamardihi	-	-	-
14.	Paudi Bhuinya Development Agency, Barkote	-	-	-
15.	Hill Kharia and Mankidia Development Agency, Jashipur	-	-	-
16.	Lodha Development Agency, Moroda	43,45,697	4,015	1082.37
17.	Chuktia-Bhunjia Development Agency, Komna	19,35,721	1,261	1535.07
	Total	**6,46,67,924**	**45,699**	**1415.08**

Source : Monitoring Cell, Scheduled Caste and Scheduled Tribe Department, Government of Orissa.

The data in the above table show that during 1993-99 the average annual per capita investment in respect of the Kutia Kondh Development Agency, Lanjigarh, is the highest and that of the Bondo Development Agency, Mudulipada, is the lowest among all the agencies. The disparity between the highest and the lowest per capita expenditure is Rs. 3164.85.

Central Place Theory and Planning for Tribal Development

The micro project approach was initiated during the Fifth Five-Year Plan for the primitive tribes. Since then it has been followed for the development of the primitive tribes irrespective of its usefulness as a strategy for planning and implementation of various developmental schemes. It is too late now to evaluate this strategy and find out its effectiveness or otherwise in achieving desired results. There are recently developed alternative strategies which appear to be more realistic, appropriate and effective in bringing about change and development among the primitive tribes. One of such alternatives was applied in a tribal area for identifying functional gaps and inter-regional functional inter-linkage, which are of utmost importance in a scientific planning for a tribal area.

This mode of approach to tribal development goes by the name of the planning based on central place theory and growth centre concept. The concept and the techniques involved in this strategy are as follows.

The following paragraphs deal with the techniques of identifying at various levels the basic planning units and functional hierarchy which were used for planning development of tribal regions in Keonjhar district.

Village is the smallest unit which can be identified in a surveyed area. In some backward areas village boundaries cannot be identified on a map. However, so far as the social facilities and the supply of inputs are concerned, village boundary may not signify any importance. People depend upon distant villages or towns for getting their requirements. Moreover, due to the limitation of resources it will not be possible to regard village as the lowest unit of planning. At higher level, a group of clusters of villages will form next higher unit of planning which would sustain higher order of functions. Thus, there should be hierarchy of planning units starting from the lowest level planning units to the highest level planning units. And higher the planning units, higher is the order of functions which they sustain.

The lowest level planning unit, with a small group of villages within its hinterland and a central village as its focal point and with functional inter-linkages with other central places, should be ideal for planning development at the grass-root level. This unit may provide the base for meaningful aggregated estimates of resources as well as needs, and for the implementation of location specific programmes. The exercise in this regard is to identify the central places and to delineate hinterland boundaries of each central place. It is already observed by experts that villages maintain linkages with other settlements for their requirements. Depending upon the nature of services and specializations, the inter-village linkage varies from village to village. A person may send his child to a village at a distance of two km for primary education, to a second village at a distance of 10 km for high school education and to a third place at a distance of 25 km for college education. A village may, therefore, be at the centre of many concentric circles with progressively increasing *radii* depending on the nature and degree of specialization of functional linkages.

The plan based on this concept is published in the book *A Integrated Tribal Development Plan for Keonjhar District, Orissa including the Juangpirh and Bhuinyapirh* brought out by the National Institute of Rural Development, Hyderabad. It was a consultancy assignment given to the NIRD at the instance of the Ministry of Home Affairs (now Ministry of Tribal affairs), Government of India by the Tribal and Rural Welfare Department of the Government of Orissa. The plan was prepared by Dr. N. Patnaik who was then serving at the NIRD as the Director of Anthropology. It was a pioneering effort in plan formulation for tribal regions employing the recently developed techniques of the Integrated Area Development Planning evolving within the spatial framework the location specific development priorities for the plan area. As an experiment this plan can be utilized for the development of Juangpirh and Bhuinyapirh of Keonjhar District, Orissa.

5

Conclusion and Agenda for Future Action

IT is only after Independence that the needs and the problems of the tribals were recognized and systematically addressed. The Constitution of India has enunciated several provisions to redress their problems and for their development. However, since the Fifth Five-Year Plan, special emphasis was given to tribal development, by introducing Tribal Sub-Plans (TSPs).

Areas of concentration of tribal population were identified and separate administrative units were established in 20 States and Union Territories for effective implementation of the Tribal Sub-Plan strategy. The Integrated Development Approach was evolved as the main thrust of the Tribal Sub-Plan strategy during the Fifth Plan and the concept of Integrated Tribal Development Project/Agency (ITDP/ITDA) was conceived as the lowest unit of this approach. One Integrated Tribal Development Project covers an area of a *Tahsil* or a Block or more in which the Scheduled Tribe population is 50 per cent of the total population or more. During the Sixth Plan, the Tribal Sub-Plan approach was extended to Pockets of concentration of Scheduled Tribe population containing 50 per cent or more Scheduled Tribe population within a total population of 10,000. These Pockets are known as Modified Area Development Approach (MADA) Pockets. Cluster approach was also adopted during the same plan to cover Pockets of tribal concentration containing 50 per cent or more Scheduled Tribe population within a total population of about 5,000.

Apart from these strategies of tribal development, the government specifically initiated the Micro project approach for the Primitive Tribes during the Fifth Plan. The Primitive Tribes were found to live in secluded regions. The Dhebar Commission Report identified them as the most backward tribes among all the tribes. The Primitive Tribes are generally characterized by the pre-agricultural level of technology and extremely low level of literacy. As many as 75 Scheduled Tribes have been identified as Primitive Tribal Groups (PTGs) in 15 out of 20 Tribal Sub-Plan States/Union Territories.

In Orissa alone 13 out of 62 Scheduled Tribes have been identified as Primitive Tribal Groups (PTGs). In the early part of this book, we have discussed the tribes of Orissa in general and ethnography of all the Primitive Tribal groups of Orissa. In the subsequent chapters, discussion and analysis have been carried out about strategies for tribal development in general and developmental strategies for Primitive Tribes of Orissa in particular.

Over the years, the Micro Projects have taken up various programmes and schemes for the socio-economic development of the Primitive Tribes. The Government of India has provided funds to finance the Micro Projects under the Special Central Assistance (SCA). This assistance has been considered as an additive to the State Plan Funds. It is seen that a considerable amount of funds have been provided under the provision of the Special Central Assistance.

To assess the impact of the development schemes of the Micro Projects on the Primitive Tribes, two case studies were carried out in two Micro Projects of Orissa, namely Saora Development Agency of the Gajapati district and Juang Development Agency of the Keonjhar district. The case studies are given in the following paragraph, in which the impacts have been assessed, problems and shortcomings have been identified and accordingly a number of suggestions have been made for future action.

Saora Development Agency

The Saoras are still in primitive stage in spite of their practice of settled and terraced cultivation. Their annual growth rate of population is only 1.01 per cent. Tradition-bound customary laws seem to exist in their society.

The Saora Development Agency has been working for the last 21 years. So far it has been able to provide benefits and facilities to 675 Saora households of 25 villages. The programmes of development are broadly of two types. These include income generating and individual benefit schemes, and infrastructure and community development programmes. Now it is to be seen what is the impact of various development schemes on the Saoras under these two types of programmes. This study was carried out in 2 villages namely Baunsuri and Jamudiha.

THE IMPACT

The impact of the Saora Development Agency has been measured in terms of the above-said programmes. For example, the impact of the income generating schemes has been measured through the total annual income of the beneficiaries and that of other schemes such as individual benefit schemes and community development programmes are assessed in terms of the nature of the facilities that are provided to the people under these programmes.

The Income level of all the beneficiaries in 1998-99, estimated earlier, indicates that none of them have crossed the poverty line. The poverty line was fixed at Rs. 12,500.00 by the National Council of Applied Economic Research for the year, 1998-99. In fact, all of them are much below the poverty line; the highest income among them being Rs. 870.000.

Apart from the benefits from the income generating schemes, the Saoras have been provided many facilities which include housing, drinking water, health measures, street light, community centres and roads.

It is found that the beneficiaries have been supplied with tin roof-sheets which most of them used in their own houses.

The villagers have been provided with dug wells and tube- wells in each village. Now they get drinking water from these wells and do not depend on the stream water anymore.

Through the provision of health facility such as financial help in case of illness, the Saora Development Agency has been able to induce many Saoras to adopt the modern medical facilities in place of their traditional system of treatment.

The study shows that the villages are provided with street light, and therefore the streets are lighted at night. It is a facility which the Agency provided after the Rural Electrification Scheme was implemented.

Community centres of the Saora villages are built and maintained by the Saora Development Agency. By providing this facility, the agency helps the Saoras in many ways. The Saoras congregate at this centre to observe the Community and ritual festivals which they cannot do elsewhere. The Community centre helps in this way so that the unity among them is encouraged and their traditional culture is preserved. This centre is also used for storing purposes and for recreation of the villagers. Thus the Community centres serve many purposes.

The Saora Development Agency has built 36.5 km roads and 15.63 per cent of the total roads existing in the project area. The study also reveals that in one village, an open culvert and in another village a part of the road has been built by the agency. These schemes have facilitated inter-village communi-cation including Chandragiri and other nearby villages.

The income level of the beneficiaries and the facilities available to them, indicate that the impact of the Saora Development Agency is not impressive, given 21 years of its operation. The Agency needs to achieve success in many areas of development. But there are some problems and short-comings which are found to be the main hurdles for the Agency to achieve a higher level of development. These problems and shortcomings have been found in the staffing pattern of the Agency, budgetary provisions and allocation and implementation of different schemes. These are mentioned below.

THE PROBLEMS AND SHORTCOMINGS

1. Staffing pattern : The Saora Development Agency has two executing bodies, namely, the governing body and the office staff. The governing body prepares action plans, reviews past performances and monitors the operation of the agency. The members of the governing body include representatives of people, technical and administrative personnel from various government departments and other organizations. The inclusion of the members from various departments seems to be justified considering the task of the governing body.

However, the problem lies at implementation level. The staff seems to be inadequate given the number of schemes and beneficiaries. The Agency does not have a single technical personnel of any programme in its staff having minimum education up to matric level. Therefore none of them are able to impart technical skills and guidance to the beneficiaries in the programmes such as agriculture, horticulture, animal husbandry and soil conservation programmes, etc. The *amin* and the chainman are the only field staff who execute the programmes and guide the beneficiaries in all matters concerning development schemes even though they do not have technical knowledge in any programme. The inadequacy of the staff can be clearly observed when the total number of staff members (8) is compared with the total villages (25) and the total household beneficiaries (675). A rough estimate shows that the ratio between the staff members and the household beneficiaries is 1 : 84. Another shortcoming of the Saora Development Agency is that for quite sometime it did not have a full-time Special Officer. Lacking any administrative head the progress was slow and half-hazard.

2. Budgetary provisions and allocation : It is seen that in the last 21 years, there was upward and downward trend in the budgetary provisions for the Saora Development Agency. Due to this factor, the Saora Development Agency did not have a consistent expenditure pattern and budgetary allocation. For instance, during 1994-95 and 1997-98, no fund was allocated to the programme of supply of bullocks while there were funds for input assistance and supply of agricultural implements under the agriculture programme.

Some of the programmes, such as animal husbandry and small-scale and cottage industries did not have any allocations of funds during the above-mentioned years.

The Saora Development Agency allocates funds for amongst three heads, namely, income-generating and individual benefit schemes, infrastructure and community development programmes, and establishment charges. During 1994-95 and 1997-98, 37.99 per cent of the total fund was spent on the income generating and individual benefit schemes and 29.84 per cent was allocated to infrastructure and community development programmes while 32.16 per cent was incurred on establishment charges. It shows that a sizeable amount was given for establishment charges. Although the expenditure in the establishment charges is essential, it has no direct bearing on the development of the people and therefore the funds allocated to this head should be as minimum as possible.

Moreover, the Agency's annual per capita expenditure for the households is only Rs. 1178.32. Given the underdeveloped conditions of the Saoras, this amount is very small.

3. Implementation of schemes : There are seven schemes, each under the income generating and individual benefit programmes, and the infrastructure and community development programmes. Each scheme has a number of sub-schemes which are equally beneficial. There are 26 such sub-schemes and these were introduced and discontinued at different times. The study has found inconsistencies

in the distribution of benefits under some of the programmes. For example, none of the beneficiaries have received any benefit under the agriculture programme, although all of them carry on agriculture as their primary occupation. Similarly, they have been given benefits under only one scheme of horticulture, although there are many schemes in this programme and the agro-climatic conditions of the area are most suitable for horticulture. The beneficiaries have not been able to derive much benefit from this source although land and irrigation facilities were provided by the Agency. Moreover, due to non-availability of input assistance, the people approach the local business men for help and get exploited at the time of harvest.

The study also found that two beneficiaries have sold their goats to purchase bullocks. Had they been supplied with bullocks, they would not have sold the goats and could have earned more by rearing them. So what is indicated is that there has been a lack of integrated approach and foresight in the matter of introducing schemes of development. This is the reason why some schemes cause failure of other schemes under the same programme.

Moreover, it was found that none of the beneficiaries have been given large amount of land for which they are not able to do farming on a large scale and produce more. The Saora Development Agency has not organized any training or demonstration programme on improved agricultural practices, application of improved seeds and fertilizers. The agriculture programme would have been of great help to the farmers in improving their economic condition.

Among the community development programmes, education is one programme by which the people have been least benefited. During 1994-95 and 1997-98, the expenditure on this programme was highest compared to that of other programmes. About 22 per cent of the total budget was spent on education. But neither any educational institution nor any literacy centre have come up in both Baunsuri and Jamudiha. Only five girls of Jamudiha have received the benefit of studying at free of cost. The literacy rate in the Agency area was 20.02 per cent. These figures indicate that literacy has not been promoted by the Agency among the people of this area. *Gyan mandiras* which have been built under this programme are not used for any educational purpose. These centres are only used for community activities.

As far as rural electrification is concerned, the villages are provided with street lights only. Household connections have not been provided to them as yet.

In the provision of other facilities, such as roads and health, minor irregularities are found out. For instance, an open culvert has been built by the Saora Development Agency in Baunsuri village for facilitating communication, but the villagers are still facing communication problem during rainy season because water flows over it. Similarly, it was found that two beneficiaries have not been provided with medical facility although they required it and one of them has not received any housing facility.

Juang Development Agency

In the following, the impact of the Juang Development Agency on its people have been examined. Some of the problems and shortcomings are also given.

The study found that a large number of people carry on shifting cultivation as one of their main occupation in two villages namely Guptaganga and Kadalibadi. This practice alone supports the view that the Juangs are still in primitive stage. In its 21 years of existence, the Juang Development Agency has provided benefits and facilities to 1393 Juang households of 32 villages. Like the Saora Development Agency, this Agency has provided benefits to the people through the income generating and individual benefit programmes, and infrastructure and community development programmes. The impact of these programmes on the people has been analysed in the following.

THE IMPACT

The impact of the income generating schemes has been measured through the total annual income of the beneficiary that he receives from the utilization of such schemes. It was found that none of the beneficiaries have crossed the poverty line during 1998-99. Their average annual income was Rs. 4,315.00 which was much below the national poverty line index.

So far as the community development programmes are concerned, the Juangs have been benefitted by such programmes as health measures, communication, community centre, and training and exhibition programmes. Many of the programmes have also failed or delivered less facility. These programmes include drinking water, housing, rural electrification and education.

The study reveals that all the beneficiaries have been provided with medicines and treatment during their illness. Like the Saora Development Agency, the Juang Development Agency has been able to introduce modern medicines and treatment in place of their traditional system.

The Juang Development Agency has built 35.5 km roads in the area under its operation. Guptaganga and Kadalibadi are also connected with Gonasika Delivery centre by the roads built by the Agency.

The community centre facility has been provided by the Juang Development Agency either through construction of buildings or repair of the same. It is found that construction and repair of *Mandaghar* has been taken up by the Agency in Guptaganga and Kadalibadi respectively. By taking up such schemes, the Juang Development Agency has helped to strengthen unity and restore the values of traditional institutions among the Juang.

Training and demonstration programmes have been organized by the Agency to orient the beneficiaries with new skills and ideas.

Especially the training regarding the use of improved seeds and the application of fertilizers were of some help to those who carry on agriculture as their occupation.

For drinking water, the Juang Development Agency has provided tube-wells in the villages. But due to iron content the people do not use this water. They use stream water as they were doing before. So there seems to be no impact of this programme.

The data shows that out of 65 households in Guptaganga only 11 households have been provided with housing facility by the Juang Development Agency. Moreover, the study shows that only one person out of six studied beneficiaries has been benefitted under this scheme. So it appears that this programme has not been taken up in large scale. Only a few have been benefitted.

Under the rural electrification programme, the villages had earlier been provided with only street light. These lights have gone out of order since long back. The provision of household connections is also not in the scheme. Therefore like the other above-said programmes, this programme has also had no impact on the people.

The study shows that nine *chatasalis* (vernacular schools) have been built under the education programme of the Juang Development Agency to impart vernacular education to the Juang children. At present these institutions are functioning under the Agency and are promoting literacy among the children. However in the rest of the villages including Guptaganga and Kadalibadi, such institutions have not been established. In 1983-84, a literacy centre for adults was opened in each village. But those centres were closed down after a year. Its impact is not yet known.

Like the Saora Development Agency, the Juang Development Agency has some problems and shortcomings for which its impact has neither been substantial in terms of annual income nor in terms of the community-based facilities. The problems and shortcomings are found in the staffing pattern of the agency, budgetary provisions and allocation and at the implementation level. These are analysed below.

THE PROBLEMS AND SHORTCOMINGS

1. Staffing pattern : In case of the Juang Development Agency, the members of the governing body include representatives of people, technical and administrative personnel from the different government departments.

But the agency does not have adequate personnel like that of the Saora Development Agency. There is not a single technical personnel in the staff of the agency. The staff members including the special officer have education up to matriculation. None of them is, therefore, able to give technical guidance to the beneficiaries. Given to the programmes and the number of beneficiaries the staff is also inadequate. There are only eight members in the staff in comparison to 16 programmes of development and 1993 household beneficiaries. The ratio between the staff and the household beneficiaries is 1 : 174. This ratio speaks of inadequacy of staff and calls for the review of the staffing pattern.

2. Budgetary provisions and allocation : Like the Saora Development Agency, this Agency shows uneven trend in its budgetary provisions over the past years. Such fluctuations seem to cause inconsistencies in the expenditure pattern of the Agency. It is found that some of the income generating schemes, namely, small scale and cottage industries, additional income generating schemes, animal husbandry and small businesses, have not been allocated budgetary funds for the period between 1994-95 and 1997-98. Among the community development programmes, the training, exhibition and cultural programme was also not given any fund during the same period.

The income generating and individual benefit schemes have been allocated only 16.72 per cent of the total expenditure during 1994-95 and 1997-98, while 41.94 per cent has been spent on the infrastructure and community development programmes. During the same period, as high as 41.35 per cent of the total expenditure has been incurred in the establishment charges. If the expenditure in the establishment charges is carried on in this scale, there will be little left for development programmes.

It is also seen that the per capita expenditure of the Juang Development Agency for households is only Rs. 690.70. This amount is much less as compared to that of the Saora Development Agency.

Moreover, it is found that the Juang Development Agency has spent only 34.88 per cent of the total expenditure on the programmes of the priority areas while the Saora Development Agency has spent 62.1 per cent during 1994-95 and 1997-98. It was recommended by the Working Group on Development and Welfare of Scheduled Tribes during the Eighth Five-Year Plan that maximum importance should be given to these programmes which include primary education, health, income generating schemes and minimum needs programmes, such as drinking water, road, employment, housing and rehabilitation and rural electrification. These programmes need to be given a major share of fund continuously till the benefits of these programmes reached to all the people.

3. Implementation of scheme : The practice of shifting cultivation among the Juangs indicate that they have not been provided with enough plain lands for settled cultivation. It is found that 49 people of Guptaganga and 24 of Kadalibadi carry on shifting cultivation exclusively. This study also reveals that only two out of six beneficiaries have been provided with small amount of lands. This study shows that the land reclamation scheme has not been properly implemented for the people to rid off shifting cultivation.

In other programmes such as agriculture, the bullocks have not been supplied to all the beneficiaries for which they face difficulty in cultivating their lands.

Under the horticulture programme, the guava garden of Guptaganga was raised by the Juang Development Agency. But no maintenance was provided by the Agency although it has schemes for such provisions. Therefore, the garden has been almost destroyed and the benefits of this programme could not reach the people. It shows how one scheme of the programme cannot deliver benefits without the implementation of the ancillary schemes.

Other income generating programmes, such as small-scale and cottage industries, additional-income-generating schemes and small business, have covered a small number of people and their impact on the people is insignificant.

So far as drinking water is concerned, the tube-wells have been provided in the villages. But the water is not used due to iron content in it. So drinking water problem persists in spite of spendings on this programme. So far the Juang Development Agency has not taken up any alternative scheme to solve this problem.

Like the Saora Development Agency, the Juang Development Agency has not been able to provide substantial benefits and facilities to the people under the education programme. The study shows that none of the households have been given any facility for the education of the children. The *chatasalis* which were established for the vernacular education of the children, were closed for sometime in the past due to shortage of funds. Moreover, there was no programme for adult literacy except one literacy centre in 1993-94.

The Juang have benefitted less from the rural electrification programme than that of the Saoras. The Juangs have been deprived of both street lights and household connections, although the villages have been supplied with electricity.

The programme of public distribution seems to be of no use for the people. They have not ever received the essential commodities under this programme.

Programmes such as training and construction works have not been entirely successful. For instance, the people of Kadalibadi have been given training under the agriculture demonstration programme while the villagers of Guptaganga have not received any such benefit. Similarly, the construction work are of no use for the villagers of Guptaganga because the store house of the *Mandaghar* (community centre) which was constructed by the Juang Development Agency has already collapsed.

These are some of the problems and shortcomings which need to be looked into urgently.

Agenda for Future Action

Interestingly most of the problems and shortcomings are same in both, the Saora Development Agency and Juang Development Agency. They need similar kind of remedies to their problems. Some suggestions are given below for future action of both the agencies and all the Micro Projects in Orissa at large.

1. Both the agencies and other Micro Projects should be provided with adequate staff. The staff must also include technical personnel, as per the need of the various programmes.
2. Basic facilities should be provided to the staff in the Agency area so that they need not have to live away from the Delivery Centre of the Agency. For instance, due to non-availability of essential commodities, communication and health problems, the office staff of the Juang Development Agency live at Keonjhar. They are not able to attend to the needs of the people in time. So the government should provide these facilities in the areas wherever they are necessary. The Working Group on Development of Scheduled Tribes during the Seventh Plan has also emphasized on this aspect.
3. No post in the Micro Projects should lie vacant. The work of each staff should be subject to scrutiny. The personnel must be held accountable for the failure of the programme they carry on.

4. The poor budgetary provisions in both Saora Development Agency and Juang Development Agency are reflected in their respective per capita expenditure for households. So there should be an increase in the budgetary provision of the Micro Project which will ultimately hike the per capita expenditure for house-holds.
5. It is to be seen that no programme or scheme is discontinued due to shortage of funds. It is found that many programmes have not been allotted funds even when the beneficiaries expected benefits from those programmes. In this regard the recommendations of the Working Group on the Development of the Scheduled Tribes during the Eighth Plan should be given importance according to which the provision of social service or infrastructure should not be delayed or avoided even if the per capita cost is high.
6. Now attention should be given to the expenditure pattern of the Micro Projects. It is seen that in both the Micro Projects, the expenditure on the establishment charges is quite high. A maximum limit should be fixed for this expenditure over which budgetary funds should not be provided. It should be made an all out effort to see that maximum funds go to the income-generating and community development programmes.
7. Programmes which are recommended by the Working Groups such as minimum need programmes and programmes of priority area, etc., should be provided with requisite funds.
8. The study shows that the programmes have failed at the implementation level mainly due to the lack of integrated approach among the schemes and programmes. Measures, such as regular review of the implementation of schemes, should be carried out by the governing body.

9. Land ownership and provision of irrigation are must for those who carry on agriculture. Provision of these facilities in large measure would certainly encourage the people to adopt settled cultivation in place of shifting cultivation.
10. Funds must be kept separate and the staff should remain alert to remove the irregularities that are found in various programmes. Empathetic and competent people should be inducted in the staff who should have willingness to work among these under-privileged people.
11. Education is one programme which seems to have delivered the least in both the Saora Development Agency and Juang Development Agency. The Micro Projects should start various programmes such as adult literacy classes, primary education and provision of other facilities at free of cost. The work on education must continue at the war-footing speed.
12. The study shows that the people lack awareness regarding many things. For instance, the Saoras question regarding the value of education of their children. Similarly, in the Juang area, the people seem to hold on to old habits and attitudes which stand in their way of development. Therefore, frequent awareness programme should be held in these areas to give right education to the people and aware them about the benefit of various programmes of the Micro Projects.
13. Electrification of the village streets as well as the houses should be carried out.
14. Training programmes should be organized frequently for the staff and the beneficiaries. The training programmes for the staff should aim at promoting motivation. The training programmes for the beneficiaries should be more of participatory type. The views of the beneficiaries should be given importance in evolving strategies for their development.

15. Lastly, comprehensive evaluation and review of each Micro Project should be carried out to learn about the shortcomings, so that appropriate measures could be taken up accordingly for the future development of the primitive tribes.

Visuals

1. A Birhor House (Kumbha) made out of Sal twigs and leaves.

2. A Birhor woman with her child.

3. A Birhor selling ropes in the local market.

4. Didayi houses in foothills (Oringi village, Malkangiri district).

5. Didayi house with pigsty (Oringi village, Malkangiri district).

6. Didayi village goddess (Gainsiri).

7. Didayi woman.

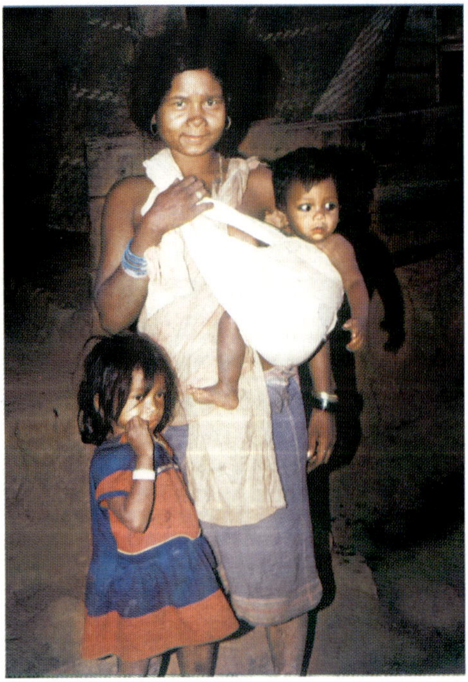

8. Didayi woman with her children.

9. Didayi woman.

10. Didayi woman.

11. An old Didayi woman with a child in the swing.

12. Didayi harvesting paddy.

13. Didayi woman using a Mortar and Pestle
for husking food grains.

14. Didayi grinder used for grinding *ragi* and paddy.

15. Didayi goat pen.

16. The Author with a Didayi in his tobacco field.

17. Young Bondo girls stitching
their clothes (Mudulipada-Bondo hills).

18. The Author, his wife and Dr. Ali with Bondo girls.

19. The Author's wife and workers with Bondo girls.

20. A Dongria village (Khambesi, Rayagada district).

21. Dongria houses (Khambesi, Rayagada district).

22. A group of Dongria women with their traditional dress.

23. A Dongria woman with her typical ornaments and hand-made scarf.

24. A Dongria with his axe.

25. A Dongria with his child.

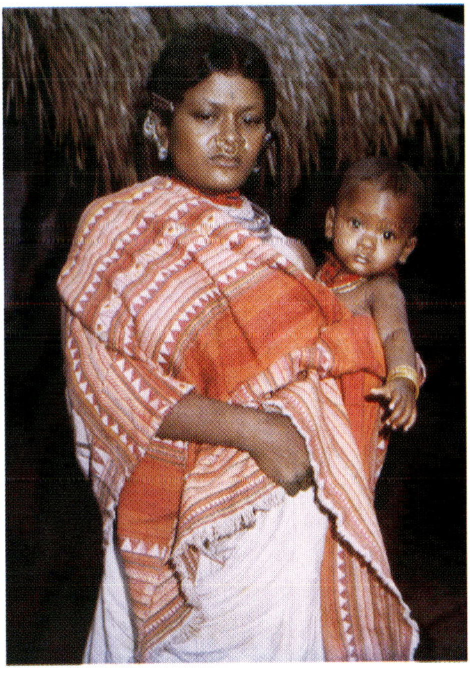

26. A Dongria woman with her child.

27. Dongria village shrine (Sadar Kudi).

28. Instruments and implements inside the shrine (Sadar Kudi).

29. Engraved wooden pillar supporting the beam of the roof of the shrine (Sadar Kudi).

30. A scene of ritual inside the shrine (Sadar Kudi) for goddess Dharani penu.

31. Dongria art.

32. Dongria musical drum.

33. Dongria women performing dance.

34. Dongria kedu festival.

35. Dongria grain bins.

36. Pineapple cultivation in a hill slope by Dongrias.

37. Banana plantation in a hill slope by Dongrias.

38. A Dongria on the way to market with two bunches of banana.

39. A Juang Settlement (Gonasika, Keonjhar district).

40. A Juang house in village Gonasika, Keonjhar district.

41. A Juang dormitory (Manda Ghar).

42. A Juang.

43. An old Juang woman.

44. Juang boys.

45. Puspunai festival observed by the Juangs and goat meat offered to the deity (Gainsiri) distributed among the inhabitants of the village.

46. A weekly market at Suakati with Juangs visiting for marketing.

47. Juang wood carving on a pillar in the Manda ghar.

48. A Hill Kharia settlement (Nuasahi, Similipal forest, Mayurbhanj district).

49. A Kharia house.

50. A Kharia house.

51. A Kharia woman with her child.

52. A Kharia child husking *ragi* on her mortar and pestle.

53. Inside the Kharia house showing a goat pen.

54. Barehipani water fall in the Simlipal hills, near a Kharia settlement.

55. A Kutia Khond village (Koraput district).

56. A Kutia Khond village.

57. A scene of Kutia Khond village street with village goddess (Dharani Penu) installed in the middle of the street.

58. A Kutia woman in front of her house.

59. A Kutia Khond old man.

60. A group of Kutia Khond women in their traditional dress.

61. A Kutia Khond woman with her child.

62. Weekly marketplace at Belghar.

63. Weekly marketplace at Belghar with Kutia Khonds visiting for marketing.

64. A Paudi Bhuinya with his fishing trap.

65. A mother and child (Lanjia Saora, Gunapur, Koraput).

Glossary

Aba	Father
Adasbetta	Dormitory for unmarried girls of Dongria
Allmai	Daughter heir
Amba Nua	Ist mango eating
Ansir	Co-operative labour system of Saora
Arua	White or raw rice
Assan Pinda	Narrow Verandah in front of house
Aswina	Months of September-October
Ayu Pinda	Earthen platform to keep cooked food, vessels, pots
Bada Naik	Head of confederacy
Badia	Real gatherers of arrowroot
Bagdir	Door made of twig woven in leaves
Bandhu	Cognatic villages
Bansa	A clan
Barga	Non-inter marrying
Barika	Village messenger
Barongsum	An old Saora word for mountain God
Barusum	Deity of hills
Basumata	Mother earth
Bedia	Lineage group

Bewar	Shifting cultivation
Bhadrab	Months of August-September
Bhal Bhai	Village elders or corporate body
Bhutas	Ghosts
Birha	Confederacy over village
Birinda	Families related to one another by blood
Bis Majhi	Asst. to secular head or village priest
Bissoyi	Mutha head
Bodam budha	Procreators
Budhi Mai	Supreme deity of Birhors
Buita	One who presides over all religious ceremonies and ritual activities
Burha Kania	Widow marriage
Buya	Religious head man of Saora
Byakra	Medicine man of Lodhas
Changu	A flat musical drum
Charpai	Cot
Chatasalis	Vernacular School
Chindal or Began	Social boycott
Daki Kania	Marriage between a man and a divorced woman in Juangs family
Dakua	Village messenger of Lodhas
Dangua	Messenger cum watchman
Dapa	Backroom
Dehuri	The priest
Devtas	Gods and Goddesses (benevolent deities)
Dhangadas	Unmarried boys of Bhuinya

Dhangdis	Unmarried girls of Bhuinya
Dharam Devta	Sun god
Dharani Devata	Earth Goddess
Dharani Penu	Earth Goddess
Dhira and Dandia	Headman of confederacy, a eldest, wisest *Pradhan*
Digar Kania	Marriage by capture
Disari	Astrologer-cum-medicine man
Durbarghar	Bachelor's dormitory of Paudi Bhuinya
Ejo	Central room
Gadalsum	Deity in charge of grass
Gaita	Village headman
Genuar	Place where menhirs are erected in memory of dead person
Gomango	Secular head man of Saora
Goti	Bonded labour
Gram panchayat	Local administration
Gusi	Cloth used by Didayi men
Harijan	Scheduled Caste
Hena	Two mortars
Ingersin	Boy's dormitory
Jani	Village priest
Jarasabara	Worshipper of Lord Jagannatha in history
Jatawali	A rotary quern
Jatra Kudi	Goddess of village Dongria Khond
Juangpirh	Juangs inhabited in Keonjhar district

Kandadaya	Inner chamber
Kangerki	Male member dormitory
Karja	A ceremony in memory of dead people
Karji	Asst. Village Headman
Karma Thakur	Deity of Birhors
Katariya	Who sacrifices animals
Kendu	A forest fruit (*Diospyros melanoxylon*)
Khandayats	A caste
Khappars	Tiles
Kisalo	Cloth used by Didayi women
Kitunganji	Collective form of deity
Kondanake	Household shrine
Kotebalipenu	Male deity
Kuda	The clan
Kudi	Hut of Earth Goddess
Kulbanji	Stands for shadows and human soul
Kumbha	Huts which are made by Birhors
Kurha	Head of the council of Bhunjias
Kutumb	Agnatic villages
Kutumb Sabha	Council of agnates related to one another by blood
Labosum	Earth God of Saora
Lodhasabar	Other name of Lodha
Logo Bir	Supreme deity of Birhors
Mai	Mother
Majag or Darbar	Bachelors' dormitory of Bhuinya family
Majang	Bachelor's dormitory of Juanga

Mala	Cobra
Mana Mani	Love Marriage
Mandaghar	Bachelors' dormitory of Juang family
Margasir	Months of November-December
Mariah	Buffalo sacrifice
Markam	Moiety
Mathiar	People bearing surname barge
Mati	Earth
Mukhya	Headman of camp
Murdhana Khunta	First pole that is fixed on ground for house construction
Muttah	A group of villages
Naek or Padhan	Secular village headman
Naya	The priest
Nayak	Village headman
Netam	Moiety
Ora bonga	Clan deity
Paiks	Soldier
Pallasi	Priest of the village
Palua	Arrowroot
Parha or Birha	Confederacy over village
Patra	Paik caste in Kutia Khonds
Patta	Ownership of land
Patua	People of leaf dress
Pausa	Months of December-January
Penu	Common term for deities and spirits
Pir	A kind of forest grass

Pirha	A group of villages of Bhuinya
Piri	Local grown grass
Pradhan	Hereditary Secular Chief of the village
Pujari	Priest
Ringa	Self woven small piece of skrit
Rusani	Ancestors of Juangs
Sahukars	Local traders, money lenders
Samudhi	Affinal relationship
Selanidigo	Girl's dormitory
Selanki	Unmarried girls are called in Juangs family
Shaman	Village priest
Sindibor	Village Assembly
Sita Kunda	A place
Sitala	Goddess of epidemics
Sudapuradan	Big soul
Sunadei	Supreme deity of Bhunjias
Taada	Birhor camp
Taila	Slash and burn method of cultivation
Talia or Chharidar	Village priest or Lodhas
Thakurani	Earth goddess of Kharia
Tumba	A dried shell of bitter gourd fruit
Tupa	A small baskets made by Birhors
Unku	Tiger
Wadi Kania	Child marriage
Zamindar	Landlord

Bibliography

Adhikary, Ashim Kumar, *Society and World View of the Birhor, Nomadic Hunting and Gathering Community of Orissa*, Calcutta, Anthropological Survey of India, 1984.

Adibasi, No. 3, 1963-64 (1st January 1964), p. 182.

Aiyyapan, A., *Porjas: Report on Socio-Economic Conditions of Aboriginal Tribes of Provinces of Madras*, Madras, Government Press, 1948.

Archer, W.G., "Hill of Flutes: Love and Poetry in Tribal India;" in *A Portrait of the Santals*, London, George Allen and Unwin, 1974.

———, *Mara Hapram Reak Katha* (in Santali), Santal Pargana, Banerjee Press, 1969.

———, *The Blue Grove: The Poetry of the Uraons*, London, George Allen and Unwin, 1940.

———, *The Dove and the Leopard: More Oraon Poetry*, Calcutta, Longmans, Green & Co., 1948.

Bag, Dhanapati, *In the Midst of Santals*, Calcutta, Subarna-rekha, 1987.

Bage, Marsallan, *Phanomenologie der Munda — Religion*, Berlin, Freie University, 1960.

Baines, Athelstane, *Ethnography: Castes and Tribes*, rpt. 1976, Delhi, Concept Publishing Company.

Banerjee, Gagan Chandra, *Introduction to the Kharia language*, Calcutta, Bengal Secretariat Press, 1894.

Banerjee, P., "A Comparative Study of Oraon Physical Characters," in, *Bulletin of the Department of Anthropology, Government of India*, 9 (2), Calcutta, 1960.

Basu, P.C., "Racial Affinities of Mundas," in *Transactions of the Bose Research Institute*, 8, 1933, pp. 211-47.

Basu, Sunil Kumar, *The Mundas: A Profile*, Calcutta, Cultural Research Institute, 1987.

Behera, D., *The Bhanjan and the Khonds of Orissa*, Calcutta, Punthi Pustak, 1987.

Bell, R.C.S., *Orissa District Gazetteers: Koraput District*, Cuttack, Orissa Government Press, 1945, p. 45, 68, 78-79.

Bhaduri, M.B., "The Aboriginal Tribes of Udaipur State, (Central Provinces)," in *Man in India*, 21, 1941, pp. 92-126.

Bhalla, V., "Blood Group Distribution Pertaining to ABO, MNSs and Rh-Hr Systems in the Indian Sub-Continent: An Ethno-Serographical Variation," in *Anthropologist*, 4, 1966, pp. 67-86.

Bhattacharjee, P.N. and Kumar, N., "A Blood Group Genetic Survey in the Dudh Kharias of the Ranchi," District Bihar, India, in *Human Heridity*, 19, 1969, pp. 385-97.

Bhattacharya, K.N. and Biswas, Makhan, "Select Genetic Markers in Lashadweep," in *Man in India*, 58 (1), 1978, pp. 65-70.

Bhattacharya, P.N., "A Genetical Study of the Santals of Santal Parganas," in *The Anthropologist*, Special Volume, 93, 1969, p. 104.

Bhattacharya, S., *Ollari: A Dravidian Speech*, Delhi, Manager of Publications, 1957.

Bhavani, Enakshi, *Folk and Tribal Designs of India*, Bombay, D.B. Taraporevala Sons and Company, 1974.

Bhowmick, P.K., "The Munda and their Way of Living in West Bengal," in *Adibasi*, Bhubaneswar, 1, 1966.

Biswas, P.C., *The Santals of Santal Parganas*, New Delhi, Bharatiya Adimjati Sevak Sangh, 1956.

Bodding, P.O., *Traditions and Institutions of the Santals*, Oslo, A.W. Brog, Boktry, 1942.

Bulu Amam, A.R.H., "The World of Birhor," in *Heritage*, 2 (1), 1986.

Campbell, A., *Santal Folk-Tales*, Pokhuria, Santal Mission Press, 1891.

Campbell, Johan, *A Personal Narrative of Thirteen Years Service Among the Wild Tribes of Khondistan for the Suppression of Human Sacrifice*, London, Hurst & Blackett, 1864.

Chandrasekhar, A. (ed.), "Village Survey Monograph on Godabavalasa," in *Census of India*, 1961, Andhra Pradesh, vol. II, part VI, Delhi, Manager of Publications, 1967.

Chatterjee, A.N. and Das, T.C. , *The Hos of Saraikella*, Calcutta, Calcutta University, 1927.

Choudhury, S., *et al.*, "Study of Blood Groups and Haemoglobin Variants Among the Santal Tribe in Midnapur District of West Bengal," in *American Journal of Physical Anthropology*, 26, 1967, pp. 307-12.

Culshaw, W.J., *Tribal Heritage: A Study of the Santals*, London, Butterworth Press, 1949.

Dehon, P., *Religion and Customs of the Uraons*, Calcutta, Asiatic Society of Bengal, 1906.

Deka, U., "Genetic Variation Among the Populations of Koraput," Paper presented at the Seminar on Human Variations in India, Calcutta, Anthropological Survey of India, 1977.

Deka, U. and Pattojoshi, P., "Genetic Study of Gadaba of Orissa," in *Man in India* 55 (3), 1975, pp. 227-34.

Dalton, E.T., *Descriptive Ethnology of Bengal*, Calcutta, Government Press, 1872, rpt. 1960, Calcutta, Indian Studies: Past and Present, Firma K.L. Mukhopadhyay, rpt. 1978, Tribal History of Eastern India, New Delhi, Cosmo Publications.

———, *Ethnology of Bengal*, p. 207.

Das, A.K. and Raha, M.K., *The Oraons of Sundarban*, Calcutta, Tribal Welfare Department, West Bengal, 1906.

Das, G.N., "A Note on the Hill Bondo of Koraput District (Orissa)," in *Vanyajati*, 2, 1956, p. 103.

Das, J.K., "Reports on Scheduled Tribes of Orissa (Book One)," in *Census of India*, 1961, Orissa, vol. XII, part V-B (Ethnographic Note), Delhi, Manager of Publications, 1972, pp. 64-69.

———, "Reports on Scheduled Tribes of Orissa (Book One)," in *Census of India*, vol. 12, part V-B, 1961, Delhi, Manager of Publications, 1963, Delhi, Manager of Publications, 1963, pp. 23-29.

Das, S.R., *et. al.*, "Blood Groups (ABO, MN, Rh) and ABH Secretation, Sickle Cell Trait and Colour Blindness in Gadaba and Bareng Paroja of Koraput District in Orissa," in *Bulletin of the Anthropological Survey of India*, 11 (3&4), 1962, pp. 145-51.

———, *et. al.*, "Blood Groups (A1 A2 BO, MN, Rh) and ABH Secretion in the Pareng Gadaba, Ollaro Gadaba and the Bonda Paroja of Koraput District in Orissa," in *Acta Genetica et Statistica Medica.*, 16, 1966, pp. 169-89.

———, "Sickle Cell Trait in Koraput District and Other Parts of India," in *Acta Genetica et Statistica Medica*, 17, 1967.

Das Gupta, B.K., "Social Mobility Movements Among the Tribes of Eastern and Central India," in *Journal of the Indian Anthropological Society*, 8 (1), 1978, pp. 11-18.

Das Gupta and Narendra Kumar, *Problems of Tribal Education and the Santals*, New Delhi, Bharatiya Adimjati Sevak Sangh, 1963.

Dasgupta, D., *Linguistic Studies in Juang, Kharia, Lodha, Mal-pahariya, Ghatoali, Pahariya*, Calcutta, Anthropological Survey of India, 1978.

Das Gupta, P.K., *Impact of Industrialization on a Tribe in South Bihar*, Calcutta, Anthropological Survey of India, 1978.

———, "The Adi Samaj Movement Among the Ho, in K.S. Singh (ed.)," in *Tribal Movements in India*, Delhi, Manohar Publications, 1983, vol. II, pp. 93-107.

Das Gupta, P.K and Khan, I.A., *Impact of Tea Plantation Industry on the Life of Tribal Labourers*, Calcutta, Anthropological Survey of India, 1983.

Dash Sharma, P., "Physical Anthropology of Oraons, Mundas and Dusadhs of Bihar," in *Journal of the Indian Anthropological Scoiety*, 11 (2), 1976, pp. 121-4.

Devi, S.S. and Naidu, J.M., "Sickle Cell Trait among Bagatha, Konda Dora and Parangi Poraja Tribes," in *Proceedings of Indian Society of Human Genetics Annual Conference*, Calcutta, 1987.

Dube, K.C., "Possible Origins of Bhunjiaand their Ethnic Relationships: A New Hypothesis," in *Eastern Anthropologist*, 16 (1), 1961, pp. 48-50.

Dube, S.C., "The Arrow Marriage," in *Eastern Anthropologist*, 2 (1), 1948, pp. 22-39.

Dutta Majumdar, N., *The Santal: A Study in Culture Change*, Calcutta, Anthropological Survey of India, 1956.

Duyker, Edward, *Tribal Guerillas: The Santals of West Bengal and the Naxalite Movement*, Delhi, Oxford University Press, 1987.

Elwin, Verrier, "An Anthology of Marriage Sermons," in *Man in India*, 23, 1943, p. 108.

———, *Bondo Highlanders*, Bombay, Oxford University Press, 1950.

———, "Notes on the Juang," in *Man in India*, 28 (1&2), 1948.

———, "Suicide Among the Aboriginals of Bastar State," in *Man in India*, 22 (4)., 1942, pp. 207-33.

———, *The Religion of an Indian Tribe*, Bombay: Oxford University Press, 1955.

———, *The Tribal Art of Middle India*, London, Oxford University Press, 1951.

Fuchs, Stephen, "Messianic Movement," in *Tribal India, Journal of the Anthropological Society of Bombay,* (NS), 12 (1), 1966-67, pp. 15-53.

———, *The Gond and Bhumia of Eastern Mandala,* Bombay, Asia Publishing House, 1960.

Ganeshprasad, P., "The Aborigines of Central India," in *Journal of the Asiatic Society of Bengal,* 27 (2). 1848, pp. 550-58.

Gausdal, J., *The Santal Khuts: Contributions to Animistic Research,* Oslo, Institute Sammenling Kulturforsk, 1960.

Gautam, M.K., *In Search of an Identity: A Case of the Santal of Northern India,* Leiden, E.J. Brill, 1978.

George, Somen E., *The Dynamics of Santal Traditions in a Peasant Society,* New Delhi, D.K. Publishers, 1979.

Ghosh, A.K., "ABO Blood Groups from Singhbhum," Bihar, in *Science & Culture,* 30, 1964, pp. 49-50.

Ghosh, G.C., "Anthropometry of the Ho of Seraikella," in *Man in India,* 47 (2), 1976, pp. 127-32.

Gini, Ashok, "Some Genetic Markers in Tribals of Eastern India," in *Acta Anthropogenetica,* 6 (2), 1982, pp. 99-106.

Goud, J.D. and P.R. Rao, "Colour Blindness and Taste Sensitivity to Phenylthio-Carbamide in Tribal Populations of Andhra Pradesh," in *Journal of the Indian Anthropological Society,* 14 (3), 1982, pp. 269-74.

Hiralal, "The Aborigines of Central India," in *Man in India,* 2 (1 &2), 1922, pp. 12-32.

Hoffmann, John Baptist, *et al.,* "Encyclopaedia Mundarica," rpt. 1990, Delhi, Gian Publishing House.

Ittaman, K.P., *Amini Islanders,* New Delhi, Abhinav Publications, 1976.

Jayakar, Pupul, *The Earth Mother,* New Delhi, Penguin Books, 1989.

KacAlpin, M.C., *Report on the Condition of Santhals in the Districts of Birbhum, Bankura, Midnapore and North Balasore,* Calcutta,

Bengal Secretariat Press, 1909, rpt. 1981, Calcutta, Firma Mukhopadhyay.

Kar, Ramendra Kumar, *The Savaras of Mancotta : A Study on the Effects of Tea Industry on the Tribal Life,* New Delhi, Cosmo Publications, 1981.

Karve, I., "Anthropometric Measurements in Karnataka and Orissa and a Comparison of the Two Regions with Maharashtra," *Journal of the Anthropological Society of Bombay,* (NS), 8 (1) 1954, pp. 456-75.

Kate, S.L., *et al.,* "Prevalence of HbE in Ten Population Groups of West Bengal," *Indian Journal of Haematology,* 2 (4), 1984.

Kirk, R.L., *et al.,* "A Genetic Study of the Oraons of the Chotanagpur Plateau," Bihar, India, in *American Journal of Physical Anthropology,* 20, 1962, pp. 375-85.

Kochar, V.K., "Village Deities of the Santal and Associated Rituals," in *Anthropos,* 61, 1966, pp. 241-57.

Kujur, Alomani Anupa, *The Oraon Habitat: A Study in Cultural Geography,* Ranchi, Satya Bharati, 1989.

Kumar, N. and Mukherjee, D.P., "A Genetic Survey Among the Desi Bhumij of Chotanagpur in Bihar," in *The Anthropologist,* Special Volume, 1969, pp. 75-84.

———, "Genetic Distance Among the Ho Tribe and Other Groups of Central India," in *American Journal of Physical Anthropology,* 42 (3), 1975, pp. 489-96.

Kumar, N., *et al.,* "Distribution of A1, A2, BO Blood Groups, ABH Secretion in Saliva and the Sickle Cell Trait Among the Oraons of Surguja District," Madhya Pradesh, Calcutta, in *Anthropological Survey of India,* 1976, Unpublished.

Kumar, N. and Bhattacharjee, P.N., "Blood Groups of the Munda of Ranchi District in Bihar (India)," in *Indian Journal of Physical Anthropology & Human Genetics,* 2 (2), 1976, pp. 201-14.

Macphail, J.J., *Three Months in Camp: Being the Daily Journal of a Medical Missionary on Tour Among the Santals,* Pokhuria, Manbhum, Santal Mission Press, 1893.

MacPherson, Samuel Charters, *Report on the Khonds of the Districts of Ganjam and Cuttack,* Madras, United Scottish Press, 1863.

Mahalanobis, P.C., *et al.*, "Anthropometric Study of the United Provinces, 1941: A Statistical Study," in *Sankhya,* 9, 1949, pp. 89-234.

Mahapatra, S., *Modernization and Ritual: Identity and Change in Santal Society,* Calcutta, Oxford University Press, 1986.

Majumdar, D.N., *A Tribe in Transition: A Study in Culture Pattern,* London, Longman Green, 1973.

———, Disease, "Death and Devination in Certain Primitive Societies in India," in *Man in India,* 13 (2 & 3), 1933, pp. 115-49.

———, "Physical Characteristics of the Hos of Kolhan," in *Man in India,* 5, 1925, pp. 83-114.

———, *The Affairs of a Tribe,* Lucknow, Enthnographic & Folk Culture Society, 1950.

———, "Racial Affiliation of Gond of Central Provinces," in *Journal of 0the Royal Asiatic Society of Bengal, Science,* 7, 1941, pp. 35-36.

———, *Races and Cultures of India,* Bombay, Asia Publishing House, 1944, pp. 125-33.

Majumdar, P.P. and J. Roy, "Distribution of ABO Blood Groups on the Indian Subcontinent: A Cluster Analytic Approach," in *Current Anthropology,* 23, 1982, pp. 539-66.

Malleswara Rao, P., *et al.*, "Genetic Studies on the Savara and Jatapu Tribe of Andhra Pradesh," in *Human Heredity,* 29, 1978, pp. 122-31.

Man, E.G., "Sonthalia and the Santhals," Calcutta, George Wyman, 1867.

Martin, W.B., *English-Santali Vocabulary*, Benaras: Medical Hall Press, 1898.

Mishra, K.K., *Social Structure and Change Among the Ho of Orissa*, Delhi, Gian Publishing House, 1987.

Mishra, U.C., *Tribal Paintings and Sculptures*, Delhi: B. R. Publishing Corporation, 1989.

Mitra, P., *Santhal Vasa*, Calcutta, Firma Mukhopadhyay, 1985.

Mitra, Parimala Chandra, *Santhali: The Base of World Languages*, Calcutta, Firma Mukhopadhyay, 1988.

Mohmmad, L., *Census of Mayurbhanj State*, 1931, 1891, rpt. 1981, Calcuttta, Firma Mukhopadhyay, vol. I, p. 224.

Mukherjee, B.N., *et al.*, "Serum Protein and Red Cell Enzyme Polymorphism in Oraon Tribe, India," in *Annals of Human Biology*, 2 (1), 1975, pp. 201-04.

Mukherjee, B.N., *et al.*, "Study of LDH Variants Amongst the Mundas in Ranchi District," Bihar, India, in *Human Genetics*, 19, 1973, pp. 285-87.

Mukherjee, B., "Trends of a Social Movement," in *Journal of the Indian Anthropological Society*, 3 (1 & 2), 1968, pp. 121-29.

Mukherjee, C., *The Santal*, Calcutta, Indian Research Society, 1948, rpt. 1962, Calcutta, A. Mukherjee & Co.

Murthy, A.S., "Religion and Society of Koyas in the Agency Areas," Andhra Pradesh, Ph.D. Thesis, Waltair, Andhra University, 1972, Unpublished.

Nag, N.G., Sukumar Singh and B.K. Roy Burman, "The Savar: A Scheduled Tribe in West Bengal," in *Census of India*, 1981, vol. I, part V-B (N), New Delhi, Manager of Publications, 1972.

Narayan, Sachindra, *Dimension of Development in Tribal Bihar*, New Delhi, Inter-India Publications, 1986.

Navalakha, S.K., "The Authority Structure Among the Bhumij and Bhil: A Study of Historical Causations," in *Eastern Anthropologist,* 13 (1), 1959, pp. 27-40.

Nayak, P.K., *Blood, Women and Territory: An Analysis of Clan Feuds of Dongria Kondhs,* New Delhi, Reliance Publishing House, 1989.

Neville, A., *The Half Clad Tribals of Eastern India,* Bombay, Orient Longman, 1972.

Niggemeyer, Hermann, *Kuttia Kondh: Dschungel - Bauern en Orissa,* Munich, Klaus Renner Verlag, 1964.

Orans, Martin, *The Santal: A Tribe in Search of Great Traditions,* Detroit, Wayne State University Press, 1965, p. 106.

Oraon, K., *The Spectrum of Tribal Religion in Bihar: A Study of Continuity and Change Among the Oraon of Chotanagpur,* Varanasi, Kishor Vidya Niketan, 1988.

Padhy, Krishna Singh and Satpathy, P.C., *Tribal India,* New Delhi, Ashish Publishing House, 1989.

Pal, Anadi, "Interstilia in Santal Foot," in *Bulletin of the Anthropological Survey of India,* 16 (1 & 2), 1967, pp. 41-56.

Panda, Santhosh K., *Indian Culture and Personality: Saora Highlanders of Eastern Ghats,* Delhi, Discovery Publishing House, 1987.

Pandey, Ajit Kumar, *Kinship and Tribal Policy: A Co-operative Study of the Mundas and Oraons of Bihar,* Jaipur, Rawat Publications, 1989.

Pareek, Ratannath, *Tribal Culture in Flux: The Jatapus of Eastern Ghats,* Delhi, B.R. Publishing Corporation, 1977.

Parija, Gurupada, *Acculturation of Sauras into Oriya Hindu Society,* Cuttack, Prajatantra Press, 1960.

Patel, Srisha, *Ecology, Ethnology and Nutrition: A Study of Kondh Tribals and Tibetan Refugees,* Delhi, Mittal Publications, 1985.

Pathak, Lalit P., "The Enticed Immigrants: Imported Tribal Tea

Labourer in Assam," 1941-1960, in *Journal of Social Sciences and Humanities*, (NEHU), 2 (4), 1984.

Patnaik, Nityananda, *Kondh of Orissa: Their Socio-Cultural Life and Development*, Bhubaneswar, Orissa Tribal-cum-Harijan Research and Training Institute, 1982.

———, (ed.), *The Bondo*, Bhubaneswar, Tribal and Harijan Research and Training Institute, 1989.

———, *The Juang*. Bhubaneswar, Tribal and Harijan Research-cum-Training Institute, 1989.

———, (ed.), *The Saora*, Bhubaneswar, Tribal and Harijan Research-cum-Training Institute, 1989.

Patnaik N., *et al.*, "Handbook on the Paudi Bhunya: An Anthropological Study of the Primitive Section of Bhunya Tribe of Orissa," in *Adibasi*, Special No. 19, Bhubaneswar, Tribal and Harijan Research and Training Institute, 1980.

Pingle, Urmilla, *et al.*, *A Genetic Study of the Five Tribal Groups of Andhra Pradesh, India*, 72 (3), 1981, pp. 339-48.

Pinnow, H.J., *Versuch einer Historischen Lautehre der Khari-Sprache* (Essay of a historical Phonetic Treatise of Kharia-Language), Wiesbaden, Otto Harrassowitz, 1959.

Piplai, C., *et al.*, "A Note on Abo, MN, Rh Blood Groups of the Tamang and Oraon Tea-Labourers of the Jalpaiguri District," West Bengal, in *Journal of the Indian Anthropological Society*, 20, 1985, pp. 66-70.

Prasad, C.B., "The Bhuinyas of Singhbhum," in *Journal of the Bihar Research Society*, 56 (1-4), 1970, pp. 272-78.

Prasad, N., *Birhor in Land and People of Tribal Bihar*, Ranchi, Tribal Research Institute, 1961.

———, *Land and People of Tribal Bihar*, Ranchi, Bihar Tribal Research Institue, 1961.

Prasad, Onkar, *Santal Music: A Study in Pattern and Processes of Cultural Persistence,* New Delhi, Inter-India Publications, 1985.

Prasad, R.N. and Sengupta, S., "Santal Rural Economy: A Study Based on Village Survey in Santal Parganas," Santiniketan, Agro-Economic Research Centre, 1973.

Puxley, E.L. (ed.), *A Vocabulary of the Santali Language,* London, W.M. Watts, 1868.

Raghavaiah, V., *Tribes of India,* Delhi, Bharatiya Adimjati Sevak Sangh, 1972, vol. II.

Rajagopal, M.V., *Andhra Pradesh District Gazetteers: Krishna,* Hyderabad, Government Secretariat Press, 1977.

Ramaiah, Pannal, *Tribal Economy of India: A Case Study of Koyas of Andhra Pradesh,* New Delhi, Light and Life Publications, 1981.

Ramdas, G., Parojas, Orissa, *Man in India,* 11 (3 & 4), 1931.

Rath, Govind Chandra, *Industrialization to Indigenization: A Study on Cultural Reformulation of a Tribe in Orissa,* Calcutta, Centre for Studies of Social Sciences, 1987.

Ray, Hinangsu Mohan, *Savara: The Snake Charmer,* Calcutta, Institute of Social Research and Applied Anthropology, 1986.

Ray, P.C., *Socio-Cultural Process and Psychological Adaptation of the Santal,* Calcutta, Anthropological Survey of India, 1975.

Ray, T. (comp.), *Santal Rebellion: Documents,* Calcutta, Subarnarekha, 1983.

Ray, Ujjwal, *et al.,* (eds.), *To be with Santals,* Calcutta, Government of West Bengal, 1982.

Ray Chaudhury, Indu, *Folk-Tales of the Santals,* New Delhi, Sterling, 1973.

Reddy, A.P., B.N. Mukherjee and R.N. Saha, "Study of PGM Polymorphism by Isoelectric Focussing Among the Munda and Kissan Tribes of Orissa," India, in *Journal of the Indian Anthropological Society,* 17 (1), 1982.

Rezeq, K.A., "Aspects of Saora Culture," in *Bulletin of the Anthropological Survey of India*, 14 (3 & 4), 1965, pp. 123-40.

Risley, H.H., *The Tribes and Castes of Bengal*, Calcutta, Bengal Secretariat Press, 1891, rpt. 1989, Calcutta, Firma Mukhopadhyay, vol. I, pp. 108-16, 350-55, 466; vol. II, p. 224 and 490.

Rout, Siba Prasad, "Hand Book on the Juang," in *Adibasi*, Bhubaneswar, 11 (1&2), 1969-70.

———, "Paroja," in *Adibasi*, Bhubaneswar, 1964.

Roy, J.K. and Roy, B.C., *Hunger and Physique: A Study of the Juang Population of Orissa*, Calcutta, Anthropological Survey of India, 1982.

Roy, P.C., "Socio-Cultural Process and Psychological Adaptation of the Munda in Culture-Contact," in *Indian Anthropologist*, 7 (1), 1977, pp. 48-56.

Roy, Sarat Chandra, "Birth, Childhood and Puberty Ceremonies among the Birhors," in *Journal of Bihar and Orissa Research Society*, vol. 4, 1928, pp. 214-31.

———, "Death and Funeral Customs of the Birhors," in *Journal of the Bihar and Orissa Research Society*, vol. 4, 1918, pp. 307-21.

———, "General account of Birhors," in *Journal of the Bihar and Orissa Research Society*, vol. 2, 1916, pp. 457-67.

———, "Gilmpses in Primitive Life, or Gleanings from an Anthropologist's Note Book: The Hos of Singhbhum," in *Journal of the Bihar and Orissa Research Society*, 15 (1 & 2), 1929, pp. 204-23.

———, *Hill Bhuinyas of Orissa with Comparative Notes on Plain Bhuinyas*, Ranchi, Man in India Office, 1935.

———, "Kinship Organization of the Birhors," in *Journal of Bihar and Orissa Research Society*, vol. 3, part 4, 1971, p. 543.

———, "Magical Practices, Omens and dreams among the Birhors," in *Journal of Bihar and Orissa Research Society,* vol. 10, 1924, pp. 209-20.

———, *Munda and Their Country,* Calcutta, City Book Society, 1912, rpt. 1950, Bombay, Asia Publishing House.

———, "Oraon Religion and Customs," Ranchi, in *Man in India,* Office, 1928, rpt. 1972.

———, *Oraon Religion and Customs,* Delhi, Gian Publishing House, 1985.

———, "The Aborigines of Chotanagpur," in *Man in India,* 26 (2), 1946, pp. 120-36.

———, *The Birhor: A Little Known jungle Tribe of Chotanagpur,* Ranchi, Man in India Office, 1925, rpt. 1978.

———, *The Oraons of Chota Nagpur: Their History, Economic Life and Social Organization,* Ranchi, Author, 1915.

———, "The Religion of Birhors," in *Journal of Bihar and Orissa Research Society,* vol. 4, Part 4, 1918, p. 455.

———, "The Marriage Customs of Birhors," in *Journal of Bihar and Orissa Research Society,* vol. 4, 1918, pp. 62-90.

———, "The Social Organization of the Birhor," in *Journal of the Bihar and Orissa Research Society,* vol. 3, 1917, pp. 367-71.

———, "Totemism account of Birhors," in *Journal of Bihar and Orissa Research Society,* vol. 2, 1916, pp. 250-64.

Roy, S.C. and Roy, R.C., *The Kharias,* Ranchi, Man in India Office, 1937.

Roy, U.K., "A Semi-nomadic Tribe of West Bengal," in *Bulletin of the Cultural Research Institute,* 12, (1&2), 1976, pp. 8-14.

Roy Chaudhury, P.C., *The Creation of the Santal Parganas in Bengal Past and Present,* Calcutta, 1962.

Roy Chaudhury, S.K., "ABO Blood Group and Haemoglobin Variant in the Central District of Orissa," in *Man in India,* Sl (3), 1971, pp. 245-51.

Russell, R.V. and Hiralal, *The Tribes and Castes of the Central Provinces of India*, London, MacMillan and Company, 1916, rpt. 1975, Delhi, Cosmo Publications, vol. I; II pp. 20-24; & III, p. 445.

Sachchidananda, *Directed Change Among the Birhors'* in *Eastern Anthropologist*, 18 (3). 1965, pp. 172-76

———, *The Changing Munda*, New Delhi, Concept Publishing Company, 1979.

———, *The Munda: A Re-study*, Patna, A.N. Sinha Institute of Social Studies, 1978.

Saha, N.K., *On Role Analysis: A Study of Inter Personal Relation Among the Santals in a West Bengal Village*, Calcutta, Prantik, 1972.

Sahi, L.N., "Bhumia Marriages," in *Man in India*, 23 (2), 1943, pp. 173-74.

Saran, A.B., *Murder and Suicide Among the Munda and the Oraon*, Delhi, National Publishing House, 1974.

Sarkar, S.S., "ABO blood Groups from Palamau Bihar," India, in *American Journal of Physical Anthropology*, 7 (4), 1949, pp. 559-62

———, "Analysis of Blood Group Data with Special References to Oraons," in *Transactions of the Bose Research Institute*, 1981, 15, 1942, pp. 1-15.

———, "Blood Groups from Orissa," in *Science and Culture*, 22, 1956, pp. 180-81.

———, "Blood Group Investigation in India with Special Reference to Santal Parganas," Bihar, in *Transactions of Bose Research Institute*, 12, 1937, pp. 89-101.

Sarkar, S.S., *et al.*, "Further Studies on ABO Blood Groups," Orissa, in *Science and Culture*, 25, 1960, pp. 694 95.

Sen, Suchibrata, *Santals of Jungle Mahals*, Delhi, Ratna Prakashan, 1984.

Senapati, N., *Orissa District Gazetteers: Sundargarh*, Calcutta, Orissa Government Press, 1975.

Sharma, Krishnan, *The Kondhs of Orissa,* New Delhi, Concept Publishing Company, 1979.

Shukla, B.R.K. and Tyagi, D., "Morphogenetic Comparison of Two Tribal Groups of Ranchi," in *Indian Journal of Physical Anthroplogy & Human Genetics,* 1975, 1, pp. 56-66.

Singh, Bhupinder, *The Saora Highlanders: Leadership and Development,* Bombay, Somaiya, 1984.

Singh, C.P., *The Ho Tribe of Singhbhum,* New Delhi, Classical Publications, 1978.

Singh, K.S., *Birsa Munda and His Movement 1874-1901: A Study of a Millerarian Movement in Chhotnagpur,* Calcutta, Oxford University Press, 1983.

———, "Introduction to the Hoffman," in J.B., *et al.,* (eds.), Encyclopaedia Mundarica, rpt., 1990, Delhi, Gian Publishing House.

———, *Introduction to Tribal Law and Justice, A Report on the Santal,* W.G. Archer, New Delhi, Concept Publishing Company, 1984.

———, *The Dust Storm and the Hanging Mist: A Study of Birsa Munda and His Movement in Chhotanagpur,* 1874-1901, Calcutta, Firma K.L. Mukhopadhyay, 1966.

Singh, K.S., *Tribal Society in India: An Anthropohistorical Perspective,* Delhi, Light and Life Publications, 1985.

———, *Tribal Society in India: An Anthropohistorical Perspective,* Delhi, Manohar Publications, 1985.

Singh, L.B., *Santal Youths: An Unseen Talent,* New Delhi, Wisdom Publications, 1988.

Sinha, A.P., *Religious Life in Tribal India: A Case Study of Dudh Kharia,* New Delhi, Classical Publications, 1989.

Sinha, D.P., "Research and Development in Anthropology: A Case of Birhor Settlement," in *Journal of Social Research*, 2 (1 & 2), 1959, pp. 98-103.

———, "The Birhor and their World View," in *Adibasi*.

———, "The Hill Kharias of Purulia: Impact of Poverty on a Hunting and Gathering Tribe," in *Memoir* no. 59, Calcutta, Anthropological Survey of India, 1984.

Sinha, S., Space, "Time and Ethnicity: Field Study Among the Bhumij of Barabhum," in *Journal of the Anthropological Society of Bombay*, 9 (2), 1974, pp. 155-62.

Sinha, S.C., "The Nature of Hindu-Bhumij Interaction," in *The Journal of Asiatic Society of Bengal*, 28 (1), 1967.

Sinha, S.P., *Life and Times of Birsa Bhagwan*, Ranchi, Tribal Research Institute, 1964.

Skrefsrud, L.O., *A Grammar of the Santhal Language*, Benaras, Medical Hall Press, 1973.

Sreenath, J. and Ahmed, S.H., *All-India Anthropometric Survey: South Zone, Andhra Pradesh (An Analysis of Data)*, Calcutta, Anthropological Survey of India, 1989.

Srivastava, S.L. and Panda, Kumud C., "Paroja and Kondha Tribes of Kondha Para of the Village Vejhigura," in *Journal of Social Research*, 22 (1), 1979, pp. 42-48.

Subha Rao, A.V., "Culture and Society of the Gadabas of Andhra Pradesh," Ph.D. Thesis, Calcutta, Calcutta University, 1975, Unpublished.

Sudhakar Babu, P., P. Veerraju and J.M. Naidu, "A Note on the Sickle Cell Trait in a Tribal Population of Andhra Pradesh," in *Indian Anthropologist*, 10 (2), 1980, pp. 125-29.

Suryanarayan, M., Marriage, "Family and Kinship of the Saoras of Andhra Pradesh," Ph.D. Thesis, Waltair, Andhra University, Unpublished.

Thakur, Rudranand, *The Social Matrix of a Tribal Village*, New Delhi, Archives Books, 1989.

Thurston, E., *Castes and Tribes of Southern India*, Madras, Government Press, 1909, rpt. 1975, Delhi, Cosmo Publications, vol. II. pp. 242-52; vol. III, pp. 453-55; vol. IV, p. 37, 207-22; vol. V, p. 443.

Thusu, K.N., "The Pengo Parojas of Koraput," Calcutta, Anthropological Survey of India, 1977.

Thusu, K. N. and Jha, Makhan, *Ollar Gadba of Koraput*, Calcutta, Anthropological Survey of India, 1969.

Toppo, Sita, *Dynamics of Educational Development in Tribal India*, New Delhi, Classical Publications, 1979, 1983.

Troisi, J. (ed.), The Santals: Readings in Tribal Life, New Delhi, Indian Social Institute, 1979, vols. I-X (mimeo).

Van Exem, Albert, *The Religious System of the Munda Tribe: An Essay in Religious Anthropology*, St. Augustine, H. Volker and Kutturen, 1982.

Venkataramamurti, Gidargu, *Saora-English Dictionary*, rpt. 1986, Delhi, Mittal Publications.

Vidharthi, L.P. and Upadhyay, V.S., *The Kharia Then and Now: A comparative Study of Hill Dhelki and Dudh Kharia of the Central Eastern Region of India*, New Delhi, Concept Publishing Company, 1980.

Walter, H., *et al.*, "Genetic Markers in Eight Endogamous Population Groups from Andhra Pradesh (South India)," in *Zeitschrift fur Morphologie and Anthropology*, 72 (3), 1981, pp. 325-28.

Yamada, R., *Cultural Formation of the Mundas: Hill Peoples Surrounding the Ganges Plain*, Tokyo, Tokyo University Press, 1970.

Index